AF605799

Between Exile and Exodus

Between Exile and Exodus

Argentinian Jewish Immigration to Israel, 1948–1967

Sebastian Klor

Translated by Lenn Schramm

WAYNE STATE UNIVERSITY PRESS
DETROIT

ISBN 978-0-8143-4367-8 (hardback); ISBN 978-0-8143-4368-5 (ebook)

Library of Congress Cataloging Number: 2017942856

Wayne State University Press
Leonard N. Simons Building
4809 Woodward Avenue
Detroit, Michigan 48201-1309

Visit us online at wsupress.wayne.edu

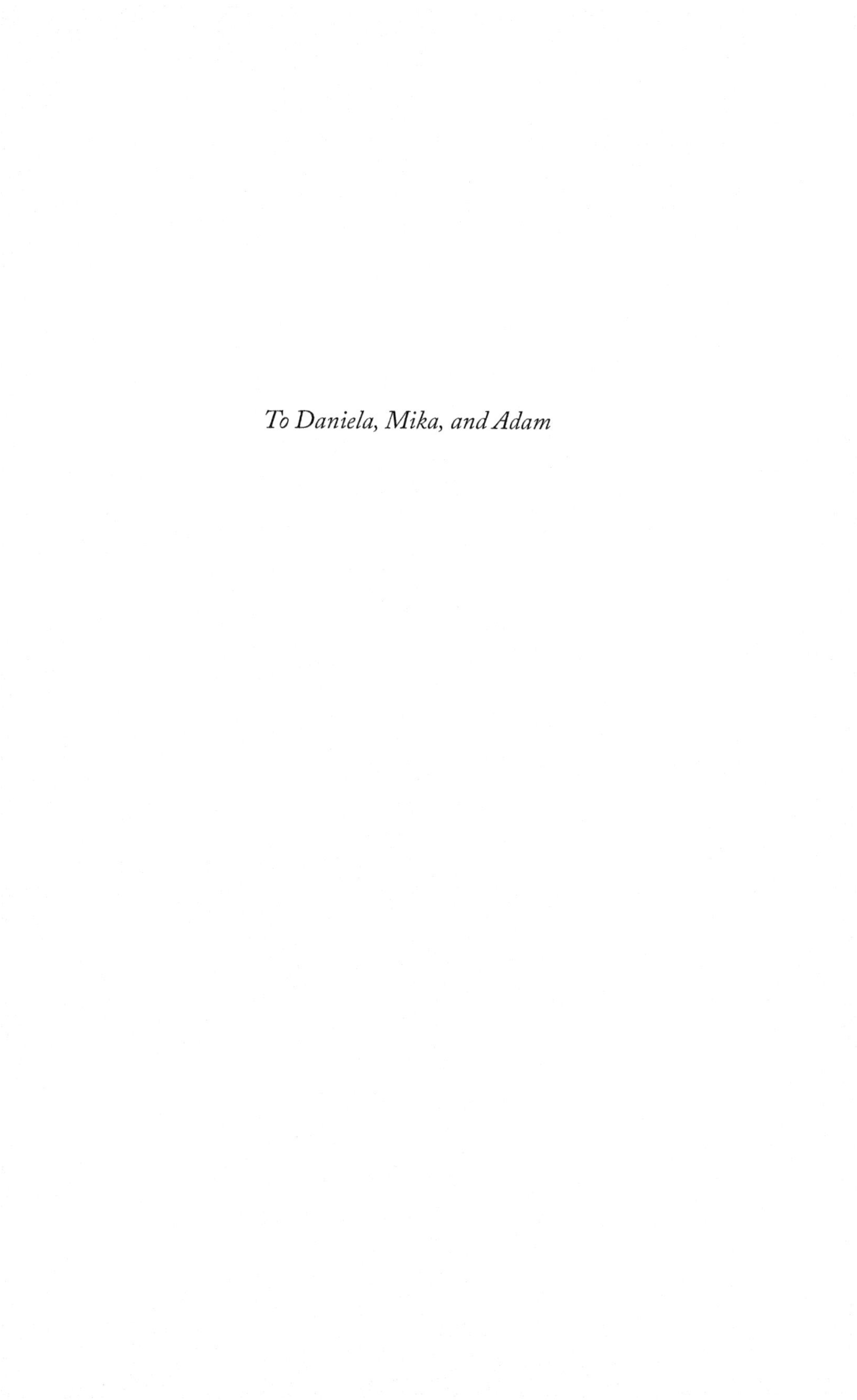

To Daniela, Mika, and Adam

CONTENTS

FIGURES

TABLES

ACKNOWLEDGMENTS

This book is the product of a scholarly, personal, and family odyssey that lasted a decade. The complex task of research and writing was not exclusively my professional occupation, but the stuff of my life—a life that began in a doubly different hemisphere (both southern and western), in Argentina, and now continues here in Israel (northern and eastern). Somewhere along the road—in the town of Pardes Hanna, to be precise—my daughter Mika, then five years old, asked me why I was spending so much time at the computer and what I was writing. I told her that I was telling the story of people who, like me, had at some point in their lives chosen to leave Argentina and move to Israel. Her curiosity was aroused. "Abba, am I Argentinian?" "You can be if you wish," I said. I confess that to this day Mika's question resonates within me; evidently the answer is not so simple. I truly hope that one day she will find the answer (or at least part of one) in this book.

And now that my labors are done, it remains only to thank those individuals and institutions without whose help and support it would never have seen the light of day. First on the list is the University of Haifa, whose generous stipend to me during my doctoral studies in the Department of Israel Studies made my research possible. I am also grateful to Yad Tabenkin, the Kibbutz movement's research, ideology, and documentation center, which gave me a grant from its Menahem Oren Fund. The employees of the Central Zionist Archives, the Israel State Archives, the Kibbutz Movement Archive in Ramat Ef'al, the YIVO archives in Buenos Aires, and the Mark Turkow archives of the Buenos Aires Jewish community generously made their materials available to me.

My path as a scholar was shaped by my doctoral advisors, Professors Gur Alroey and Dr. Leonardo Senkman. They held my hand from my first days in the academic world. There are no words to describe what I gained from their experience, lectures, advice, criticism, and support. With regard to Gur, I do not know where to begin; my gratitude and debt to him are inexpressible. We have been conducting a dialogue for more than ten years now, and it will certainly continue for many more. His vibrant mind and acuity are my model and inspiration as a scholar. His generosity and friendship exceed anything that might be expected. I will be eternally grateful to him.

I also have a huge debt to the Schusterman Center for Jewish Studies at the University of Texas, where I was a postdoctoral fellow in 2013–15, with support from the Israel Institute. Its programs brought me into contact with accomplished scholars and students whose intellectual curiosity is unbounded. Among them is my good friend and colleague, Professor Ami Pedahzur. I am profoundly grateful to him for supporting and encouraging me and finding the funds that allowed me to complete the manuscript. The Schusterman Center became my academic home in every sense. The intimate atmosphere that prevails there, in large measure thanks to the efforts of the senior program coordinator, Galit Pedahzur, and the scholarly energy invested in the Center's activity provided me with the ideal conditions to write the book. Many colleagues read the drafts and made important comments that certainly improved the finished product, including Professor Gary Freeman, Professor Robert Abzug, Professor Naomi Lindstrom, Professor Yoav Di-Capua, and Professor Gabi Sheffer.

I wish to thank the anonymous reviewers of Wayne State University Press for their helpful and constructive comments. I have no doubt that their observations upgraded the manuscript, and for that I am deeply grateful. I also want to express my gratitude to the editors with whom I worked at Wayne State University Press while preparing this book for publication. Special thanks to Kathryn Wildfong, the editor in chief; Kristin Harpster, the editorial, design, and production manager and the production editor of my book; senior designer Rachel Ross; and Dawn Hall, the copyeditor. It was an extraordinary experience for me to work with them and the rest of the team at Wayne State University Press.

I would like to thank Lenn Schramm for his close reading of my Hebrew text, useful comments and suggestions, and professional translation that makes it available to a wider audience.

In his monumental *Literature or Life*, the Spanish writer Jorge Semprún, who lived most of his life in France and wrote mainly in French, wrote that the land of his birth and mother tongue were not a matter of choice for him. A man's roots, as an idea, are even less his own. After he left Spain he no longer had a mother tongue—or rather, he found himself with two, placing him in a rather delicate family situation. Having two mothers, or two homelands, is not conducive to a simple life. So too for me.

Finally, I pay special tribute to Hilla and our three children, Daniela, Mika, and Adam, who have been my full partners in writing and life. Thanks to them, I now have a home far away from home.

INTRODUCTION

The State of the Research

Israel is a classic country of immigration. Israeli society has and continues to be shaped by the waves of immigrants who streamed to its shores, both before and especially after independence. Until the early 1970s, immigrants constituted a majority of the country's Jewish population. Even today, almost a third of its Jewish residents were born elsewhere.[1] Despite the centrality of the migration process for Israeli society, it is astonishing to discover that historians have never carried out a systematic and focused study of the phenomenon.

In Israeli society, Jewish immigration to Israel continues to be referred to as aliya, "ascent," and is viewed as an exceptional phenomenon without parallel in the history of nations. Jews "ascend" or "make aliya"* to Israel, but immigrate to every other destination in the world. By the same token, yerida or "descent" (emigration from Israel) is viewed as a negative phenomenon that undermines the exalted ideal; that is, as a social and national failure. The concept of aliya as bearing ethical significance and unlike every other migratory process took root in Zionist thought even before the establishment of the state.[2]

This unique perception continued to be cultivated by Israeli society after independence. Today, too, the public discourse about immigration to Israel deals mainly with experiences, emotions, fears, and hopes—but especially with myths. The storm generated in early 2015 by the Facebook page "Olim to Berlin" is only the most recent evidence of this. Against the background of the high cost of living, young Israelis began circulating information about jobs in Berlin, German-language classes, and began attending meetings to explore the possibility of moving there. Israeli public opinion roundly castigated this initiative

*The process is *aliya*; the individual is an *oleh* (plural *olim*). The corresponding terms for emigration from Israel are *yerida* and *yored* (*yordim*).

of the twenty- and thirty-something generation. At the same time, though, (former) Israelis who live in the United States have established organizations that enjoy support and recognition from the Israeli government and the Jewish Agency. In October 2014, the New York correspondent for *Ha'aretz* and its *The Marker* financial supplement reported on this in an article titled, "No Longer a Scrap Heap of Weaklings." The writer used this phrase, coined by Yitzhak Rabin in the 1970s to castigate yordim, in his survey of the fundamental difference with the current generation of Israeli emigrants to North America, a generation that is not ashamed of its Israeli identity and even basks in the warm embrace of both the Israeli establishment and the local Jewish community.[3]

This discourse must be understood against the background of the demographic, economic, security, and institutional changes in Israeli society since 1948. A country that practiced strict food rationing in its infancy is now "the start-up nation," a world leader in the high-tech industry, and ranked nineteenth in the UN Human Development Index (HDI) for 2014.[4] The "normalization" of Israeli society is also reflected in how Israelis see themselves. Today, yordim are increasingly viewed as constituting a foreign diaspora of the sort that other countries have and that can even provide various benefits to the mother country, Israel.[5]

A similar development has taken place in the social science literature on the history of Israeli society and Jewish immigration to Israel. A review of Zionist historiography indicates that aliya has usually been examined through the prism of the development of Jewish society in Israel. Immigrants were and continue to be perceived instrumentally, as a tool for building and consolidating Israeli society. The good of the national entity always takes precedence over the good of the human collective. This is true for the pre-State periods as well as for independent Israel. With regard to both eras, the immigration process is usually studied against the background of Zionist policy and as a function of the financial, social, and political development of Jewish society in Israel. As a result, the immigrants are evaluated exclusively in terms of their contribution (or lack of contribution) to the Yishuv (the pre-State Jewish community of Palestine) and the state and relegated to the margins of the research.[6]

By way of illustration, when the Jewish population of Israel reached the one-million mark in late 1949, government and Jewish Agency officials decided to celebrate the festival of Hanukkah under the sign of "The First Million." December 19, 1949, the fourth day of Hanukkah, was proclaimed a special holiday in the country and in the Diaspora—"Ingathering of the Exiles Day."[7] In his address to the Israeli parliament, the Knesset, Prime Minister David

Ben-Gurion said that his government had set the doubling of the country's Jewish population within four years as its lodestar.[8] Israel Radio devoted all its programs to the topic of the first million[9] and began its broadcasts that day with a speech by Yitzhak Rafael, the director of the Jewish Agency Aliyah Department:

> We went through difficult stages of aliya until we reached the first million. Thirty years ago, the Yishuv numbered only 56,000 persons. From 1919 to the end of this November [1949], 753,000 people made aliya and they, along with natural increase, make up the million. . . . From the establishment of the independent state in May 1948 through today, 333,000 persons have made aliya, or some 17,000 a month. . . . And if we merit to see aliya continue at this pace in the future, and if we take natural increase into account, we will reach the second million within four years. . . . This vast aliya comes from 52 different countries, from almost every Jewish diaspora. Jews overcame the difficulties of leaving and the obstacles to crossing borders. The message of redemption reached the most remote and distant Jewish communities. . . . They have come from lands of distress and from comfortable situations; they have come from Eastern and Western Europe, from North and South America, from Afghanistan, from India to Ethiopia. The aliya movement has become that of our entire people. The mass aliya is built of and rests on two fundamental trends, whose combination provides the driving force that pushes and the people and demands that they move towards Zion, with great and expeditious speed.[10]

The doubling of Israel's Jewish population in its first three years was unprecedented in the history of nations, and certainly in such complex economic, social, and security circumstances.[11] The composition of Israeli society continued to change beyond recognition, with the arrival during the 1950s of more than half a million newcomers from Muslim countries. "This is the pioneer* aliya of recent years" is how Baruch Duvdevani, director of the Aliyah Department, described the mass immigration from North Africa in a lecture he delivered at the conference of department employees in 1956, and added:

*"Pioneer" represents the Hebrew *XXalutz*, which referred to the enthusiastic young people, mainly from Europe, who immigrated to Palestine in the first four decades of the twentieth century to till its soil and were taken as the epitome and ideal of Zionist endeavor.

> These immigrants are going to Lakhish, Ta'anakh, to every out-of-the-way place, to Eilat. Here in Israel all of us—the aliya family—are working with these immigrants, helping them get organized. But here [in the department] we are involved mainly with paperwork, dealing with people's files, with words written in ink. We relate to the file and do not see the live individual.[12]

The account here, set against the background of the mass immigration of the early 1950s, is based on Aliyah Department documents, articles published in its house organ, press clippings, and memoirs. All these faithfully reflect how Israeli society related to the immigrants, and especially the perception of the newcomers as a means to build and bolster Israeli society. But conspicuously absent from the press reports, memoirs, statistics, and scholarly research on Jewish immigration to Israel are the immigrants themselves, the protagonists of this historic drama.

The mass immigration from Muslim countries and the resulting demographic transformation of Israel's Jewish population led scholars to focus on the differences between the immigrants who came en masse in the 1950s and those who arrived from Eastern Europe before the establishment of the state. These scholars developed various and rival theoretical and analytical approaches. For the purpose of their research, they relied on a sweeping classification by continent—Asia-Africa or Europe-America—and other dichotomous categories, such as "Western Jews/Eastern Jews" and "countries of distress/wealthy countries." Such broad categories were appropriate to the issues of interest to scholars, mainly social topics related to the cultural and structural influences of immigration on Israeli society, and especially the differences between Ashkenazim (Jews from Europe and the Americas) and Sephardim (Jews from Asia and North Africa) with regard to mobility and social justice.[13]

Immigration and absorption have been examined mainly against the background of Israel's melting pot ethos, security problems, and ethnic fissures. In other words, the hundreds of thousands of immigrants who were processed before being dispatched to transit camps, agricultural settlements, and development towns were studied in a functional manner in light of Israeli policy, but they were neglected as individuals and relegated to the margins of social research, deemed unworthy of examination and study in their own right.[14]

The theoretical assumptions of the quantitative research and the broad categories employed in it perpetuated the perspective of the immigrants as a homogenous mass and blurred the differences between olim from different countries.

The classification by continent, for example, did not take account of the huge impact of a person's specific country of origin on the immigration process; their psychological background was ignored even in extreme personal circumstances. The treatment of all the "wealthy countries" as a single unit was based on the classical Zionist assumption that immigration from them was unrelated to economic or political problems or anti-Semitism and was spurred exclusively by ideological and personal considerations and on the notion that aliya was the only way to prevent assimilation and the loss of Jewish values.

This outlook is also evident in studies of the Jewish Diaspora as an ethno-national exile (a prominent research category in the social sciences). In the Zionist perspective, the topic of migration is limited by the dichotomous notion of "Center" and "Diaspora." That is, the Jews, as a distinct ethno-national group, reside in their "host countries" in a state of exile, constantly dreaming of returning to their spiritual and symbolic center.[15]

The Jewish Latin American context can serve as a fascinating basis for a consideration of these issues. We are fortunate to possess a broad and diverse body of research on Latin American Jewry in general and on its Argentinian branch in particular. Space is lacking here to list it in detail, and I will mention only a few articles and volumes published in the last decade that reflect the fierce and fruitful debate among scholars who deal with Latin American Jews and hyphenated identities.[16] The crux of the debate has to do with the relative weight of the Jewish ethnic and the local civic components of the collective identity of the various Jewish communities there. Are they Latin American Jews or Jewish Latin Americans?

One approach that is common in Jewish studies today emphasizes Jewish particularism and focuses on topics such as the impact of anti-Semitism on the Jewish communities, the relations between the Jewish communities of Latin America and international Jewish organizations, and of course and especially, with Israel.[17] Another approach, found more in Latin American studies and in Diaspora studies, challenges the particularist approach on the grounds that it leaves out large groups, such as those who are not affiliated with Jewish organizations; pays insufficient attention to the local component of the Jews' identity in various countries; and downplays comparative aspects, both with other ethnic groups and with Jewish communities elsewhere.[18] In other words, unlike the particularist approach that focuses on their Jewishness, the ethno-national approach highlights their Latin American identity.

By contrast, the focus on hyphenated identities extends to more general aspects; it serves as the basis for a comparison between Jews and other ethnic groups and also includes sectors that tended to be left out of the scholarly ambit, such as unaffiliated Jews, women, and Jews of Middle Eastern origin.[19] The analytical categories have been broadened, too. In recent years, a third approach has made its appearance; it calls for adopting transnational categories for understanding ethno-national diasporas and holds that the ethno-national approach pays too little attention to the tension between Jews' diaspora identity and civic identity. This method assumes that ethnic minorities can feel a bond to multiple centers and multiple national identities. The adoption and application of diaspora and transnational categories to the study of Latin American Jewry can (according to this school) contribute to a better understanding of both regional aspects and global aspects.[20] In effect, this approach tries to return the focus of the discussion to Jewish particularism.

I will not propose to render a verdict in this fascinating methodological debate. However, it informs what follows, mainly due to the underlying conceptual paradigm, which raises two main questions. First, we will be able to determine the extent to which the Jews who left Argentina for Israel were motivated by their Jewishness and their Argentinidad (Argentinian identity). Second, we will compare the motives of Argentinian Jewish emigrants who chose Israel with those who opted for other destinations and with non-Jewish emigrants.

Historical research on Jewish immigration to Israel has tended to adopt the broad dichotomous categories and the conclusions of quantitative research without question and to rely mainly on retrospective ideas that emerge from the research topics. By contrast, it has given only limited consideration to the cultural, political, economic, social, and psychological variations among the immigrants who came to Israel from different countries. But immigration always plays out in a particular social and cultural context and should not be isolated from it. The decisive importance of the local level in every immigration process was demonstrated long since in the general literature on migration, and especially Jewish migration. Nevertheless, the historical literature about Jewish immigration to Israel is dominated by studies that adopt the continental and other binary categories as their basis and pay little if any attention to the regional factor. As a result, the immigrants' old world is neglected and relegated to the official statistics—a black box in most studies.

This may explain why some groups of immigrants to Israel have never been the subject of serious academic treatment. Those from Argentina—about 70,000 since 1948—are among these neglected groups. A survey of bibliographic references to South American Jewry finds very few studies of their immigration to Israel.[21] The handful of quantitative studies generally present basic figures, assembled from Central Bureau of Statistics data on the number of immigrants since independence, and an analysis of the composition and characteristics of the immigration from Latin America. The studies' authors focus on the immigrants' successful absorption in Israel.[22] There are three reasons why the Latin American public in Israel has been an "invisible community": their Zionist ideology, their successful integration in the job market, and their lack of prominence in the public eye.[23] The historical facets of immigration from Latin America have been studied only in fragments, generally related to the members of the Zionist youth movements, and have tended to stress the importance of Zionist ideology as their main motive for immigration.[24]

The immigrants from Latin America, especially those from Argentina, were accounted as coming from wealthy countries. This is reasonable in light of the changes that overtook the Jewish world as a whole and Latin American Jewry in particular during the Holocaust and the first years thereafter. However, I do not believe that these vague and dichotomous assumptions can explain the process in any depth. This complexity was quickly discerned by Jacob Tsur, the first Israeli minister in Buenos Aires (1949–53). Soon after his arrival there, the diplomat assessed that this broad distinction between countries of distress and wealthy countries was inadequate for the case of Argentinian Jewry:

> This diaspora does not belong to either of the two groups of the exile in our time: this is not a country of distress, it is not poor and it is not persecuted; but it is also not a wealthy country, in the accepted sense of the term. On the surface, the Jews' economic and political status is stable. They live in relative ease. There is antisemitism, sometimes overt and sometimes covert, but the Jews' civil rights are not infringed. On the contrary, the authorities are cordial to them and frequently emphasize their affection for the Jews and appreciation of the role that they play in the country.[25]

The Israeli diplomat discerned the problematic nature of the sweeping categories and understood the complexity of the situation, even in the early stages of his mission. In this book, we will encounter the fact that Argentinian Jewry was accounted secure and well off in a country that actually had many of the characteristics of "a country of distress."

The survey above highlights the need to make the immigrants themselves the focus of analysis, worthy of independent treatment and study—the individual immigrant as the central axis of the research. But his or her story must be placed against the background of the macro and quantitative picture, in the broad historical context of both the country of origin and the country of destination. Through its case study of Argentinian Jewry, this book creates a more appropriate fusion of the micro level of the individual with the macro social level reflected in quantitative research. In this way, the picture that the historian attempts to uncover transcends the anecdotal, and the immigrant is brought to life rather than being drowned in dry statistics.

We also see the need to study Jewish immigration to Israel using the research methods and tools of the various disciplines that focus on migration, on the assumption that aliya, too, can be assessed and measured objectively, with neutral and comparative research instruments. The widespread assumption that aliya is propelled chiefly by ideology, rather than social and economic factors, keeps us from seeing the full canvas of the motives behind it. Although we cannot ignore the importance of ideological and ethical variables, I believe they should be assigned a more moderate role and given a more complex interpretation. Historians of Jewish immigration to Israel have shown that ideological olim were always a small and unrepresentative minority of all immigrants and that it is possible to "make aliya" to other destinations and not just Israel.[26]

The analytic intent of this book is to uncover the variety of factors that drove Jews to move from Argentina to Israel and that motivated the bureaucracy that helped them do so. Here, as in other cases, this book endeavors to steer clear of all the binary and value-driven categories that are so widespread in the study of Jewish immigration to Israel.

This is why I have tried to limit my use of the term "aliya." The Israeli scholar Gur Alroey distinguishes olim from (im)migrants and traces the semantic evolution of these terms in Zionist thought.[27] He rejects the argument, common today among historians, that "aliya" can have a neutral sense. Alroey holds that it is value laden and ideological; on the one hand, it assigns a national motivation to every Jew who comes to Israel, while on the other hand it blurs or even effaces the other factors behind their migration. This is a classic case of mobilizing language in the service of a national movement. A historian is not obligated to accept the national terminology without question and should study Jewish immigration to Israel (pre- and postindependence) by the normal standards of migration studies. Alroey proposed a typological distinction between these two terms for relocating to a new country, whether the destination is Israel or somewhere else.

Zionism starts with the fact that those who make aliya are leaving their current home in fulfillment of national ideology, whereas migrants do so to improve their economic condition and would like to continue their previous life in their new home. Olim do not come from the impoverished strata of Jewish society, and their aliya is not meant to solve their individual distress. It is the weakening of the bonds of Jewish society that propel olim, and not their shaky economic condition. Another difference between olim and immigrants has to do with their attitude toward their country of origin. Olim reject the social values of their former home and wish to build a new society that champions new values. Immigrants, by contrast, continue to identify with their former society and are not necessarily interested in changing or reforming their new home. These differences influence both groups' absorption in the new country. Immigrants maintain their link to their country of origin for many years and have a strong propensity to live among others with the same background. Olim, by contrast, sever their ties with their former home and its values and are more readily absorbed in their new environment.[28]

I accept Alroey's stricture. In this book, I apply the typological distinction between olim and immigrants to examine the diverse motivations that led Jews to leave Argentina for Israel. As will become evident, the vast majority who did so in the 1950s and 1960s are a better fit for the immigrant designation. I will examine all the reasons for their relocation to Israel in an attempt to differentiate, to the extent possible, those who were propelled by their Zionism from those for whom ideology was not the prime mover in their decision.

The Research

On the basis of the historiographical survey, we can say that no real research has been done about the historical issues related to Israeli policy on immigration and its application to Argentina, the motives of the Argentinian immigrants and the path that brought them to Israel, and the number and socioeconomic profile of the immigrants. This book probes complex issues through the lens of the Jews who left Argentina during Israel's first two decades (1948–67). Employing quantitative and qualitative databases that were constructed for this project and methodological tools that are in common use in the social sciences, the book tries to answer specific historical questions related to the various stages of Argentinian Jewish immigration to Israel.

Immigration is ultimately an individual and not a collective experience. The only way to understand it is from the perspective of rank-and-file immigrants, with their individual and subjective motives.[29] We must never forget that the decision to leave home is a subjective choice. This, indeed, is what makes the phenomenon so fascinating. But the story of the individual migrant must be understood in the broader historical context of both the country of origin and the country of destination. In this book, consequently, the unique perspective of the individual is combined with the macro dimensions—social, economic, and historical—which are also crucial. If we fail to combine these two dimensions the individual picture never escapes the level of anecdote, while the quantitative data alone cannot provide a deep explanation of the phenomenon. This book's integration of the macro and micro dimensions sets the two research methods, quantitative and the qualitative, in the proper relationship. I will expand on my unique methodology below after reviewing the most important historical questions that emerge from these research issues and the historical sources from which this book draws.

When dealing with the question of the immigrants' motivation, I will try to respond to four specific questions: What role did financial and political factors, both in Argentina and in Israel, play in spurring Argentinian Jews to move to Israel? To what extent was anti-Semitism in Argentina a factor in their decision? Where did Zionist ideology fit into their overall considerations? What place did a formal Jewish education occupy in them? Two key questions are raised in an attempt to get to the bottom of the issue of Israeli immigration policy and its application in Argentina: What principles shaped Israeli immigration policy during the first two decades? What role did the policies devised in Jerusalem and their actual implementation play in Argentinian Jews' decision to immigrate to Israel? With regard to the scale of Argentinian Jewish immigration to Israel, I will look closely at the numbers, with regard to both the overall traffic and the size of the Jewish community in Argentina, in order to identify the factors that influenced its scope. Finally, Israeli immigration policy is juxtaposed with the composition of the Argentinian immigrants to ask two key questions: What was the immigrants' demographic, economic, and social profile (sex, age, ethnic origin, family status, family composition, education, and occupation)? Was Argentinian Jewish immigration to Israel selective?

A Critical Appraisal of the Sources

The decisive element that shaped and organized the aliya apparatus was the Aliyah Department of the Jewish Agency. In its files, deposited in the Central Zionist Archives in Jerusalem and the storerooms of the Jewish Agency Logistics Center in Tserifin, I found the routine correspondence between department officials in Israel and in Argentina, the reports submitted by department representatives and emissaries, publications and news items, survey results, and much more. The Aliyah Department newsletter, *Dappei Aliyah*, is a treasure trove of primary sources and of great historical value. A total of sixty-nine numbers were published between April 1949 and the last issue in June 1968. Its columns contain rich and diverse quantitative and qualitative information: surveys of the aliya situation as of various dates, articles about immigration and absorption reprinted from periodicals published in Israel and abroad, excerpts of speeches and presentations at various forums that dealt with these twin topics, including the Zionist Congresses, sessions of the Zionist General Council, meetings of the Coordinating Committee and the Zionist Executive, press conferences, and the Knesset plenum and committees. One of the regular sections of *Dappei Aliyah* summarized the news from the department and its offices abroad; another summarized authoritative information about customs matters—vital information for future immigrants.

It was the representatives of the Aliyah Department who came into contact with potential immigrants on an individual basis and organized their move to Israel. They also received the files of candidates from other departments, including the Economic Department and the Youth and Hehalutz Department, for approval by the head of the office in Buenos Aires. After the files were assembled there they were forwarded to Jerusalem for final approval. The Aliyah Department handled all the technical details related to the move. Medical exams were arranged in cooperation with the consulate, which was also responsible for issuing Israeli visas at the department's recommendation. The department handled travel arrangements and negotiated with the Buenos Aires offices of steamship lines to obtain discounts on the cost of the ocean passage, which was usually paid for by the Jewish Agency and the Argentinian Jewish institutions. A few immigrants paid their own travel expenses. The Aliyah Department shepherded them until they reached Israel. When they landed, they became the concern of the Absorption Department.[30] The documentation of these activities helped me locate and collect personal information about the immigrants from Argentina.

The Economic Department and the Youth and Hehalutz Department were also active in Argentina. The former worked with wealthy potential immigrants and tourists, providing them with information about the options and prospects for setting up industrial and commercial enterprises in Israel. The Economic Department also offered advice and support for dealing with the Israeli bureaucracy, including import licenses, permits for new factories, acquisition of land for factories, and the transfer of capital and investments in productive branches of the economy. The Aliyah Department, along with the Youth and Hehalutz Department and the emissaries of the Zionist youth movements, strove to instill a Zionist spirit in the hearts of young Jews and provided physical and ideological training for their members. The Professional and Technical Workers Association (PATWA) focused on conveying information about work conditions in Israel, employment possibilities, and guidance to skilled craftsmen and university graduates. PATWA also worked with Jewish students.[31]

Another actor that merits attention here is the Israeli diplomatic mission in Argentina—the legation and then, from 1955, the embassy. In addition to their regular assignments, its staff members came in contact with the Jewish community and influenced it significantly, including with regard to immigration to Israel. "In our diplomatic endeavors we cannot ignore the factor of aliya, which is crucial for the future of our work," wrote Jacob Tsur in the detailed report he drafted soon after taking up his post at the legation.[32] Tsur was the top Israeli diplomat in Buenos Aires from mid-1949 to 1953, when he was succeeded as minister by Arie Kubovy (ambassador from 1955). Yosef Avidar and Moshe Alon were the other Israel ambassadors to Argentina during the period covered in this book. All of them paid serious attention to the topic, maintained close contact with Jewish Agency officials, and sent routine reports to Jerusalem. This correspondence is found mainly in the Israel State Archives in Jerusalem.

In Argentina, the Jewish Agency, along with the legation and later the embassy, worked in accordance with the instructions and policies formulated in Jerusalem pursuant to the general lines specified by the Zionist Congresses. The Zionist General Council (the deliberative organ of the World Zionist Organization [WZO] between congresses) defined day-to-day policy and directives for the work of all WZO departments in Israel and abroad. The Zionist Executive oversaw the actual implementation of the policy. The Coordinating Committee, composed of representatives of the Zionist Executive and the Israeli government, was established in May 1950 to organize, plan, and carry out decisions related to immigration, absorption, and settlement; its chairman was the prime minister.[33] These were the bodies that defined Israeli policy in these domains. This policy will be the focus of the present study, because the various Jewish Agency departments adhered to it and they, especially the Aliyah Department, supported the waves of Jewish immigration to Israel, including from Argentina.

Here we should note that the documents left behind by these actors do not present the whole story. Their observations, reports, and surveys were drafted or conducted in accordance with ideological, financial, and political considerations that must always be kept in mind. Another reason why these sources paint only part of the picture is that the reports in which the representatives of the various departments summarized their work and the immigration process rarely referred to their contacts with the local community. This means that the voices of local Jews are silent. To balance this, I supplemented the official documents with other sources and invested great effort in systematically scanning the archives of the Argentinian Jewish press for items about the Jewish Agency in general and about immigration to Israel in particular. It must not be forgotten that only about 5% of Argentinian Jewry left the country for Israel during the period covered here. I have also drawn on letters written by immigrants, their retrospective impressions as embodied in memoirs, and oral documentation. To my delight, I found there is an extensive and almost unknown body of memoir literature that holds great value for scholarship. I also collected abundant oral testimonies for this study, both in Israel and in Argentina.[34]

Methodology

The core of this study is an examination of Argentinian Jewish immigration to Israel using a combination of macro and micro methods; that is, looking at the social, economic, and historical dimensions while also observing the individuals as they experienced this complex process. Every aspect of the immigration process is considered on both planes. Using quantifiable macro data, it examines how large-scale events in Argentina and in Israel during the period under scrutiny influenced the migration pattern. The frequent economic and political crises, the manifestations of anti-Semitism in Argentina, and the wars in Israel exemplify the macro-scale events that impacted the process. On the micro level, the individual and family aspects of Argentinian Jewish immigration to Israel are examined, from registration at the Jewish Agency office until arrival in Israel. Cross-checks of the quantitative data against the qualitative information provided by the immigrants themselves supplied the most complete, comprehensive, and detailed picture of the process under discussion.

In light of the book's goals, and to ensure the success of this combination of the micro and macro, I built two databases, quantitative and qualitative. The quantitative database contains reports, publications, newspaper clippings, memos, surveys and proposals submitted by emissaries, the minutes of meetings, information manuals for immigrants, and the impressions of senior visitors from Israel and the Zionist movement with regard to immigration and absorption. These are supplemented by the information found in the Aliyah Department newsletter (*Dappei Aliyah*), the reports of the Israeli diplomats in Argentina, and the aggregate quantitative data found in studies, censuses, reports, and surveys. The qualitative database incorporates the individual details of immigrants, as found in records that originally served administrative purposes. From these sources, I assembled a database with the personal details of 10,487 Argentinian Jews who settled in Israel between 1954 and 1967.[35] In addition to names, the database lists the immigrant's age, family status, occupation, financing of their immigration, date of immigration, the name of the ship on which they sailed, the agency that organized their immigration, where they were absorbed in Israel, and the type of visa they received. The qualitative database is fleshed out by memoirs, contemporary press reports, personal archives, letters by immigrants, and oral documentation.

Building a database of this kind is a difficult and complex undertaking—but also challenging and important. The first step was to locate the information in the various archives; not all the documents of the several Jewish Agency departments have found their way to the Central Zionist Archives.[36] The second step was to encode the information and enter it into the computer, a process that took about a year. The work, as noted, was complex and tedious, but paid off in the end. Processing and summarizing the data revealed trends and patterns that make it possible to see both the macro picture and the individual dimension. As a methodological tool, the database of individuals brings to life the people behind the numbers and the estimates and helps us get to know various aspects of individual immigrants and their families before, during, and after the move from Argentina to Israel. This provides a deeper understanding of the immigration process, with its various stages and aspects.

The patterns and trends that emerged from analysis of the data allowed me to realize one of the main goals of the book and understand the patterns of Argentinian Jewish immigration to Israel. An accurate picture of the demographics of the immigrants from a particular country or era, and a breakdown by age, sex, family status, occupation, and more, can tell us about their motives. All research on migration has to confront these issues, especially quantitative studies. They are almost always based on aggregate data, faceless and nameless, and the individual migrant is reduced to a number. My database of individuals makes it possible to see the people hidden behind the numbers and to learn about them and their families. In addition, the use of such abundant and diverse data supports questions and conclusions that are unlikely to come up when only aggregate data are available.

The methodology employed means that the book can take the immigrant's own perspective as a central unit of analysis. I believe that this approach is essential for understanding the immigration process in all its complexity. Through these individual life stories, we can better comprehend the patterns that are reflected in the dry quantitative data. A life story allows us to see and assess the decisive importance of "chain migration," a phenomenon known from other studies of migration.[37] Direct contact with immigrants—the interchanges and relationships with family, friends, members of the same trade or profession, or comrades in the same Zionist youth movement, both in Argentina and in Israel, were decisive for the immigration process.

Perceiving such basic relationships requires the systematic collection of primary sources that reflect the perspective of the immigrants and their families, including letters, memoirs, and oral testimonies. Such sources make it possible to analyze the information and document the full range of their closest relationships. Detailed study of the various cases allows us to trace the process in a different way. In methodological terms, we may ask whether an individual instance is a representative case that can teach us about the whole, or unique and idiosyncratic. The only way to answer this question is to place it against the backdrop of the overall or macro picture. The database of individuals proved to be an effective tool as well, because it allowed me to identify the "immigration chains" from Argentina to Israel.

The full potential of a database of this kind can be realized only by supplementing its contents and checking them against the aggregate data provided by other quantitative sources, including aggregate data on Jewish immigration to Israel, data on the demographics of Argentinian Jewry as found in academic studies, national censuses, and publications of the Central Bureau of Statistics. The juxtaposition and analysis of the information from all these sources provide the quantitative macro picture of the demographics of the Jewish immigrants from Argentina during the period in question. To understand, for example, the immigration patterns of skilled tradesmen, we have to look at the occupational profile of the Argentinian Jewish immigrants in contrast to that of the Argentinian Jewry as a whole. Only then can we understand, for example, why tailors were more likely than farmers to make the move.

Structure of the Book

Any study of migration, I believe, must anchor its analysis in the country of origin, because that is the place that determines the entire process. The social structure of the Argentinian Jewish immigration to Israel, that is, the immigrants' demographic and socioeconomic profile, was rooted in their origins, as was their future and absorption in Israeli society. Accordingly, chapter 1 focuses on what Jewish immigration to Israel meant in the country of origin—that is, on Argentina as a separate geographic entity that the immigrants left behind. It profiles the Jews of Argentina in demographic, economic, and social terms, identifying the main changes and developments that took place among them in various domains and strata, from the community's birth in the late nineteenth century until the 1960s. These details are necessary for the subsequent investigation and serve as the quantitative and qualitative underpinnings of what follows.

Any discussion of the process must be solidly grounded in an analysis of its motives. In the period studied here, several factors were at work in Argentina and Israel. In Argentina, there were both negative factors that pushed the migrants to leave and positive factors that encouraged them to stay put. In Israel, the positive factors pulled immigrants to leave Argentina, while the negative factors militated against their doing so. In chapter 2, against the background of these general assumptions, and drawing on an analysis of sources I collected, I assess the balance of the forces that impelled and deterred Argentinian Jewish immigration to Israel during the first two decades after independence. I weigh the impact on migration of the economic and political situation in Argentina as compared to the weight of Zionist ideology.

The discussion centers on anti-Semitism, which aroused and continues to arouse special attention in the Argentinian context, both in scholarship and in public opinion. In all likelihood this can be traced to five topics of the postwar and post-Holocaust period: Argentina's reputation as a refuge for Nazi criminals during the Perón era, the 1960 abduction of Adolf Eichmann by Israeli agents, the fecklessness of the Argentinian authorities in dealing with ultranationalist and anti-Semitic movements and organizations during those years, "the special treatment" of Jews during the sinister military dictatorship that ruled the country from 1976 to 1983, and, finally, the two murderous terrorist attacks in Buenos Aires in the 1990s. Thanks to the prominence and nature of those events, anti-Semitism received sensationalist coverage in the media, which makes it hard for scholars to accurately assess its strength. Against this background, the question of anti-Semitism in Argentina during the period covered in this book is a special challenge and has to be near the center of our discussion of the push factors that propelled immigration to Israel. Still, pace the common view, anti-Semitism does not seem to have been near the top of the list of the factors that motivated Argentinian Jews to leave for Israel. At most it expedited the process in unfavorable economic and political circumstances.

Chapter 3 focuses on the immigration policies of newly independent Israel through a critical analysis and systematic look at the documents left behind by the policy makers. The goal is to identify the main principles that were at work in this domain. Chapter 4 places the actual immigration against the backdrop of that policy, reconstructing the work patterns of the bureaucracy that organized and channeled the process and evaluating its influence. With those patterns in view, in the rest of the book we will be able to assess the extent to which Israeli immigration policy and its implementation influenced the scope and social composition of the immigration from Argentina.

Chapter 5 deals with two main quantitative aspects of the Argentinian Jewish immigration to Israel—its size and its sociodemographic makeup. The chapter is based on the aggregate statistics from the censuses, for example, cross-checked against my database. It begins with a systematic and critical analysis of the figures for all Jewish immigration to Israel during the period under study. In this light, the movement from Argentina is considered both in absolute numbers and as a percentage of the country's Jewish population. This examination highlights the factors that affected the scale of the phenomenon. The chapter continues with a sociodemographic analysis, based on the patterns and trends extracted from the database. Armed with this knowledge of the immigrants' distribution by ethnic origin, age, sex, hometown, occupational stratum, and place and region of absorption in Israel, we will be able to determine the selection criteria that Israeli policy imposed.

The findings in this chapter suggest a selective migration, spurred by economic circumstances in Argentina. More than 60% of the immigrants were at their peak work capacity. They were mainly lower-middle-class and blue-collar workers (at a time when two-thirds of Argentinian Jews held white-collar positions).

In order to understand the process more fully, we must combine the quantitative picture with microhistorical elements. Accordingly, chapter 6 looks at the people behind the numbers, assessments, and estimates and studies individual immigrants and their families in greater depth. In contrast with the quantitative research, which is based on faceless and nameless aggregate data, in this chapter I use immigrants' life stories as a unit of analysis that permits a better understanding of the patterns reflected in the quantitative data. These stories reflect the immigrants' primary relationships and their motives for coming to Israel, as expressed in several paradigmatic cases that are representative of the different circles of immigrants. Finally, the conclusion summarizes the main findings of this study.

A Note on Abbreviations and Language

For the key to source abbreviations and transliterated versions of the titles of works in Hebrew, please see the bibliography. It is taken for granted that Israeli government and Jewish Agency documents, as well as articles in the Israeli press, are in Hebrew, so the language has not been specified in the notes except where this is not the case.

1

Argentina—Host Country or Homeland?

Argentina: A Land of Immigrants

Argentina conducted a national census in 1947. That date was not accidental; rather, it marked the end of the era of mass immigration to Argentina, which had taken place between the two world wars. Those who planned the census were aware of the fundamental changes that immigration had brought to Argentina in terms of population growth and demographics. Immigration has had a decisive and unmistakable effect on the image of modern Argentina, which is a classic example of a country of immigrants: almost five million newcomers arrived between the late nineteenth century and the middle of the twentieth century, most of them from Italy and Spain.[1] So it was natural that the 1947 census counted nearly sixteen million people in Argentina, twice as many as the official census of 1914, when immigration to Argentina was at its height.[2]

Jews began to arrive in Argentina in the late nineteenth century as part of their growing exodus from eastern Europe. In the early twentieth century, this emigration became a mass movement. Nearly five million Jews left Europe for the young liberal democracies across the ocean in the hope of finding a safer and more comfortable place to live. The most important destination, which attracted more than 70% of the migrants, was the United States. About half a million went to Palestine, where they provided the human foundation for the establishment of Israel. And almost a quarter of a million Jews chose to settle in Argentina.[3]

Historical research about Jewish immigration to Argentina takes the story of the SS *Weser* as the seminal event that links the chronicles of the Jewish people and the annals of the Argentinian republic in the modern era—a sort of modern version of the American *Mayflower*. On August 14, 1889, the German passenger ship *Weser* cast anchor in Buenos Aires. On board were 136 Jewish families, almost all of them from towns and villages near Kamenets Podolsk, the capital of the district of Podolia in the southern Pale of Settlement. They had come to Argentina to work in agriculture and settle in the pampas, where they laid the foundations for the Argentinian Jewish "mother of the colonies"—Moisés Ville.[4]

The SS *Weser* was important for the future of Jewish immigration to Argentina for two main reasons: First, its passengers were an organized group who paved the way for other Jews looking to escape their misery by means of emigration and settlement on the Argentinian frontier. Second, the *Weser* set the precedent for the establishment, in 1891, of the Jewish Colonization Association (ICA) by the Baron Maurice de Hirsch, a German Jewish philanthropist who worked intensively to find a way to facilitate Jewish emigration from eastern Europe. Baron Hirsch saw settlement in Argentina as a prime solution to the Jewish problem in Russia.[5]

With their fare paid by Hirsch, tens of thousands of Jews sailed for Argentina, which gradually became an alternative destination for eastern European Jews who wanted to turn to farming. By 1896, the year the baron died, his settlements in Argentina were home to some 7,000 people who lived on 910 farms in four large colonies.[6] In numerical terms, the settlement enterprise peaked in 1925, when 5,802 Jewish families (more than 33,000 people) were living in these colonies.[7] Those numbers are not large, but, as we shall see, their importance is greater than they would suggest.

From the outset, the Jewish settlements in Argentina were marked by rapid population turnover. The agricultural colonies served as a way station for many Jewish immigrants who never planned to settle there in the first place, as well as for those who did not prosper as farmers. According to one estimate, some 50,000 Jews passed through the agricultural colonies of Argentina.[8] Many of them left the settlements for a new home in the country's developing urban centers. As a result, many farm families had relatives in the cities, who encouraged more of their members to move there. By the late 1890s, there were active "out-migration chains" from the settlements to the major towns, involving both singles and families. These chains led directly to the emergence and expansion of the Jewish communities all over Argentina, and notably in Buenos Aires, Rosario, Santa Fe, Córdoba, La Plata, Tucumán, Mendoza, Concordia, and Paraná.[9]

Alongside the organized and official immigration under the auspices of the ICA, the 1890s saw a significant stream of Jewish urban immigrants who arrived on their own; most of them settled in Buenos Aires. The majority were from eastern Europe, mainly Russia and Galicia, with a substantial minority from Romania.[10] Jews of Oriental descent also came to Argentina: from Morocco (mainly Tangiers), Gibraltar, and Tetuán; from Syria and Lebanon (mainly Aleppo and Damascus); from Turkey (Rhodes and Saloniki); from the Balkans; and a few who left Ottoman Palestine. At first, these groups immigrated in modest numbers, but during the first two decades of the twentieth century their number grew, fed mainly by those fleeing the districts scarred by the tumultuous events in the Ottoman Empire in those years.[11]

The wave of immigration to the Americas, especially by Jews, was renewed at the end of World War I. Almost a million and a half immigrants came to Argentina between the two world wars. For Jews, Argentina became an important destination during the 1920s. Jewish immigration to Argentina during that decade averaged 7,520 a year, most of them from the new countries established after World War I (chiefly Poland and Lithuania). There were also many Jews among the immigrants from Syria and North Africa: about half of all Turkish and Syrian immigrants counted in the Argentinian 1960 census who arrived in those years, as well as a quarter of the immigrants from Italy, the Balkan states, and Africa. Argentina was the third-most-important destination for Jewish migrants in the 1920s, after the United States and Palestine.[12]

Despite the limits on immigration imposed by Argentina in the 1930s and 1940s, more than 40,000 Jews entered the country then. These waves produced an additional sector, comprised of German-speaking Jews from central Europe.[13] After the Holocaust, survivors arrived in modest numbers, mainly to be reunited with relatives already living in Argentina, and despite the obstacles posed by the country's strict immigration rules.[14] The Sinai Campaign and the Hungarian Revolution, both in the autumn of 1956, stimulated Jews from Egypt and Hungary to flee to Argentina. The nationalist revolutions in North Africa brought Spanish- and French-speaking Jews to Argentina in the late 1950s and early 1960s. After this, however, Jewish immigration to Argentina effectively came to an end.[15] Moreover, this is when Jews began leaving Argentina for other countries.

This survey of the history of Jewish immigration to Argentina makes it clear that ethnic diversity is one of Argentinian Jewry's most prominent characteristics. From the very beginning, the community comprised members of various Jewish ethnicities, from different countries, reflecting the entire Jewish spectrum. As I will show, this exerted a major influence on diverse areas of Jewish life in Argentina. It also bears mention that the dominance of eastern European Jews (more than 80%) made that group the central player in the Argentinian Jewish arena. Its original core consisted of the Jewish farmers who settled in the pampas in an organized manner. This unique historical fact had many implications for the consolidation and development of the Jewish community in Argentina.

The settlers' stories were fashioned into a foundation myth and were used to educate the second and third generations of Argentinian Jewry. They were especially important for the immigrants and/or native born who abandoned the Jewish colonies for the cities. The exceptional forms of socialization and the communal lifestyle in the colonies left their mark on the Jews who lived there. Even though the experience of the Argentinian frontier was quite traumatic for some of them, most continued to feel a spiritual charge and showed a distinct inclination toward public involvement.[16] As a result, for many Jews Argentina was more than just the land to which they had chosen to immigrate; many Jews took its landscapes and history to heart as a major element of their collective identity. This fact is clearly reflected in the memoir literature of the Jewish settlers in the Argentina. "Brothers! The Land of Israel will be here," wrote Mordechai Alperson, one of the founders of Colonia Mauricio, in the 1920s.[17] This utopian element extended beyond the boundaries of the rural settlements and doubtless influenced the cooperative and communal nature of the urban Jewish communities as well.

The Sociodemography of Argentinian Jewry

The national census of 1947, which was the first to include a question about religion, yielded an estimate of a quarter of a million Jews in Argentina. Those who took a close interest in the number of Jews in the country rejected this figure, asserting that many Jews had reported they had "no religion" and chose to conceal or avoid stating their religion. The results of the census were also at variance with the higher estimates by local institutions and by leading scholars in the field of Jewish migration, including Jacob Lestschinsky and Arieh Tartakower.[18] In the early 1960s, Ira Rosenwaike rechecked and corrected these estimates and drew a plot of the growth of the Jewish population of Argentina from the beginnings until 1947. Rosenwaike's findings refuted his predecessors' exaggerated numbers and showed that the results of the 1947 census were not far off. Rosenwaike concluded that the Jewish population in Argentina before the establishment of Israel was 265,000 to 275,000.[19]

The next national census in Argentina, in 1960, also asked about the respondents' religion. It identified approximately 276,000 Jews in Argentina, age five and up. This time, too, the findings provoked controversy among scholars; the same skepticism about the data was voiced again, especially by the leaders of the community. This time, however, it was decided to overcome the deficiencies; in 1961, the Buenos Aires Jewish Community (AMIA, Asociación Mutual Israelita Argentina) established a department for social research, which began methodical statistical tracking of Argentinian Jewish demographics.[20] Two Israeli demographers, Sergio DellaPergola and Uziel Schmelz, reviewed the data in the early 1970s and came up with an estimate of 286,000 Jews in Argentina in 1948.[21] By cross-checking the results of the 1960 census against the records of marriages and deaths kept by AMIA's Social Research Department in the early 1960s, they reached a figure of 310,000 Jews living in Argentina in the 1960s.[22]

These findings sharpened the debate between demographers and historians about the number of Jews in the country. The controversy itself is not relevant to our discussion, but it is important to note that the disparity between the figures computed by the two scholars and the estimates by local and international groups (including the American Jewish Yearbook) increased in the 1960s. According to local and international estimates, there were 400,000 Jews in Argentina in 1960, and over the course of the decade the community grew to half a million.[23] Here it is worth noting that most of the primary sources I consulted and various knowledgeable individuals, including the emissaries of Jewish and Zionist organizations, diplomats, community activists, local leaders, and Argentinian immigrants to Israel, relied on the same inflated estimates that, as the scholars had demonstrated, were overblown and had no basis in fact.

The exaggerated estimates camouflaged the decisive turning point in Jewish migration to and from Argentina in the late 1950s and early 1960s. As can be seen in figure 1, the Jewish population of Argentina grew significantly until the early 1960s, but its numbers had begun to decline by 1970. The sharp decrease that begin during that decade reflects a demographic contraction with several causes, including the significant drop in Jewish immigration to Argentina in the 1950s and the fact that Jews began emigrating in the 1960s in large numbers, with many of them going to Israel.[24]

According to current estimates, there was negligible Jewish emigration from Argentina before the 1960s, and only a trickle to Israel: fewer than 5,500 Argentinian Jews immigrated to Israel between 1948 and 1960 (slightly less than 500 a year). The scope of Jewish emigration from Argentina increased in the 1960s, including more than 14,000 who came to Israel.[25] From a research perspective, the lack of additional statistical information about Jewish emigration from Argentina to places other than Israel is sorely felt, because it would provide the basis for interesting comparisons. Nevertheless, the primary sources I studied clearly demonstrate what was going on. Yehoshua Wolberg, a senior official of

Figure 1: The Jewish population of Argentina, 1900–1970

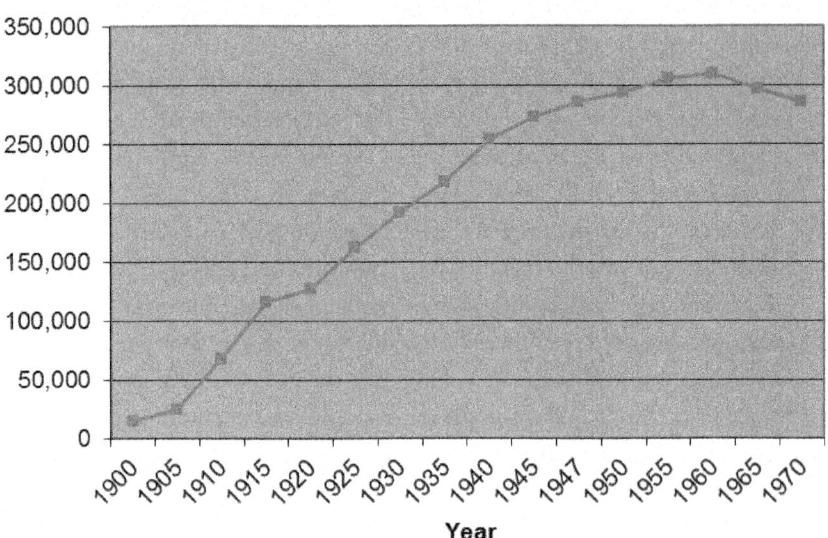

Source: Sergio DellaPergola, "Demographic Trends of Latin American Jewry," in *The Jewish Presence in Latin America*, ed. Judith Laikin Elkin and Gilbert W. Merkx (Boston: Allen and Unwin, 1987), 92.

the Jewish Agency Aliyah Department in Jerusalem and director of its Latin American desk, prepared a comprehensive report when he returned to Israel from Argentina in October 1963. He noted the increasing emigration of "Argentinian Italians returning to their homeland," which he saw as analogous to the departure by Jews.[26] With regard to the latter, Wolberg added as follows:

> According to information I received, every month approximately 2,000 Argentinian citizens file requests for immigrant visas to the United States. About 1,200 of them are granted. Slightly less than a third, or 350 of them, are Jews. Jewish emigration to Brazil has also just begun, but I have not yet had time to determine its scope.[27]

According to unofficial data in an Aliya Department file, 13,000 engineers, physicians, and university professors left Argentina for the United States in 1964, among them 3,000 Jews, most of whom had relatives in the States.[28] In October 1965, Wolberg drafted another document in which he emphasized that, as of that date, the number of Jewish emigrants from Argentina to the United States exceeded the number of those who chose Israel as their destination.[29]

The data presented above point to the fact that emigration from Argentina during the 1960s was substantial not only among Jews, although Jews were represented disproportionately to their percentage of the general population. According to academic studies of the subject, emigration from Argentina increased in that decade, mainly to other countries in Latin America but also to the United States.[30] According to one estimate, around 94,000 Argentinians were living outside their country in 1960—more than 60% in Latin countries and 40% in the United States. Only a decade later, in 1970, in excess of 183,000 Argentinians were living outside Argentina.[31] On the assumption that the data in the primary sources are credible, a realistic estimate of the total number of Jewish emigrants from Argentina in the 1960s would be around 40,000. Another matter that warrants further discussion is the question of ethnicity and homeland and relates to Wolberg's understanding of Argentinian Jewish immigration to Israel: Argentinian Jews may return to their homeland as similarly and naturally as Argentinians of Italian ancestry return to theirs. This outlook corresponds with the view of Argentinian Jewry as an "ethno-national dispersion" and as "ethnic migrants" when they move elsewhere.

As noted, the waves of immigrants who came to Argentina were the main reason for its explosive population growth. The immigrants also made a decisive contribution to the geographical distribution of the population. Most of them—more than 80%—settled in the Humid Pampa, the region that includes the provinces of Buenos Aires, Entre Ríos, Santa Fe, Córdoba, and La Pampa. As can be seen from table 1, the pattern of Jewish settlement in the late nineteenth century was similar to that of the population as a whole. This is because during those years, agricultural settlement played a key role in the absorption of Jewish immigrants.

Table 1. Geographic distribution of Jews in Argentina, 1895–1960

Year	Absolute number*	Place of residence, percent		
		Buenos Aires (city)	Buenos Aires Province	Other provinces
1895	6,085	12.4	11.0	76.6
1947	249,326	66.7	13.1	20.2
1960	291,877	66.4	17.1	16.5

Source: U. O. Schmelz and Sergio DellaPergola, *The Structure of Latin American Jewry: The Demography of the Jews in Argentina and Other Countries in Latin America* (Tel Aviv: David Horowitz Institute for the Study of Developing Countries, Tel Aviv University, 1974), 148.

*The data are based on the national censuses of 1895, 1947, and 1960.

Later, though, the Jews tended to stay in Buenos Aires; by 1947, two-thirds of them lived there. In that year, according to the census, there was a Jewish presence in fifty-one provincial cities, small towns, and rural settlements, in addition to the dozens of farming communities in the traditional districts of Jewish settlement.[32] In 1960, Argentinian Jewry was overwhelmingly urban. Only a small fraction still lived in the rural sector, although more than a quarter of the population as a whole did so. Of the 291,877 Jews counted in the census, 231,955 (79.5%) were living in greater Buenos Aires—as against the 34% of the population as a whole.[33] In 1960, Jews made up 6.5% of the population of the city itself and 1% of its suburbs—overall, 3.4% of the metropolitan area.[34] That year there were also significant concentrations of Jews in Entre Ríos (3%), Santa Fe (5.1%), and Córdoba (3.1%) provinces. The other provinces were home to smaller numbers.[35]

From these statistics, it is clear that Argentinian Jewry experienced a major process of urbanization that began in its earliest days and had chosen to settle in the major urban centers, primarily Buenos Aires. In the 1960s, there were large communities in the main urban centers—Rosario, Córdoba, La Plata, Santa Fe, Tucumán, and Mendoza—and smaller communities in the capitals of the other provinces. However, even though there were organized Jewish communities in more than 120 localities in the 1960s, the geographic dispersion of Argentinian Jewry was quite limited. It was concentrated in Buenos Aires, quite unlike the pattern of the general population. It is important to add that the geographic concentration of Argentinian Jewry left most Argentinians with a mistaken impression of the Jewish presence in the country, which they thought to be significantly larger than the actual figure of 1.5%.

The number of Jewish immigrants to Argentina and the immigrants' geographic concentration generated far-reaching economic changes. Because of their urbanization and concentration in the main cities, notably Buenos Aires, most Jewish immigrants engaged in various skilled trades and commerce. From the outset, the Jews in Argentina joined the urban proletariat and lower middle class as skilled tradesmen, laborers, and peddlers who sold on the installment plan. A large proportion of the immigrants, who had been employed in petty commerce in their countries of origin, returned to this occupation. A peddler who managed to amass an adequate sum usually opened his own business and often became a supplier to other peddlers. Skilled tradesmen, too, pursued economic independence and stability; many of them advanced from small workshops to small factories that employed new immigrants.[36]

From the beginning of the Jewish presence in Argentina there was a marked process of deproletarization. The process was well under way in the early 1930s but picked up steam during and after World War II. During the war, Argentinian Jewry achieved greater economic security thanks to the general industrialization of the country. This process accelerated after the war, during the regime of General Juan Perón, and had a strong effect on the Jews. The Peronist regime's centralized economic policy and protectionism stimulated a vast expansion of local industry and the domestic market. The Jews' economic base improved drastically, and many of them moved upward into more lucrative and prestigious fields and occupations; a large number opted for the liberal professions. This process, together with the end of Jewish immigration, led to a decrease in the number of Jewish laborers; the few Jewish immigrants who arrived from Central Europe in those years naturally went into middle-class occupations.[37] The reverberations of these changes are evident in a memo on South American Jewry submitted to Israeli prime minister David Ben-Gurion in late 1952.

> The processes of proletarization, which existed only in Argentina (in 1917–1932) and Uruguay (in 1925–1935), ended long ago, and the transition to middleman occupations of all kinds was rapid and comprehensive. Only in Buenos Aires are there still Jewish laborers in various field[s]—between 20,000 and 52,000 (out of a total Jewish population of about 200,000). Peddling, the main livelihood of Jewish immigrants throughout the continent, has died out, too, after playing its part in the local economy. The Jews have moved into commerce, industry, and the liberal professions. In commerce and banking, there are quite a few paper-pushers; but there are not many in industry: the most "proletarian" category is that of owners of workshops and small factories. There is no specifically Jewish economy. The penetration into the crevices of the local economy has ended. A large stratum of native-born merchants and industrialists has emerged and is fusing with broad circles of the Spanish, Italian, and even German immigrants who engage in the same occupations.[38]

The data of the 1960 census make the deproletarization of Argentinian Jewry even more conspicuous. They show that the Jews of Argentina enjoyed socioeconomic mobility and had advanced from the proletariat to the middle and upper middle class. In 1960, two-thirds of all employed Jews were working in commerce, light industry, clerical positions, and the liberal professions—the white-collar fields typical of the middle class. The petty commerce and skilled trades that had been dominant in the past receded in the wake of the economic boom that promoted Jews to the status of merchants and industrialists. The Jewish presence was mostly felt in the wholesale and retail trade in clothing, footwear, textiles, leather goods, and furs as well as furniture. In these sectors, Jews became producers and factory owners. There was also a prominent Jewish presence in the liberal professions, notably medicine and engineering.[39]

In light of these data, scholars have placed special emphasis of the deproletarization of the Jews and their successful integration into the Argentinian economy. But one cannot ignore the fact that nearly 25% of the Jewish workforce in the 1960s belonged to what might be called the manual laborer class—mainly traditional skilled tradesmen. This sector of Argentinian Jewry has hardly been studied. The interesting point that I will expand on later is that the main potential for Jewish migration from Argentina to Israel in those years rested with this group, composed of tens of thousands of Jewish artisans, a group that, unlike the overwhelming majority of Jews, was not upwardly mobile and had not managed to find its place in the Argentinian economy.

The Social Image of the Jews of Argentina

Even though most Argentinian Jews were not affiliated with the community, its formal organizations can be taken as an analytical unit to study the structural changes that took place during the Jews' integration into Argentinian society. In these changes, we can see the internal ideological dimension that was decisive for the construction of their collective identity. In other words, the institutions and organizations established by the Jews in Argentina reflect the way they saw themselves. I do not intend to offer a full exposition of the organizational system of Argentinian Jewry. My ambition is much more modest and extends only to an attempt to locate the main elements of the collective identity of the Jews in Argentina as expressed in this system.

The Jewish community organizations in Argentina coalesced in a country whose constitution promised equal rights for all citizens and residents but did not anchor the rights of its component ethnic groups as such, because it had adopted the social model of the melting pot (in Spanish, *crisol de razas*). Theoretically, such a society had no room for ethnic organizations recognized by law. But there were no legal restrictions on voluntary associations, so the various ethnic groups were able to maintain their unique identities and operate community institutions, funded by private sources and not the state budget. Thus, organized Argentinian Jewry was and continues to be based on voluntary associations whose content, goals, scope, and strength depend exclusively on the public forces that its leaders can inspire and mobilize. The Jewish organizations in Argentina were based on free and individual socialization and were recognized as mutual assistance organizations, unlike the Jewish communities in eastern and central Europe before World War II, where the community organization (the kehillah) was anchored in law, and the Jews were recognized as an ethnic minority.[40]

The community organizations of Jews in Argentina started out as Landsmannschaften (associations of people from the same town, district, or province), in which immigrants from the same place in the Old Country congregated and socialized. When they arrived in the New World, the immigrants naturally looked for a common element that could unite them on the basis of language, culture, and traditions. Shared geographical origin created the infrastructure needed to express solidarity. The community institutions dealt with a broad variety of topics; in particular, they helped immigrants in their first stages of absorption and provided assistance to the needy. They also established the frameworks required for maintaining Jewish cultural life and passing it on to the coming generations. The material comfort that the Jews enjoyed, especially after World War II, fostered an extensive and ramified mix of organizations that provided services in various domains and comprised hundreds of political, economic, social, cultural, and religious associations, both in the capital and in the cities of the interior.[41] Little by little, this broad spectrum of institutions found its place in the traditional community structure, in keeping with the patterns the Jews had brought from their countries of origin but modified to suit the new situation. Eventually these led to an umbrella organization that incorporated the various institutions and groups that provided services in the fields of welfare, health, religion, education, security, political representation, and more.

Within the organized Jewish community in Argentina, it is common to distinguish two large sectors that coalesced separately, as a function of the cultural and social differences that set them apart from each other: the Ashkenazim (from central and eastern Europe) and the Sephardim. Among the latter, there were also internal divisions by country of origin: those originally from Morocco and North Africa, those from Syria (mainly Aleppo and Damascus), and the immigrants from Turkey and the Balkans. Each group organized separately and saw to its own needs with regard to religious services, education, and welfare. The separation and division between the Ashkenazi and Sephardi sectors derived from their significantly different worldviews. Whereas Sephardi communities highlighted the religious element of their Jewish identity and built their institutions accordingly, the organized Ashkenazi sector cultivated a secular cultural approach.[42]

Eastern European Jews, who made up the vast majority of Argentinian Jewry, established dozens of Landsmannschaften. These fulfilled their members' needs in two main channels: first and foremost, they served as philanthropic agencies that supplied welfare services and guaranteed basic subsistence, but they also satisfied the cultural and ideological needs related to the spiritual ideas that the Jews brought with them from the Old Country. This found expression in the emergence of multifarious political, cultural, economic, and educational organizations. The Landsmannschaften did not establish community umbrella organizations because the Ashkenazi Burial Society, established in 1894, filled the traditional role of the kehillah. From the second decade of the twentieth century, this institution had a monopoly on burial services, which proved to be extremely profitable even in the largely secular Jewish society. As noted, this many-branched system of organizations was gradually incorporated into the traditional structure of a kehillah. The process picked up speed in the second half of the 1930s and reached its peak in 1949, when the Ashkenazi Burial Society was reconstituted as the Ashkenazi Community of Buenos Aires (known by the Spanish acronym AMIA). By this time, the organization included not only immigrants from eastern Europe but also those from Germany and central Europe and had become a central institution in the lives of Jews in Buenos Aires and in the entire country. AMIA was organized on a political basis, a fact that had many ramifications for Jewish public life in Argentina.[43]

A significant fraction of the Jewish Ashkenazi immigrants to Argentina were politically aware (mostly had a proletarian consciousness), with a tradition of partisan activity in various factions—Jewish and non-Jewish, Zionist and non-Zionist. There was also a stratum of intellectuals, Yiddish- or Russian-speaking, atheist and in fact antireligious, who wished to coalesce around the ideology they had supported in their countries of origin, according to the European organizational model. By the end of World War I there were strong core groups of revolutionary socialists, Bundists, anarchists, Territorialists, and Zionists. After the Russian Revolution, and particularly during the 1920s, the Communists, too, enlarged their ranks. These groups' ambitions gave rise to extensive partisan political projects in the form of cultural organizations, libraries, and schools. The parties soon became the dominant factor in the Argentinian Jewish street, inasmuch as they competed for support in the main institutions of the Ashkenazi community, most of which were run on a democratic basis. These institutions became the main theater in which the parties contended for influence and control, both in the capital and in the cities of the interior.

The partisan system seems to have been the latent source of Argentinian Jewry's political power. Aside from control of the organized community in Buenos Aires and in the provincial cities, party representatives held senior positions in the other economic, cultural, and educational organizations and institutions, and even in the DAIA (the representative umbrella organization established to combat anti-Semitism). As a result, there was a fierce struggle to "conquer the community," which mainly pitted the Zionists against the Communists. Within the Zionist camp, too, there was a bitter struggle between the bourgeois Zionist Federation and the socialists. All those battles were waged in Argentina in the name of political ideologies and groupings whose centers were elsewhere—in eastern Europe, in Palestine, and in the United States. It was this political conflict that led to the conversion of the Burial Society into a community organization that provided extensive services going far beyond its traditional role, particularly in the fields of education and culture. The most important change in this context was the triumph of the Labor Zionist parties in the battle for control of the community, notably after the establishment of Israel.[44]

The political divisions among Argentinian Jewry were surprisingly similar to those that existed in the Yishuv in Mandatory Palestine and subsequently in Israel. All the Zionist parties in Argentina, including the Revisionists (and then Herut), as well as representatives of the Zionist Youth Confederation and of the Women's International Zionist Organization (WIZO), were affiliated with the Zionist Central Council (Consejo Central Sionista) of Argentina, a democratic umbrella organization founded in 1943. After the twenty-fourth Zionist Congress, held in Jerusalem in early 1956, and pursuant to its decision, the Zionist Central Council was reconstituted as the Argentinian Zionist Association (Organización Sionista Argentina or OSA). This body, like its predecessor, functioned as the local arm of the international Zionist movement and was the arena for activity by the various parties that represented Argentinian Jewry at the Zionist congresses and sessions of the Zionist General Council.[45]

The triumph of Labor Zionism in Argentina must also be understood against the background of the changes in the Jewish world as a whole, and in Argentinian Jewry in particular, during the Holocaust and the first years afterward, and with greater force following the establishment of Israel. The Jewish world after World War II was very different from that which preceded it. The horrifying results of the Nazi genocide of the Jews led to the physical and spiritual decline and weakening of European Jewry and the emergence of American

Jewry as the major force in the Jewish world. The undermining of Great Britain's status in the Middle East and its increasing dependence on the United States, mainly with regard to the future of Palestine, created a new political horizon for the leaders of the Yishuv and the Zionist movement, who operated in the shadow of the carnage of the Holocaust and the diktats of the White Paper, which placed draconian limitations on Jewish immigration to and land ownership in Palestine. This can be seen from an article published in the organ of one of the Zionist youth movements in Argentina after the elections for the twenty-second Zionist Congress (the first after the Holocaust), which met in Basel in December 1946.

> The tragic results of the Holocaust of European Jewry opened the eyes of many Jews. But there is no doubt that it was mainly the young people who felt the trauma caused by these events, particularly the events in Palestine. Jewish youth began to fulfill their moral obligation. Young people evinced an increasing desire to cultivate their national consciousness, which made itself felt especially during the elections. The young people participated actively and enthusiastically. . . . In the provinces, all the work was delegated to them. . . . They have proved their political maturity and are now beginning to sound their voice in the national life of the Jewish people. . . . The victory of the Labor Front strengthened the popular democratic nature of our community. This proves that the Jewish masses in Argentina, who identify with Zionism, are aware that the building of the Jewish national home was made possible only by the Jewish proletariat and that it was the workers' parties in Palestine and the General Federation of Labor that endowed the Yishuv with its social and national character.[46]

With these developments in the background, the Zionist idea provided a source of identification for the Jews of Argentina, an axis for organization and a focus of legitimacy. One manifestation of this can be seen in the fund-raising drive conducted in Argentina for the newborn State of Israel. The United Appeal for the Defense and Consolidation of the Jewish State, representing Keren Hayesod (the international fund-raising arm of the Zionist Organization), the Jewish National Fund (which acquired land in Palestine), and the Haganah (the Jewish self-defense organization in Palestine), was created in April 1948. To run the campaign, the Haganah sent a delegation to Argentina, headed by two prominent representatives of the agricultural settlements, Yaakov Uri and Haviv Zerubavel. This fund drive was a rousing success; all sectors of the Argentinian Jewry, including the anti-Zionist left, rallied to the cause and gave generously. The minimum contribution was set at 2% of one's capital or half a month's salary. The organizers' expectations were high, and the proceeds came to some forty million pesos (around $3.5 million).[47] "We eliminated voluntary donations, contributions, and the like, and levied a tax. We told the Jews: you must pay a tax of 2% of your assets to the State of Israel," recalled Yaakov Uri at a meeting of the Zionist General Council in late August 1948, and added: "We didn't visit the Jews in their homes. The people came to our offices and brought their balance sheets with them."[48]

The sum collected and Uri's remarks to the Zionist General Council reflected Argentinian Jewry's unreserved identification with the Jewish national struggle and give an idea of the relationship that prevailed between the national center in the Land of Israel and the Jewish diaspora in Argentina (even though it is hard to ignore Uri's patronizing attitude). Israel's central place in the collective identity of Argentinian Jews went far beyond the fiscal contribution and was reflected in various levels of their organizations; the educational, cultural, and political institutions; and the internal life of the community. Moreover, the Zionist and national component of the collective identity of the Jews of Argentina served as a nucleus of legitimacy vis-à-vis Argentinian society as a whole.

At this stage, we can identify another element that emerges from a case study of Argentinian Jewry: it is a Jewish community with a strong national and Zionist character. On the surface, we might expect this to have stimulated the Jews of Argentina to move to Israel en masse. But this did not happen. In fact, only a small minority chose to relocate to Israel between 1948 and the Six-Day War. The national and Zionist aspect of the collective identity of Argentinian Jews did not prevent them from displaying, prominently and in various ways, their affiliation with the Argentinian nation. In order to delve more deeply into this, in the next few pages I will focus on Jewish education, because this field constituted a central axis of the organized activity that determined the priorities of the Jewish community during the emergence of its collective identity, from its earliest years in Argentina.

The secular schools that were established on an ideological and political basis left their mark on the collective identity of Argentinian Jewry. The pioneers in this domain were from the Marxist-Zionist and Yiddishist Left Po'alei Zion party, which, in the early 1920s, established a chain of five schools for the children of laborers (Yiddish: arbeter shul'n) in the densely populated Jewish neighborhoods of Buenos Aires.[49] Their curriculum emphasized Yiddish culture. In early 1934, Po'alei Zion members established the Central Organization of Secular Yiddish Schools (Tzentral Veltlej Idishe Shul Organizatzie or TZVISHO). Its founding conference endorsed the principle of Jewish secular education and emphasized its humanistic character, which included the social and national themes found in Jewish literature and culture.[50] Under the auspices of TZVISHO, a network of four Scholem Aleijem schools was established in the Jewish neighborhoods of Buenos Aires.[51] Years later, Jaime Finkelstein, a TZVISHO stalwart, described the new path they charted:

> The nationalist and socialist sentiments that pervaded the new Jewish educational model in Eastern Europe influenced the new Jewish school in Argentina. The ambitions and hopes for the creation of a new world, a new Jew, served as a source of faith and inspiration, too. But not everything was the same. The social reality, the general culture, the Jewish cultural environment, and the living conditions were utterly different from those in Eastern Europe. So it was clear that the Jewish school on the new continent could not be a copy of the school in Poland and would have to find its way to preserve the original sound, which would blend harmoniously into the new Jewish education. I do not know whether, back then, any of us would have been able to clearly define the nature of this chord and how it was supposed to reverberate in the daily educational work. I know that we did not sit idle and that we poured a lot of feeling and energy into our search for new paths.[52]

The establishment of TZVISHO set off a fierce controversy in the Argentinian Jewish street. The Guezelschaft far Idishe Veltleje Shuln (the Secular Jewish Schools Association), founded by Bundists, refused to join the organization, asserting that a network of secular schools had been in existence since 1931 and there was no need for another one. The Guezelschaft operated one of the largest Jewish schools in Buenos Aires, the I. L. Peretz School. The Jewish Communists, too, had their own Méndele Mojer Sforim school network; accordingly, they too declined to participate in TZVISHO and maintained their separate educational activities. The official Zionist authorities, headed by the Zionist Central Council, which was controlled by the liberal General Zionist party, related to the whole matter with a certain degree of suspicion.[53] Regarding the rivalry among the ideological streams, Finkelstein added:

> In certain domains, Left Po'alei Zion and the Jewish Communists collaborated. However, our competition with them was very intense. The

> Zionist parties, such as the [bourgeois] Zionist Federation, Ze'irei Zion Youth, and even Right Po'alei Zion, ignored the Yevsektzia. They had no contact with it and went so far as to complain that we were becoming friendly with Communists. Our argument was different: Despite the sharp differences of opinion, we had common interests; in addition, a boycott did not strike us as an appropriate tool for ideological battles. The Yevsektzia fought against all streams of Zionism. But it saw us, Left Po'alei Zion, as a competitor. This was first of all because we were active in the same milieu of Jewish workers; and second, because we paraded ourselves in front of everyone as no less socialist than they were.[54]

The establishment of TZVISHO reflected the need, which was beginning to be felt in Argentina, for the Jews to unite and provide a supportive setting in which children could obtain an adequate knowledge of their Jewish heritage. This development, as Finkelstein noted, reflects the influence of the Old Country, but the goal, so it seems, was to reexamine Jewish identity in a context that was fundamentally different from that of eastern Europe. This explains how other ideological streams got involved in education. A prominent example is the founding of the Jaim Najman Bialik School as a Hebrew and Yiddish institution, with a bond to both modern Jewish nationalism and Jewish tradition. Another example is the establishment of the Escuela Integral Hebrea Natan Gesang, which integrated (hence the term "integral school") Jewish and general studies in a way similar to the North American Jewish day school. A similar trend was evident in the religious schools, which were under the authority of the Educational Committee of the Congregación Israelita de la República Argentina (CIRA—the first Jewish community organization in the country, founded in 1867). As a result of modernization, some of the latter abandoned the traditional model of the talmud torah (the Jewish elementary school of eastern Europe, which taught religious subjects almost exclusively) and turned into formal and progressive schools, with a greater emphasis on national and secular subjects in the curriculum. It is important to note that all these institutions depended financially on supporters and parents as well as on the savings funds and the credit cooperatives.[55]

Despite the ideological differences and controversies that swirled around education, the secular Jewish education system jelled in the 1940s and attracted more pupils. This change was also related to the increasing impact of another educational committee, founded in 1934 as part of the Burial Society in Buenos Aires.[56] From then on, the Burial Society's involvement in educational matters increased. The number of schools affiliated with this committee surged in the 1940s and included the left-wing Bundist and Communist educational organizations. Most of the institutions in this system were supplementary or parallel schools, as they were called in Argentina, which held classes in the afternoon or on weekends. This system offered a solution to the Jewish secular identity of most Argentinian Jews; its cultural-national alternative to the religious and traditional pattern did not contradict the sought-after integration into civil society and enabled the younger Jewish generation to see itself as legitimately both Argentinian and Jewish.[57]

The establishment of Israel generated an extremely significant change in Argentinian Jewry, which was soon reflected not only in the political dimension but also in the educational arena. Israel emerged as a new factor in the Jewish national identity; this led to a major change in the Jewish schools' climate and curricula.[58] Support for Israel became the common property of most Jews in Argentina; the new country's role as the exclusive center of Jewish national life was unchallenged. The domestic situation in the Peronist era pushed in the same direction, especially after the regime recognized Israel in early 1949. The relations between the countries were actually a problem, "precisely because of the [Peronist] regime's eagerness to demonstrate its support for Israel in public," wrote Jacob Tsur, Israel's first minister to Argentina, in his memoirs, and added:

> As time passed and the date for the opening of the legation in Buenos Aires grew closer, the picture clarified. President Perón tried to exploit his relations with Israel as a means to win the hearts of the Jews, first in Argentina, and then in the United States. . . . The emphasis on his sympathetic attitude towards the Jewish state was meant to cleanse his name and purge the stain of a fascist and antisemitic regime that had clung to him since the war. The diplomatic mission in Buenos Aires ostensibly had an open path before it, but to complicate matters, the president, as I feared, tried to carry out his plan by means of a sycophantic Jewish organization [the Organización Israelita Argentina or OIA], which the Jewish community was united in opposition to. So the legation had to try and walk between the drops: maintain good relationships with the president and his government but also not hurt the feelings of the organized Jewish community.[59]

"Whatever the reasons and motivations for this position—it is a great thing for Argentinian Jewry and South American Jewry as a whole," editorialized one

Tel Aviv newspaper about Argentina's recognition of Israel.[60] Indeed, it provided Argentinian Jewry with another source of legitimacy in the public sphere. This can be illustrated by a representative anecdote from Jacob Tsur's memoirs. When he arrived in Argentina in late July 1949, he was shocked by the intensity of the feelings that he aroused among Argentinian Jews and the crowd that welcomed him in Buenos Aires on that wintry day. A few days later, when he submitted his credentials, the Jewish community celebrated the great day. "Throngs of Jews waved the Israeli and Argentinian flags. . . . The excitement was indescribable."[61] The fact that the Jews of Argentina could wave the Israeli and Argentinian flags in public and at the same time, with no sense of contradiction or inferiority, amazed and impressed the diplomat.

It is no coincidence that the Burial Society was officially transmuted into a kehillah that year and reorganized as AMIA. Its centrality in Jewish public life has been substantial since then, along with its involvement in education. AMIA's importance was expressed in its attempts to unite the communities of all the cities, which was crowned with success in 1952 with the establishment of the national umbrella organization, the Council of Jewish Communities in Argentina. This federation of all the communities was intended to provide essential Jewish services more efficiently. At first, thirty-eight communities were affiliated with it. By the end of the decade, 104 communities had joined; and by the late 1960s the number had risen to 130. The establishment of the council triggered attempts to unite the network of CIRA schools in the provincial cities with that in the capital and its environs, which were overseen by the Buenos Aires community. The merger was completed in late 1956; since then, the Central Education Committee has served as the umbrella organization for all streams of Jewish education in Argentina, except for the Communist schools, which retained their independence. AMIA's central role in the Council of Communities and the Education Committee reflected the fact that, starting in the 1950s, it was the keystone of Jewish public life in Argentina. By that time, the entire Ashkenazi sector depended on it for financial support, welfare services, and other social needs that went far beyond the traditional activities of the original Burial Society, including Jewish education.[62]

The material well-being enjoyed by a large segment of the Jewish community in Argentina made its mark in the field of education: starting in the second half of the 1950s, the kehillah dedicated about half its revenues to purposes other than burial and welfare, including education, culture, and programs for youth. At this stage, AMIA covered about 40% of the expenses of the Central Education Committee schools and even opened and funded its own educational institutions: two teachers' colleges founded in the 1940s, one in Buenos Aires and the other in Moisés Ville. It also established the Hebrew College (Midrasha Ivrit) to train teachers for Jewish secondary schools.[63] An important change that influenced the content and scope of Jewish education came in the late 1960s, when the government lifted the restrictions on private degree-granting institutions, thereby opening the field of general education to private initiatives. Henceforth, the Jewish schools were private institutions. This change allowed groups that worked in Jewish education to refashion the complementary system into "integral" schools. However, this possibility was not completely realized until the late 1960s, when a fundamental reform in the government education system pushed the balance toward integral Jewish education in schools subject to oversight by the authorities and with partial funding from them.[64]

The investment in the Jewish education system paid off and was reflected in a steady rise in enrollment. In 1942, there were only 6,300 pupils in Jewish schools throughout the country; the number grew to 8,500 in 1950 and surpassed the 15,000 mark in 1957. According to a detailed report drawn up in Argentina at the start of the 1963 school year and submitted to Zalman Shazar, who was then head of the Department of Education and Culture in the Diaspora at the Jewish Agency, there were 125 Jewish schools in Buenos Aires alone (at the preschool, elementary, and secondary levels), with a total enrollment of nearly 15,000 children. According to the same report, there were another ninety-two schools in the provinces, with more than 4,000 students. Close to 300 students were enrolled in the Teachers' College in Buenos Aires, and another 200 in the Center for Jewish Studies in Moisés Ville.[65] In the words of the report to Shazar, "the Jewish education network in Argentina has grown and become more stable in recent years. Its public prestige has increased, the caliber of its teachers has risen, and young and dynamic forces have joined the ranks. Everyone ranks education as one of the main priorities of Jewish public life in the country." However, the data collected in advance of the report pointed to a major problem that was facing the education system in the early 1960s: fewer than 20% of all Jewish children were involved in formal Jewish education.[66]

In other words, the vast majority of Argentinian Jews did not attend Jewish schools of any sort. The mode of education adopted by the Jews in Argentina during the period covered in this study was that of supplementary (afternoon and Sunday) schools. It should not be forgotten that in the early 1960s, most Argentinian Jews below age forty-five had been born in the country and educated in its public schools. As is clear from the research by Schmelz and DellaPergola, a large percentage of the Jews had a secondary education; a growing number, particularly among those younger than forty-five, had earned a university degree.[67] This had immediate ramifications for the collective identity of Argentinian Jewry. By the time of the 1960 census, Argentinian Jews were more similar to the general population than to their immigrant parents.

A majority of the Jews saw Argentina as their homeland and country and not as one possible destination for immigration, "a host country" for "temporary residents." This element in the collective identity of the Jews in Argentina was no less prominent than the national and Zionist element. They saw no contradiction between their unqualified identification with the State of Israel and their affiliation with the Argentinian nation. According to a prominent figure in Córdoba in the 1950s and 1960s, "one cannot be a Zionist and turn one's back on Judaism, and one cannot be a Jew and remain apathetic to the Zionist ideology." He maintained that Jews should wage a persistent and honorable battle in professional life, in business, in industry, in the economy, in education, and in the arts so they could respect Jewish and Zionist ideals. In his words, "only this way can we be Jews; only this way can we be free; only this way can we be Argentinians."[68]

I will conclude this chapter by quoting from the autobiography of Dr. Carlos Meirovich, also of Córdoba and the grandson of one of the earliest settlers in the pampas.[69] To understand his motives for staying in Argentina, when his fellow scientists had no qualms about emigrating in search of better professional opportunities, he begins that work with a description of his life, including his family's collective biography. Meirovich is certain that the key to his personal identity is to be found in this journey to his roots and memories; this is the source of his desire and impulse to document his family's history. An intellectual, physician, and capable scientist, a Jew, but first and foremost an Argentinian, he wrote as follows:

> I think that Argentina is the beloved daughter of Israel, my distant motherland. I see no contradiction between my being Argentinian and my being Jewish. On the contrary, I believe that the two elements complement and enrich each other. Once, someone asked me if I would feel more Jewish, or a better Jew, if I emigrated to Israel. My response was that I probably would not. Being a Jew involves a process of internal construction that is not significantly dependent on the physical environment, but on an endogenous force that drives it. Is there a contradiction between being Argentinian and a Zionist at the same time? The answer, again, is no. Zionism is, first and foremost, a spiritual dimension. Every Argentinian can be a Zionist, both Jews and non-Jews. The

> antisemites should make no mistake: like many other Jews, I feel tremendous love for my homeland, for my country—Argentina; and at the same time I feel that everything that happens to the Jewish people, its suffering and its achievements, is happening to me. . . . I see Argentina as my homeland and Israel as the mother of my homeland.[70]

In theoretical terms, this is a model of identity that resembles the American hyphenated-identity paradigm.[71] But unlike the case of American Jewry, which emphasizes the religious element, Argentinian Jewry highlights the ethnic, cultural, civic, national, and supranational elements. Religious apathy and a lack of a strong religious awareness characterize the Jews in Argentina, most of whom moved away from religion and some of whom even opposed it actively. In the period discussed here, Argentinian Jewry presents a version of secular Judaism that has strong cultural and ethno-national characteristics. This model undermines the classic Zionist dichotomous assumption that Diaspora Jews have only two options in their "host" countries: total assimilation, on the one hand, or separatism and ghettoization, on the other hand. The case of Argentinian Jewry proves that there are other alternatives. On the basis of the short survey and data presented above, we may conclude that here we have a Jewish community that integrated but did not assimilate. Moreover, the majority of Argentinian Jews did not isolate themselves in a Jewish ghetto but found their place in the society around them while maintaining and reformulating their specific Jewish identity.

2

The Pintele Yid and the Economic Calculation

The Factors behind Argentinian Jewish Immigration to Israel in the 1950s and 1960s

The Motives for Argentinian Jewish Immigration to Israel in the Perón Era

The documents I collected include profound analyses of the economic, social, and political situation in Argentina and its impact on its Jews, especially on those who were inclined to immigrate to Israel at various times. Soon after he took up his post in October 1949, Jacob Tsur, the first Israeli minister to the country, drafted a comprehensive report on the possibilities of organizing large-scale aliya from Argentina and other countries of South America.[1] Tsur wrote to the Foreign Ministry that there seemed to be good prospects for emigration from Argentina at the moment. Although Argentinian Jews felt a bond to their homeland, its language, and its culture, he did not believe these ties were as strong as the identity of American or French Jews, for example; hence, they would find it easier to adapt to the conditions of life in Israel than immigrants from the other "tranquil" countries, as he called them.[2] He asserted that the Jews in Argentina were pervaded by a sense of insecurity and feared that anti-Semitism would come to rule the country; as a result, they spoke about leaving the country as a real possibility. But "this has not yet taken the form of a mass movement," Tsur stated, and added:

> It must be remembered that despite the monetary crisis, things have not reached the point here where people have to run away. The Jews

> lead a fairly comfortable life and are not willing, in today's conditions, to uproot themselves from their homes and go to meet the unknown, merely out of a yearning and love for the Land of Israel. The time may come when a regime of antisemitic persecution comes to power in Argentina; there is no lack of signs of this. But it can be said that large-scale aliya would be more valuable to us now than at a time when those Jews would come to us naked and bereft of everything, fleeing persecution.[3]

Like Tsur, Moshe Kitron believed that processes and events in Argentina would compel the Jews to look for a safer and more permanent refuge.[4] As a boy, Kitron (born Kostrinsky) immigrated to Argentina from Pinsk in 1927. For the next twenty-two years, until his aliya in 1949, he devoted his life to political activities on behalf of the Po'alei Zion Party and was one of the most prominent socialists in Argentina in the 1930s and 1940s. Although Kitron's political career in Israel, where he became the most prominent representative of the Latin American immigrants, played out in Mapai (the socialist party led by David Ben-Gurion that was the center of all Israeli governments until 1977), he continued to be deeply involved in issues related to South America, including the treatment and absorption of immigrants from that continent. Hundreds of letters, articles, and reports preserved among his personal papers reflect his assessments and opinions about the economic, social, and political situation in Argentina and its impact on Jewish immigration to Israel.[5]

On board the SS *Santa Cruz* en route to Israel in July 1949, Kitron wrote a sort of farewell note to Argentina. "For two decades, I have learned to know and love the Latin American continent," Kitron confessed, while attempting to explain his reasons for relocating to Israel.[6] He reached the conclusion that there was no contradiction between his sincere and warm fondness for Argentina and his aliya; in keeping with Jewish tradition, he affirmed, he had loyally and honorably fulfilled his civic duties to Argentina. Nevertheless, he knew that the Jews were not one of the ethnic or cultural building blocks of the new nations of South America.[7]

On the basis of his experience, but mostly on the basis of the data he collected over the years, Kitron assessed the prospects for Argentinian Jewish immigration to Israel. In his opinion, the Jews of that country, in many ways and for various historical, political, and economic reasons, constituted the main pool for voluntary immigration just then. There were good prospects for substantial Jewish immigration to Israel, for three main reasons:

1. The national and ideological reason: In his texts, Kitron portrayed a largely Zionist Diaspora with a strong attachment to the State of Israel.[8] "This is perhaps the only sector in the world where the feeling of Jewish nationalism and Zionist sentiment are so strong as to be motives for aliya," he wrote in a June 1953 report to Yitzhak Rafael, the head of the Aliya Department in Jerusalem.[9]
2. The economic reason: The deproletarization of Argentinian Jewry reached its peak in the early 1950s. Many Argentinian Jews enjoyed a high standard of living. They had penetrated commerce, industry, and the clerical and liberal professions. "The most 'proletarian' stratum consists of the owners of workshops and small factories," he wrote.[10] Kitron saw this class as embodying the main potential for immigration to Israel.
3. The political and social reason: Argentinian law recognized and protected the Jews as equal citizens, but unlike the case of the United States, the melting pot in Argentina was not the result of historical forces but of clear and deliberate efforts by the authorities. Although the Jews in Argentina were immersed in the local language and culture, they refused to fully assimilate into its society. Kitron believed that the fact that they held on to their Jewish national identity caused those in the majority society to view them as foreigners.[11]

The assessments by Kitron and Tsur are products of their Borochovist (Marxist Zionist) worldview, a rigid determinism that saw the Jewish condition in the Diaspora as a temporary situation marked by alienation and rejection by the host society and foredoomed to a catastrophic end. They saw the Jews in Argentina as an ethnic and cultural minority that was not fully integrated into the majority society. As such, the Jews were sitting on the edge of a volcano that was liable to erupt at any moment. In their perspective, the Jews' concentration in nonproductive occupations and minimal presence in productive endeavors was a classic result of the "national competition," which inverted the pyramid in Argentina, too.[12] It is important to note that this perspective was very common in Zionist thought, among Israelis (especially socialist circles) as well as Argentinian Jews.

Nor should we detach Tsur's and Kitron's appraisals from the macro political background in Argentina. Starting in the late nineteenth century, three main factors produced dramatic changes in various domains of Argentinian society: mass immigration, secular education, and economic policy. The extremely large-scale immigration to Argentina was fed by the country's desire to become a full-fledged member of the international economic system. Given its traditional economic structure and demographics, this ambition compelled Argentina to look for capital and manpower in Europe. From the late nineteenth century through 1930, almost 3.5 million people—most of them from Spain and Italy—immigrated to Argentina with the active encouragement of its government. To help lay the groundwork for absorbing the horde of newcomers, a series of liberal and secular statutes were enacted that mandated equality before the law for all citizens and residents; these laws included the General Common Education Act of 1884 (Law 1420), which mandated compulsory, free, and secular state-funded education for all children age six to fourteen. It was one of the most progressive education statutes in the world at the time.[13]

The issues of mass immigration and secular education stirred up a stormy debate between the ideological currents that coalesced in those years with regard to the components of Argentinidad ("Argentinism"). One current believed that the Catholic religion was the core of the national identity: because it was impossible to separate the Argentinian national identity from the Catholic religious identity, state and society had to be erected on this spiritual foundation. This axiom ipso facto turned non-Catholics into a foreign element that could not be an equal partner in the nation. Another and more prominent ideological stream welcomed the non-Catholic immigrants with open arms, in the expectation that they would alter the demographic balance and populate the towns of the interior, but without doing damage to the existing ethnic and cultural foundations. This current assumed that the immigrants would abandon their unique cultural identifiers and fully integrate into the majority society, thereby helping to create the "new Argentinian" (the melting pot).[14]

Argentinian nationalism grew and blossomed from this complex ideology, which takes "Argentinian" and "Catholic" to be synonymous, even while liberal concepts are incorporated as well.[15] These ideas also pervaded the regime, especially after the military coup of September 1930 launched a neoconservative restoration that continued for over a decade. After that, nationalist, military, and civilian circles organized repeatedly to overthrow the government. In this situation, the armed forces and the Church frequently interfered in politics and encouraged ultranationalist elements, some of them with an anti-Semitic outlook, to seize control of the executive branch.[16]

The ultranationalists stepped up their activities in the 1930s and 1940s. They saw democracy as a weak form of government and looked forward to the establishment of a strong fascist state—an alternative that enjoyed widespread support in those years, and not only in Argentina. For those groups, the Jews of

Argentina were an incendiary and revolutionary element. This notion became rooted in various sectors of Argentinian society in general and sometimes made itself felt in government institutions as well. For example, the interior minister in the first military government, Matías Sánchez Sorondo, who was affiliated with an ultranationalist anti-Semitic group, appointed Colonel Juan Bautista Molina, a prominent anti-Semite and one of the founders of the fascist Argentine Civic Legion, as his deputy. The appointment of the anti-Semitic author Hugo Wast as director of the National Library and later to other posts in the military government made anti-Semitism even more pervasive in the regime. Wast's rabidly anti-Jewish novels, *El Kahal* and *Oro*, both published in 1935, helped entrench the Protocols of the Elders of Zion in Argentinian civil society.[17]

Harsh manifestations of official anti-Semitism came to the fore after another military coup in early June 1943, whose leaders included Colonel Juan Domingo Perón. The military government prohibited kosher slaughter in areas populated by Jews and tried to ban the use of Yiddish in public. The interior minister ordered the closure of Yiddish newspapers, and Jewish teachers were fired. That December, an Education Ministry decree made religion a compulsory subject in all government schools.[18] Two months before that, Perón was appointed head of the Labor Bureau, in which post he introduced far-reaching changes in the regime and in Argentinian society. He quickly asserted his control of the labor unions and cultivated their political support. This action paid off when he won a landslide victory in the presidential election in early 1946, thanks to the support of the working masses, for whom Perón symbolized the promise and hope of economic and social reforms.

Perón ran the country for the next decade. He began by instituting a centralized socioeconomic policy, statist in nature, aimed at the expansion of Argentinian industry. The government nationalized the railroads and electric utilities and established and developed a merchant marine and civilian aviation authority. The goal was a fully laissez-faire economy, even if this required huge outlays and an increase in the domestic national debt. In the political arena, Perón continued to cultivate the growing urban proletariat, his main political base, by means of benefits and grants. He curried favor with other circles, especially the Catholic Church, by means of various sops, mainly in the domain of education. Perón also kept his finger in the armed forces pie, altering the composition of its senior echelons so as to guarantee the loyalty of the strongest and most influential element in the country.[19]

Despite these achievements, Perón's regime faced increasing opposition over the years. The compensation paid to nationalize foreign economic concessions depleted the foreign currency reserves and emptied the Treasury. As a result, the national debt skyrocketed, and foreign trade plummeted; during Perón's first term, the peso fell from five to thirty-five to the dollar.[20] His authoritarian tendencies, too, stirred up resistance. The core of the opposition came from the expanding middle class, to which most of the Jews belonged. This is the background for Kitron's assessment of the economic situation in Argentina and its impact on the Jewish community. In a memorandum drafted for Prime Minister David Ben-Gurion in 1952, he wrote that the Perón regime's economic policies had failed.[21] The intensifying economic crisis in Argentina was liable to undermine the Jews' economic situation and might even lead to political ferment accompanied by anti-Semitic manifestations:

> This has long been my assessment. . . . My assumption was that we should not absolutely rule out the actuality of the dangers, but there are no signs that they will be realized in the foreseeable future. . . . By contrast, I know from letters and from conversations with olim and tourists that the feeling of the local community leaders themselves has certainly changed. In the past, they vigorously rejected my appraisal of the situation. Today, they are showing great anxiety. The economic crisis keeps spreading and hurting the Jews grievously. Most of them are still well off and maintain a high standard of living. But the prospects for the future give grounds for concern. . . . I cannot draw unambiguous conclusions from these descriptions. Perhaps the wave will pass, and South American Jews can still anticipate a period, of lesser or greater duration, of a fat and tranquil exile—but a rapid deterioration is also possible.[22]

The Perón regime vigorously curbed the anti-Semitic currents and protected the Jews' legal status.[23] This is corroborated by the findings of scholars who have studied anti-Semitism in Argentina during the Perón era. After the wave of anti-Semitism in October–November 1945, there was a clear and consistent decrease in the scale of anti-Semitic incidents as long as Perón was in office.[24] Kitron's take on this was colored by his worldview. In an article published in October 1951, he predicted that "in the case of a serious shock, the Jews will be the first victims of the outbreak, which will certainly be accompanied by acts of violence."[25]

Despite Perón's authoritarian tendencies and the fact that, at least in the early days of his regime, he relied on the support of anti-Semitic ultranationalist groups, he made sure that the new constitution of 1949 included an unambiguous ban on racial discrimination. Perón also issued frequent denunciations of anti-Semitism. His government recognized newly independent Israel and had close ties with it.[26]

The Perón government's protectionist policy was a boon for the economic situation of many Argentinian Jews, many of whom prospered in business and industry in its early years. Despite this, and notwithstanding Perón's attitude toward the Jews, many in the community had strong reservations about the regime. These may have been related to the authoritarian aspects of his regime. Argentinian Jews who were high school students at the time have never forgotten their humiliation when they were forced to leave the classroom because of the decree, enshrined in law by the Perón government, that made Catholic religious education a compulsory subject. Some noted that in the state secondary schools they were forced to participate against their will in progovernment parades and rallies.[27] The many Jewish intellectuals and students were also opposed to Peronism.[28]

Like a good Borochovist, Kitron believed that social integration and assimilation were continuing in Argentina. But alongside and in reaction to them, there was also a countervailing process, caused by the host society's animosity toward the Jews, of increased insularity and ghettoization—"more so today than 15 or 20 years ago," he wrote in one of his newspaper articles.[29] In his opinion, Hispano American culture was sufficiently developed to attract both the older and younger generations but was not solid enough to "easily digest the large clumps of these Jews."[30]

According to Kitron, there were signs of a similar process of integration and rejection in the economic domain as well: "There is a persistent and profound confrontation between the drive to expand and achieve stability felt by small and mid-sized Jewish businessmen and liberal professionals, on the one hand, and the development of the same occupations and strata among the local population."[31] In the case of Argentina, however, Kitron's conclusions were off the mark. First, its Jews became full and prominent members of civil society in the late 1950s and the early 1960s. Second, Argentina never experienced such "national" competition in business and the professions to the extent that Kitron alludes. There was no specifically Jewish economy, and Jews were represented in every branch of the Argentinian economy.[32]

The Jews began having urgent concerns about the awakening of anti-Semitism in Argentina at the time of the first uprising against the Perón regime, in June 1955. Their anxiety was prompted by the unmistakable anti-Semitic tone of the ultranationalist Catholic circles that supported the uprising. These worries naturally found their way to Israel. Isser Harel, who was then the director of the Mossad, wrote that David Ben-Gurion sent him to Argentina to help the Jews organize for self-defense should the need arise. According to his memoirs, he arrived in Buenos Aires that September, at the height of the second and successful revolt that overthrew Perón, and stayed for about a week, until it became clear that the battle was over and the Jews' safety was no longer in doubt.[33] After the fall of the Perón regime, the Catholic ultranationalists did not retain power for long; a coup in November pushed them out of the government. From that time on, the attempts to restore democratic and constitutional life to Argentina gained momentum.

Mordechai Kaufman, the director of the Aliya Bureau in Buenos Aires, referred to the stormy events and their impact on Jewish emigration from Argentina.[34] He maintained that they spurred Jews to give more serious thought to the idea. But he qualified this with the observation that "the road to a movement of serious proportions is still very long."[35] He had laughed when he read the news items about long lines at the Israeli consulate in Buenos Aires, which gave readers the impression that an "Argentinian exodus" had begun.[36] His evaluation was that such demonstrations were more psychological than practical, in light of the mounting obstacles to liquidating assets and transferring them out of the country, caused both by the near-disappearance of cash transactions in Argentina as a result of the crisis and by the rigidity of the absorption institutions in Israel. In his opinion, the main factor behind the psychological shift was that the Jews, who had been totally passive witnesses to the political unrest in Argentina, had again come to the realization that, notwithstanding their equal rights, they were excluded from the forces that shaped the country.[37] As for anti-Semitism and its influence, Kaufman wrote:

> The Argentinian people should be commended for the fact that during the utter chaos and tension, with the release of untrammeled impulses and everything that went along with this, not a single Jewish store was looted and not even one shop window was shattered. It is hard to know how matters will unfold. With the restoration of freedom of speech and the press, it is not inconceivable that there will also be expressions of antisemitism, something that Jews were spared during the Perón regime. The Jews have not yet forgotten the slogan "kill the Jew and save the homeland," which was so widespread just a few years ago, and are very sensitive to any manifestation of antisemitism.[38]

The catastrophic scenarios imagined by Tsur, Kitron, and Kaufman, which, as noted, reflected the reigning Zionist discourse in Israel and Argentina, did not come to pass; in fact, the opposite was true. As we will see in the next few sections, the economy continued to deteriorate, the political situation remained shaky even after Perón's fall, and anti-Semitism roared back; nevertheless, the number of Argentinian immigrants to Israel (about 500 a year) did not rise significantly for the rest of the decade.

The main potential for Argentinian immigration to Israel in the Perón era lay in the thousands of young people affiliated with the Zionist youth movements. In early 1954, Kaufman reported on the scope and composition of aliya from Argentina in 1953: There had been almost 450 olim, of whom 40% were halutzim ("pioneers," the term for those planning to join communal agricultural settlements in Israel) who had spent time on a training farm in Argentina and another 16% the parents of halutzim who followed them to Israel; the rest were young people, professionals, and lower-middle-class families.[39] Prominent among the middle-class immigrants were small-scale industrialists, shopkeepers, and workers in the traditional Jewish crafts, especially textiles, leather, and furniture, whom Kitron had referred to as the "most proletarian stratum."[40]

Many factors delayed and postponed the relocation of middle-class Jews from Argentina to Israel. First and foremost was the declining value of the local currency. A person worth 300,000 pesos in the 1950s was considered to be a capitalist and led the comfortable lifestyle of the upper middle class, but converting that sum into foreign currency at the official exchange rate (thirteen pesos to the dollar or twenty-six to the Israel pound) did not provide an adequate nest egg for one's future in Israel.[41] The many rumors about the threat of the nationalization of factories and seizure of private investments by the General Federation of Labor in Israel, the reports that tourists and returning residents brought back to Argentina about housing conditions and the cost of living in Israeli towns, and the rigidity of the absorption institutions in Israel were enough to make people defer or cancel their plans for emigration.[42]

The cost of passage posed another obstacle to the move. Kaufman addressed this issue in November 1955, when the fare doubled. This spike was one outcome of the Argentinian government's new fiscal policy, aimed at ending the economic crisis. Kaufman wrote that a ticket to Israel that had sold for 5,078 pesos would now cost 11,000 pesos and might reach 50,000 pesos in the future.[43] Regarding the impact of this jump on Argentinian Jewish immigration to Israel, Kaufman added:

> This change will have a significant effect on aliya by Argentinian Jews, which consists mainly of parents going to live near their children, or members of the middle class, who have disposable assets of around 150,000 pesos. If they have to spend 50,000 pesos of this on travel expenses alone (for a medium-sized family of four persons), their entire aliya is called into question.[44]

An equally difficult problem was that the shipping lines priced their tickets in dollars, but Argentinian Jews had to pay in pesos at the current day's exchange rate.[45] The inflationary policies the government adopted in those years, too, posed another effective barrier to the departure of members of the established middle class, because in such conditions they were not inclined to liquidate their assets at a significant loss and emigrate. It was evidently the policy of the Argentinian government to reduce the number of emigrants. This fact alone suggests that the push factors were on the rise in the second half of the 1950s. In the report summing up his posting, Moshe Armon, Kaufman's successor in Buenos Aires, wrote about the main factor behind Argentinian Jewish immigration to Israel. He asserted that an essential condition for it was some external push, economic, political, or otherwise—but always related to the immigrant's own situation:

> As is known, aliya from Argentina since the establishment of the state has averaged 500 persons a year, and this number will almost certainly remain stable in the coming years. In recent weeks, I have realized again that aliya by Jews from South America is largely dependent on the situation prevailing at that moment in their countries of origin. For example, when the metalworkers went on strike in Argentina, new aliya candidates showed up from among the Jews employed in the metal industry, but they stopped coming when the strike was over; and during the textile workers' strike, the textile workers were our main clients.[46]

The Large-Scale Immigration to Israel in the Shadow of Eichmann's Abduction

In May 1960, the Mossad abducted Nazi war criminal Adolf Eichmann from a Buenos Aires street and spirited him off to Israel for trial. The proceedings opened in April 1961 and went on for seven months. Eichmann was sentenced to death in December of that year and executed at the end of May 1962. The Eichmann trial aroused great emotions throughout the Jewish world, especially

Figure 2: Argentinian Jewish immigration to Israel, 1948–67

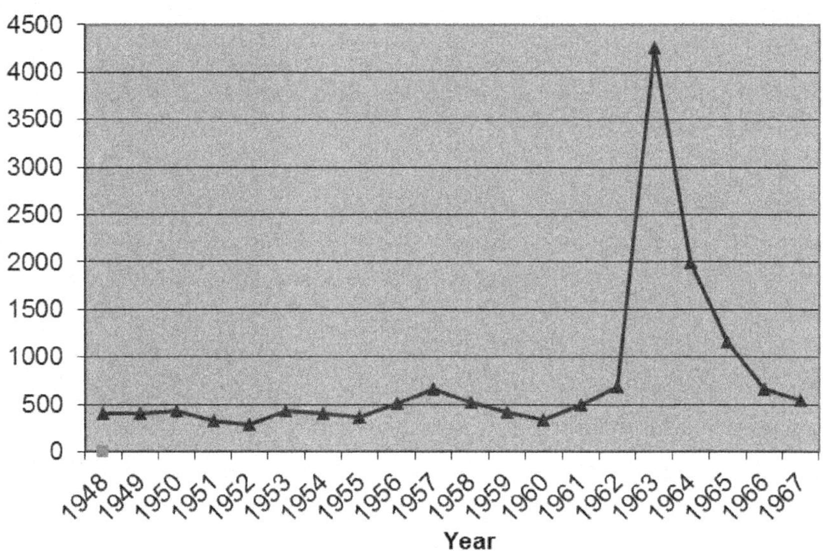

Source: Aliya to Israel, 1948–1972, Part A, Annual Data (Jerusalem: Central Bureau of Statistics, 1973).

in Israel, and had a major impact on the shaping of Jewish identity, both in Israel and in the Diaspora.[47] The Jews of Argentina were subjected to a test of dual loyalty. Argentinian society viewed Eichmann's abduction as a clear and severe infringement of national sovereignty but also as almost the only option for trying the Nazi criminal responsible for sending millions of Jews to the death camps in Europe.

During the trial, Argentina was swept by a wave of anti-Semitic attacks that were perceived chiefly as a response to Israel's violation of the country's sovereignty. As time passed, the incidents multiplied, peaking after Eichmann's execution. The assailants were right-wing ultranationalists groups whose declared common goal was to employ violence to repulse the Communists and the Jewish threat. The most vocal of them was the radical nationalist and anti-Semitic Tacuara movement. The gravest of the thirty incidents for which it was responsible took place on June 21, 1962, in Buenos Aires, when three of its members abducted nineteen-year-old Gabriela Sirota while she was waiting for a bus on her way to the university. The young woman was brutally beaten and tortured. Before she passed out from the pain she heard her kidnappers say that their actions were meant as revenge for the hanging of Adolf Eichmann.[48]

These events, as reflected in the primary sources I have examined, aroused grave concern among Argentinian Jews, mainly from early June 1962. Late that month the director of the Buenos Aires office of the Aliyah Department, Yaakov Israeli, reported to his director in Jerusalem about the press of applicants in his office. He also expressed concern that the office would not be able to deal with the "wave of aliya, which is mounting from day to day."[49] A representative of the Jewish Agency Organization Department, Menachem Gelerter, was sent out from Israel to examine the situation in Buenos Aires. In the report that he submitted to the chairman of the agency, Moshe Sharett, he recounted his conversation with one of the leaders of the Conservative movement in Argentina, Rabbi Marshall Meyer. Meyer had offered a gloomy forecast and wondered whether these anti-Semitic incidents should be seen as a foreboding of things to come, as in Germany of the 1930s.[50] In the same report, Gelerter wrote about a conversation he had overheard between a clerk in the Aliya Bureau and a potential immigrant: "I am a native-born Argentinian, third generation," the woman had said. "But when the incident occurred with the Sirota girl, I told myself, 'from now on, this land is no longer my land.'"[51]

The Israel embassy in Buenos Aires also submitted worried messages. In June 1962, one of its counselors reported back to Jerusalem on his visit to the twin cities of Resistencia and Corrientes in northern Argentina. During his four days there, several anti-Semitic events that took place in Argentina and the adjacent countries darkened the mood of the local Jews (fewer than 1,000 in each town).[52] The Israeli ambassador in Buenos Aires, Yosef Avidar, painted a similar picture. In a report to Arieh Levavi, the director of the Latin America Division of the Foreign Ministry, he surveyed the mood of the Jewish community in Argentina, two and a half months after the start of the wave of anti-Semitic events, of which the "Sirota case is the hallmark."[53] The news also made the Israeli headlines. On July 30, 1962, *Ha'aretz* described the situation in South America as it was portrayed in letters and in accounts by recently arrived immigrants from Argentina and Uruguay:

> The Jews are sunk in fear about the morrow. Parents are walking their children to school and waiting to pick them up at the end of the day. Jewish girls are afraid to go out alone. Many families are living with an unending stream of telephone threats. Jewish institutions are operating with a sense of emergency. Given this atmosphere of terror and fear, interest in aliya is increasing. Long lines have formed outside the Jewish Agency offices, particularly in Buenos Aires and Montevideo.[54]

Aliya and absorption officials in Israel saw the situation in Argentina as a new kind of challenge—large-scale Jewish immigration from a "wealthy country." For Israeli policy makers, immigration from the wealthy countries, which they saw as a monolithic bloc, was motivated by ideology or personal reasons and not based on "catastrophic" experiences—severe economic distress or hostility toward Jews—as was the case for "countries of distress." Some, though, saw the expressions of anti-Semitism as an opportunity to organize a special sailing from Argentina, which would have the grandiose nature of "an organized rescue operation." This operation, like previous large-scale missions of this sort, was given a name: Operation Shalhevet.

Starting in June 1962, the number of applicants who came to the Jewish Agency offices in Buenos Aires increased, leading naturally to an increase in the number of those who actually made the leap. The turning point was the final months of 1962. From December of that year, and throughout 1963, around 360 people immigrated to Israel from Argentina each month, for a total of almost 5,000 Jews. As can be seen in figure 2, this was a major spike, after more than a decade in which there had been fewer than 500 immigrants a year. This huge wave in 1963 presents the fascinating research challenge of evaluating the role of the anti-Semitic incidents among the various factors pushing Jewish emigration. The following pages take up this challenge.

The Motive behind the Large Wave of Argentinian Jewish Immigration to Israel

Yaakov Israeli, the director of the Aliya Bureau in Buenos Aires, was appointed to the post in January 1962. Like most Aliyah Department emissaries, he was a member of Hapoel Mizrahi, the Religious Zionist party that had controlled the department since the establishment of the State, and had limited prior knowledge of Argentina and its Jewish community. But it is clear from his descriptions that the events he witnessed made a strong impression on him. In a report sent to his colleagues in Jerusalem, on the period April 19 to May 9, 1962, he reviewed the situation in Argentina then. The week of Passover (April 19–26) had been dominated by a siege atmosphere, with the tanks of two rival generals facing off in downtown Buenos Aires, ready for battle. He was surprised to find that the Jews' reaction did not reflect this situation: "They continue about their lives as though nothing had happened. The parties took place with great magnificence and splendor and almost exaggerated public display—in front of the muzzles of the tanks ready to open fire on anyone in range."[55]

These words were written against the background of the stormy political and economic situation in Argentina. After the overthrow of the Peronist regime in 1955, Argentina began a long and complex process of democratization that continued for some thirty years. In 1958, when the candidate of the leftist faction of the Radical Party, Arturo Frondizi, was elected president, the military stepped aside for an elected civilian government, but in practice continued to monitor its actions. Banning the Peronist party was a fundamental condition for the restoration of constitutional life, but the "Red scare," exacerbated by the Cuban revolution, and the fear of Peronism did not abate.

There was also a deepening economic crisis. A cyclic depression struck in late 1961. Wages were eroded, unemployment climbed, and inflation soared. Frondizi's conciliatory approach toward Fidel Castro's revolutionary regime in Cuba worried various groups in Argentinian society, which saw him as paving the way for a Communist takeover. Manifestations of government corruption and the tension in the military between the "Blues" (moderates and "legalists," who were mainly afraid of a Cuban-style revolution) and the "Reds" (reactionaries and proponents of military dictatorship, whose main fear was Peronism) exacerbated the political ferment.[56]

The political crisis reached a peak in late March 1962, at the start of an election campaign for half the seats in Congress and the governorships of several provinces. Frondizi's decision to allow the Peronists to run heightened the tension. There were frequent demonstrations and strikes; the atmosphere was particularly stormy in the armed forces, and especially among the "Reds." In reaction to the Peronist candidates' success in the elections, the generals staged another coup on March 29, 1962, deposed Frondizi, annulled the election results, and set up a provisional civilian and military government, with the president of the Senate, José María Guido, as interim president. Yaakov Israeli described the climate among the Jewish community in early May as follows: "The dominant atmosphere in this country is saturated with a strong desire for aliya and has created a wide potential for it. We must prepare the necessary and appropriate tools for this."[57]

Two prominent leaders of Argentinian Jewry, Isaac Goldenberg and Gregorio (Zvi) Fainguersch, described matters in similar fashion.[58] At the time, Goldenberg was president of the DAIA, the umbrella organization of the Jewish organizations in Argentina; Fainguersch was an influential member of the Ashkenazi community of Buenos Aires (AMIA). Both men were politically active in the Po'alei Zion Union, which was identified with the Mapai party in Israel. On June 3, 1962 (three days after Eichmann was hanged, setting off a wave of vocal anti-Semitism), the two men contacted the head of the Jewish Agency Aliyah Department, Shlomo Zalman Shragai, and asserted that, given the recent events in Argentina, it was essential to send a group of senior officials of the Aliyah and Absorption Department to Argentina in order to expand the aliya apparatus there.[59] The two men also put together a series of practical proposals that they thought would facilitate the immigration process. It should be noted, however, that most of the proposals made in this document dealt with an issue that seems to have been the primary concern of Argentinian Jewry just then; their main anxiety had nothing to do with the "muzzles of the tanks ready to open fire" or the wave of anti-Semitic incidents, but rather the economic situation.[60]

The mixed civilian and military government was not managing to deal with the economic crisis. The period of Guido's interim presidency, which lasted for 562 days, was even stormier than the preceding years. Bankruptcies were common, unemployment kept increasing, purchasing power shrank, the value of the peso continued to plummet, and the middle class found itself eroded. The military coup had merely added to the prevalent sense of political instability. During Guido's time in office, no fewer than eighteen cabinet ministers were replaced; confrontations between the Blue and the Red factions of the armed forces became a routine scene on the streets of Buenos Aires. This was the political and economic background of the severe anti-Semitic incidents of June and July 1962. At the end of July, the Israeli ambassador, Yosef Avidar, reported from Buenos Aires that the government of Argentina was weak and unstable; Congress was paralyzed and lacked the tools to solve the country's economic and political problems: "It is clear that the antisemitic ultranationalist organizations, who assumed or even knew that the authorities or some segments of the government were sympathetic to their existence, because they are nationalists and anti-Communists, and would not suppress them, thought the time was ripe to launch a series of attacks against Jews."[61]

In the wake of these reports from Argentina, the World Zionist Organization quickly organized a high-ranking delegation to visit Argentina. It included Jacob Tsur, the chairman of the Zionist General Council, considered to be an expert on Argentina as a result of his service as the first Israeli minister to that country between 1949 and 1953. The other members were Menachem Gelerter, a Jewish Agency executive and representative of the Organization Department; Baruch Duvdevani, the director general of the Aliyah Department in Jerusalem; and Avraham Cygel, his counterpart in the Absorption Department in Tel Aviv. Their main assignment was to assess the mood of the Jews in Argentina and the prospects for large-scale immigration. Cygel concluded that the mood in Argentina was favorable for this. In his report, written in Buenos Aires in August 1962, he noted that the recent anti-Semitic events had given a "slight push to thoughts about and the inclination towards aliya."[62] The economic and political instability was in fact the main force pushing the Jews to Israel:

> There is no doubt that the difficult economic situation and the uncertain political circumstances—I would even say the economic and political panic—are liable to give a serious push to preparations for aliya. The mere fact that, thus far, 500 families have registered for aliya in Buenos Aires alone, and this in the span of only a month and a half, while the traffic to our office here continued unabated, proves this in the clearest way. And all this is still without expanded activity by the WZO.[63]

As noted, Cygel was joined in Argentina by his colleague from the Aliyah Department in Jerusalem, Baruch Duvdevani. In an internal report to Shragai, the head of the department, Duvdevani wrote that most of the Jews were concerned about their lack of a future in their country and were afraid that one day they would be forced to emigrate. He added that it was not the anti-Semitic incidents that were the main force driving Jewish emigration, but the anxiety about the shaky economic situation and the fear of far-reaching political changes, whose most extreme expression was the Cuban revolution. These changes threatened mainly the middle class, to which most Jews in Argentina belonged.[64] On the other side, Israel's attraction was growing. The news from Israel about the economic situation there was positive and encouraged relocation:

> Returning tourists have brought good news about the economic prosperity and cultural blossoming. The families that have already been absorbed in Israel are telling their relatives to follow them and make aliya; pioneer youth who have made aliya to agricultural settlements in Israel are asking their parents to join them. The repulsive force of the Latin American Diaspora, which has increased in recent years, and the attraction of Israel, which has soared in recent years, together create a ferment of unending interest in Israel as a country of individual fulfillment.[65]

In the wake of the reports from Argentina, the Jewish Agency decided to expand the aliya apparatus there and dispatched Moshe Kitron to represent the Zionist Executive. As noted previously, Kitron was the most prominent champion of Latin American aliya in Israel. The main reasons for his selection for this task involved his familiarity with the place, his knowledge of the circumstances and moods, and his personal contacts with local groups and institutions.[66] As part of his assignment, Kitron regularized the status of the Jewish Agency vis-à-vis other groups in Argentina, including the Argentinian Zionist Association (OSA), the central institutions of Argentinian Jewry, the Israeli embassy in Buenos Aires, and, when necessary, Argentinian government agencies. His brief included coordinating and supervising the work of the Jewish Agency emissaries.[67]

The many detailed reports he drafted during his mission and the newspaper articles he published frequently, in both Argentina and Israel, offer his assessments of the economic and political situation in Argentina and its impact on immigration in 1962 and 1963. The documents Kitron penned are of greater value than other sources. His familiarity with Argentinian Jewry, his vast experience in public activity, his critical perspective as well as the nature of his job and special task, turn his chronicle of these years into a treasure trove for research on the subject.

Kitron recorded his impressions of the situation in Argentina upon his arrival there in October 1962 in a letter to his colleague in the Cultural Department of the Executive Committee of the Histadrut (the General Federation of Labor), Bezalel Shahar: "You should use your imagination and try to visualize a vast country that has lost its entire political, economic, and moral conscience."[68] In Buenos Aires, Kitron began collecting the monthly data on applications and actual immigration kept by the various departments so that they could be summarized "quickly." In January 1963, he was already able to present the data for the year just ended.[69] As can be seen in figure 3, there was a sharp downturn in the number of applicants after July 1962. Kitron's conclusions about that turning point were as follows:

> The jump in the numbers for the second half of this year leaps out at you and is a direct result of the events of June/July (the violent acts by the fascist Tacuara Organization, the government's indifference to the riots, and so forth). The Jewish community replied in three ways: the bold and very respectable defense of the rights and honor of Argentinian Jewry by the Central Delegation (the DAIA); the simultaneously impassioned and disciplined self-defense by the younger generation, with the full assistance of classes of all strata of the community; and finally, the turning point towards aliya. To understand the situation, you must remember that, with regard to this turning point, the antisemitic

Figure 3: Applications and actual immigration, 1962

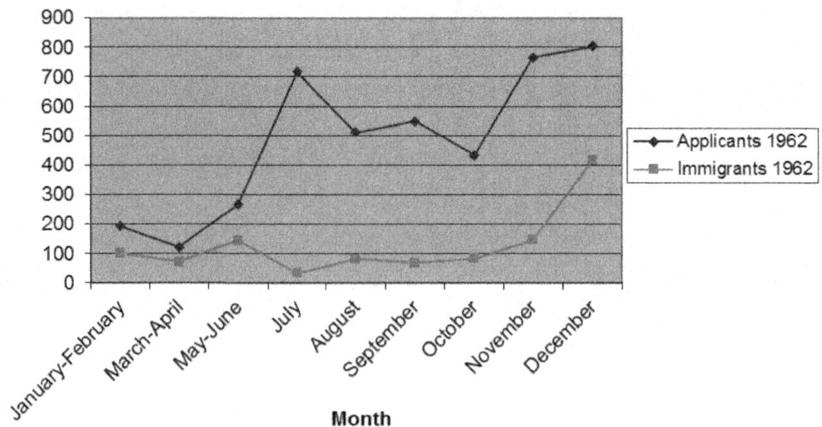

Source: M. Kitron to S. Lurie, "Report on Applications and Aliya in 1962," January 21, 1963, CZA S64/393.

incidents were merely the final push, the zenith of a prolonged and complex process.[70]

The data pictured in figure 3 show that the heavy traffic to the Jewish Agency offices in July 1962 was reflected in a sharp rise in the actual number of immigrants in the last months of 1962. That December, at the crest of the wave, Kitron submitted a detailed assessment of the situation to Shragai:

> The economic crisis in Argentina is getting worse, as are the political crisis and the social confusion. Perhaps we should change the order of the factors, but that would not change the picture, and the order in which I presented them is what counts for aliya. . . . The number of those who are talking and thinking seriously about aliya is quite large, and it is no exaggeration to speak in terms of thousands. . . . I stick to the hypothesis of 5,000 olim in 1963. . . . The tremor that shook Argentinian Jewry this past July led Jews to make a decision and brought many of them to the aliya offices. Our processing of candidates, the liquidation of businesses, and their various preparations took a few months, so that only now is the wave beginning. The peak will be this month.[71]

But one of the main factors that impeded increased Jewish immigration to Israel from Argentina was the problem of liquidating assets, because converting property into money involved significant losses. This was linked to another problem, which was particularly severe in Argentina in those days: the exchange rate.[72] "The exchange rate, which recently was 83 pesos to the dollar and has now reached 127 pesos to the dollar, makes it difficult for people to make aliya; it hurts them to have to sell for less than they would have received just a few months ago," Cygel reported in August 1962, after his visit to Argentina.[73] Kitron, too, believed that the main factor holding back increased Jewish emigration from Argentina was the economic situation of many members of the middle class, who had no possibility of liquidating their businesses or selling their possessions. As noted, another factor was inflation and uncertainty about the value of the peso (which by then had fallen to 154 pesos to the dollar). Around that time, the Argentinian authorities made further changes in economic policy; as Kitron observed, "we still have not learned what new changes there may be in the economic policy and what impact they will have." He added:

> Should there be a change, which is followed by a certain reassurance of the population, it is possible that our brothers, too, will calm down and defer the question of aliya to some future time. But most of our community leaders and businessmen believe that it is precisely then that the aliya of the true middle class will increase. The idea of aliya is too deeply rooted in their consciousness and they are waiting for a practical way to carry it out.[74]

The item that attracted Kitron's particular attention was that among the Argentinian Jewish middle class, which consisted mainly of merchants and accounted for a large proportion of the community, only a minority chose to relocate to Israel. According to Economic Department data,[75] 1,678 people had requested advice or information during the past year, but fewer than 23% of them went on to the stage of a formal application and only 8.36% actually moved to Israel in the end. The Economic Department opened 384 files in 1962, in which the applicants declared total assets of $23.5 million. But these declarations had no real meaning, because the dollar amounts of early 1962 shrank drastically with the continuing devaluation of the peso and also because most of the assets declared were real estate, at a time when property values were falling.[76]

Alongside the economic erosion in Argentina, the political situation also deteriorated in early 1963. The moderate wing's victory in the clashes between military factions in the streets of Buenos Aires in September 1962 led to a cabinet reshuffle. On January 14, 1963, President Guido hastily called for general elections, but the unsettled climate, particularly among conservative circles, forced their postponement.[77] Here is Kitron's review of the political crisis that gripped Argentina in early 1963:

> Here, as you know, there was an attempted military coup. I will not go into details that do not directly concern us; for us, the important fact is that the victory of the ostensibly legal government did not solve any question or move this country closer to a solution of its problems and an end to the prolonged and complex crisis. The confusion, distrust, and insecurity remain as they were and are even getting worse. It appears that the conjectures and calculations I presented in my survey and various letters will be proven true. According to all the indications, we should expect an increase in aliya from Argentina.[78]

In the first half of 1963, the economy was getting worse, and there were again frequent armed clashes on the streets of Buenos Aires. Anti-Semitic incidents did not cease, but they were minor and did not cause the same reverberations as those of May and June 1962. At the same time, the Jewish Agency offices saw an increase in registration for immigration to Israel. Drawing on the data about applications and immigration in the first six months of 1963, Kitron estimated that the total number of immigrants for the year would be around 5,300, but he noted that "the final numbers depend on various factors that we lack the ability to assess and calculate in advanced."[79] Kitron also noted the results of the presidential election, which finally took place on July 7, 1963, and was won by the candidate of the centrist Radical Party, Arturo Illia. According to Kitron, the election results restored the Argentinian people's sense of security and confidence in the present regime. Kitron saw this turn as a positive change that would increase Argentinian Jewish immigration to Israel, but that also raised another possibility:

> If this welcome change persists, there is no doubt that it will lead to the start of a solution to the economic crisis even before the new government begins functioning. This is not the place to assess the possible developments regarding the status of the Jewish community, particularly its political status. By contrast, it is our duty to warn that we are facing a very significant turning point for aliya as well: an improvement in the local economy might well enable many Jews to sell off their assets and businesses on reasonable terms and realize their ambition

Figure 4: Applications and actual immigration, 1963

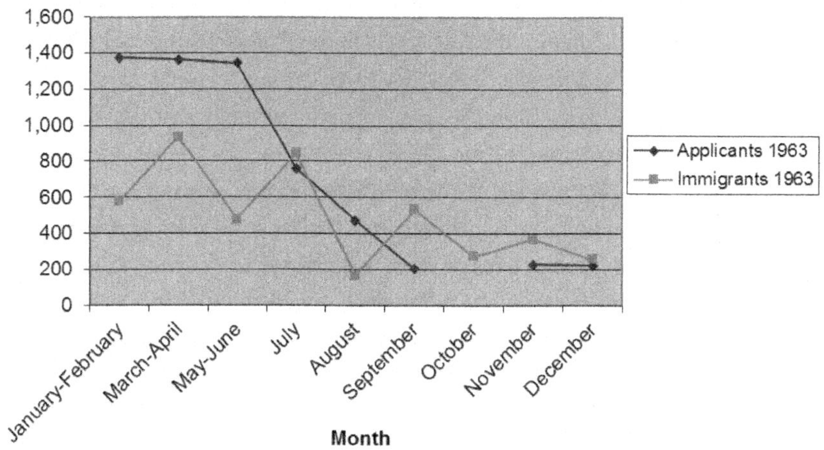

* Data on applications in July are taken from the Aliyah Department files stored in the Jewish Agency Logistics Center, files 2070–72. The data for October could not be found.

Source: M. Kitron, "Aliya from Argentina in January–June 1963," CZA S65/203; "Data on Registration, July–December," JAFI Logistics Center.

> of making aliya. In other words, it is possible that the middle class will start to occupy the place in aliya that is appropriate to its numerical and social weight in the Jewish community. And because the prospects of the other sectors and classes will improve more gradually, aliya will grow and increase. But it is also possible that aliya candidates will decide to put off the move in order to improve their situation, . . . and the pace will slow down significantly, at least for a certain period.[80]

In the end, Kitron's expectations of immigration to Israel by the middle class were not fulfilled, and this sector's attitudes did not change as he had hoped. Of the two possibilities, he envisaged, the middle class opted for the second: when the political and economic situation calmed down after the elections in early July, the traffic decreased (see figure 4).

Evidence of the change that took place after the elections in Argentina is found in a letter written by the representative of PATWA (the Professional and Technical Workers Association) in Buenos Aires:

> The past month has been one of reflection and thought about the problem of continued aliya from Argentina. As I continue to think about it,

> I reach the same conclusions that I conveyed in my previous letters to you. All the signs indicate that aliya from Argentina will return to the dimensions it had before the last crisis. Before the elections on July 7, aliya applicants had to wait at least four weeks for a personal interview with me. My workday lasted at least 10 hours without a break. After the elections there came the months of cancellations, even in cases that had been fully processed and the people were only waiting for their departure date. For the past several weeks, almost no new applicants have been coming to our offices about aliya matters. Most of our work has been reduced to handling olim who applied months ago and are continuing with their aliya plans. The change that took place in the field of aliya came so suddenly that many still cannot grasp this transformation. My impression is that after all those who are being processed today make aliya, our building will be almost empty.[81]

Kitron never wrote about the changes that took place in the latter half of 1963, because his posting came to an end in October, but it seems that he had already grasped their meaning. At a press conference for the local Jewish media, held shortly before he left Argentina, he summarized his mission as follows:

> In 5723 [1962/63], 4,400 Jews made aliya from Argentina, or nearly 1% of the Jewish community in this country. . . . The factors that energized this wave were: the economic crisis that beset Argentina in the last two years; the spiritual crisis of young Jews and their response to antisemitism; parents' concerns about their children's education; and the pull from Israel, conveyed in the messages of relatives and friends from Argentina who have settled in Israel. In addition to all these, tourism from Argentina to Israel is another factor encouraging aliya. . . . The substantial assistance and support of the Jewish community in Argentina has also been a decisive factor in the organization and processing of this wave of aliya. Antisemitism expedited the aliya process, but it was not the main factor that motivated the process.[82]

We can infer from this that it was the political turn in July 1963, which was followed by what one emissary called the "months of cancellations"—meaning a sharp drop in the number of those registering for aliya—that took Kitron by surprise. Yaakov Israeli, too, failed to anticipate that development. In light of the sparse traffic in the Jewish Agency offices and the steep decline in the number of applicants, he admitted that his appraisal had been mistaken:

> It was difficult to predict that the slight change in the political situation in Argentina would cause many of those who had registered for aliya to open their suitcases and postpone their aliya until new conditions forced them to pack again. Many believed that such conditions would return within a few months, after our Jewish brethren were convinced that the economic situation had not improved. But in fact—wonder of wonders—the economic situation is getting worse from day to day, and antisemitic incidents and outbreaks have surged again and given the Jews cause for concern and anxiety: but this time it has had no influence on aliya.[83]

"A Decrease in Aliya and Rise in Yerida"

In light of the registration figures, Yaakov Israeli predicted a sharp decline in Argentinian Jewish immigration to Israel in 1964 as compared to the previous year. The political situation had not improved, even now, and the anti-Semitic incitement had actually grown worse.[84] Between Illia's inauguration (October 12, 1963) and late July of the following year, the DAIA counted 303 anti-Semitic incidents in Argentina, which included damage to institutions, property, and people.[85] The worst was the murder of thirty-two-year-old Raúl Alterman in February 1964, for which members of the National Restoration Guard and Tacuara were responsible.[86] The anti-Semitic attacks continued throughout Illia's presidency (1964–66) and even reached new heights.[87]

The number of aliya applicants continued to decrease in the second half of 1964, even though the political and economic situation remained perilous and anti-Semitic incidents were rampant. "We are witnessing a process of classic and systematic antisemitism, which has taken on quite respectable proportions in this country," wrote Israeli in late September 1964.[88] He added that since the start of the year, "the wild and venomous incitement" of the Arab League was also felt in Argentina, and that even though the league's representative, Hussein Triki, was expelled from Argentina, his replacement was even more extreme and connected with senior Nasserist circles.[89] The political situation was also unclear:

> In the last three years, there have been three changes in the government; but there has been no change with regard to antisemitism. Even

> the current democratic government has not been able to uproot this noxious weed; by contrast, the new laws impact Zionist activities. In the meantime, the incitement has done its job and a bill sponsored by antisemites, which would mandate an investigation of Zionist activities in the country, is in practice being implemented by the Federal Police in the capital and provincial cities, where community leaders are being interrogated about their activities and the emissaries are being followed. The community leaders and heads of the DAIA believe that various activities should be camouflaged and that we should be careful about working in ways that could be interpreted as against the law, primarily in matters of aliya and the United Appeal. To a certain degree, our embassy supports this method, too, and this is liable to reduce and deter many worthwhile programs.[90]

Anti-Semitism flourished, the economic situation went from bad to worse, and the political instability continued, but the number of Jewish emigrants decreased anyway. In light of these developments, in September 1964 the Aliyah Department conducted a survey of the Jews of Buenos Aires and their attitude toward immigration to Israel,[91] in cooperation with Daniel Hofen and Dr. Perla Perez of the Department of Sociology at the University of Buenos Aires. More than fifty interviewers, most of them affiliated with the Faculty of Humanities at the university, were trained for this purpose. AMIA provided them with basic information—the vital statistics of their sample population. Various stratagems were employed to camouflage the survey's true sponsor and real goal.

> In light of the manifestations of antisemitism that have broken out, mainly in the capital, we foresaw that problems would arise, as well as some resistance to providing the requested information. Because of the subjects' natural concerns and fears, the idea was born of establishing a Jewish Institute for Social Research (IJES). On the formal plane, this alleviated the respondents' fears, because an address and phone number were included with the name. In addition, the idea was circulated that the study was being conducted for the Jewish newspapers, which were trying to track the development of Jewish life in Buenos Aires. These methods decreased the number of those who declined to answer and energized the activities on the ground.[92]

The research team managed to reach 2,000 people, broken down as follows: 4% of the respondents belonged to the working class, 31.3% belonged to the salaried middle class (clerical workers, technicians, teachers, and so forth), 60.2% came from the self-employed middle class (liberal professionals, merchants, and industrialists), and 4.5% had no defined occupation or profession. The structure and composition of the research population was fairly close to those of the Argentinian Jewish population as a whole. Of the 2,000 respondents, 593 said that they were thinking about settling in Israel—close to 30% of the sample.[93] This figure confirms my own assessment of the true potential for Argentinian Jewish immigration to Israel), based on the 1960 census and cross-checked against the secondary literature, of approximately 25%. But we must qualify this and note that Hofen's survey was based on a representative sample only.

The survey findings demonstrated that attitudes toward immigration to Israel were not directly correlated with respondents' socioeconomic situation. That is, those who had no interest in relocation and those who were considering it could be found in the same occupational categories; their respective positions were not influenced by their objective economic state.[94] Another important finding was that even though the age composition of the two groups was similar, there was a higher percentage of young people among those who rejected leaving—a rather unexpected fact, because the prevailing opinion was that the anti-Semitic manifestations impacted chiefly the younger generation. The breakdown by age is parallel to that by place of birth: the survey found that there were more young native-born Argentinians in the stay-put group.[95]

The authors of the survey drew up a series of follow-up questions for those who expressed interest in moving to Israel, asking about their assessment of their economic situation at the moment, five years earlier, and in the future.[96] Even though a correlation between a pessimistic view of one's economic situation and a desire to live in Israel might have been expected, it did not show up in the findings. The researchers concluded the "lack of significant differences does not enable us to lightly accept the notion, which is widespread in both the Jewish and non-Jewish street, that Jews with a positive attitude towards aliya reach it as a result of economic or social failure."[97] The authors of the survey viewed this assertion as refuted by their data, which showed unambiguously that positive decisions about immigration to Israel were linked mainly to the respondents' personal assessment of themselves as Jews—what the survey defined as "ideological support" for aliya.[98]

The survey also proved that there was a close relationship between a tie to Israel maintained through relatives and friends already living there and their reports back to Argentina, on the one hand, and a favorable disposition toward relocation to Israel, on the other.[99] The survey found that 45% of those considering the move had relatives in Israel, 60% of them received frequent news from their relatives, and 65% of those giving positive consideration to the idea had received positive reports about Israel. Among those who were not interested in immigrating to Israel, only 32% had relatives there, fewer than 44% received frequent news, and only 40% received positive reports.[100] These findings, too, strengthen my basic assumption about the importance of chain migration for the process.

The survey also examined the relationship between attitudes toward immigration to Israel and respondents' national and cultural sentiments. The group of questions that addressed this related to four criteria: use of Yiddish, reading Yiddish and/or Hebrew newspapers, sending one's children to Jewish schools, and membership in Jewish social or athletic clubs or youth movements. Based on their findings, the researchers concluded that there was a direct relationship between a positive attitude about immigration to Israel and a lifestyle grounded in Jewish principles. They asserted that the idea of moving to Israel grew out of a Jewish life and Jewish social circles. The most prominent datum had to do with the children's education: about 80% of those seriously interested in immigration to Israel sent their children to Jewish schools, as against only 40% of those who were not inclined to move to Israel.[101]

The survey also investigated whether those with a favorable attitude toward immigration were actually inclined to move to Israel. Only about a quarter of this group said that they had set a date for leaving. The remainder replied that they had not done so—either because they were only pondering the move or because external factors kept them from leaving.[102] Respondents who found it hard to set a date for their departure were more likely to focus on the economic problems associated with the move, whereas others were apt to highlight problems related to their family or their fear of the new situation. Among respondents who were positive about relocation, 45% believed that they were being held back mainly by economic issues. The researchers expressed their reservations about this and wrote that "we must not conclude from this that we are speaking about a financial inability to make aliya; rather, they feel a need to guarantee themselves a certain standard of living that will not be lower than what they have been accustomed to in Argentina."[103]

The last section of the survey examined the issue of "rejection of the whole idea of aliya." This is an important and valuable section, because the scholarly literature on migration naturally tends to focus on the migrants and not on those who stay put. The survey classified this group on the basis of occupation, socioeconomic situation, and age. It found that 55% of those with no interest in immigration to Israel said that the primary reason was their fear of problems in absorption and settling down in Israel; 25% cited financial difficulties; and more than 20% gave other reasons, mainly related to their age and health. Those who rejected the idea of immigration fell into one central category: they were strongly integrated into daily life in Argentina. Family, home, job, and profession were the restraining factors that worked against their leaving.[104]

According to the researchers, only a strong bond to the Jewish nation and culture could weaken the many negative factors and lead to aliya. In this context, the survey raised the question of anti-Semitic, given that the "Jewish community was and continues to witness antisemitic incitement." They maintained that the Jews of Argentina were responding to the manifestations of anti-Semitism in two ways: either recognizing its existence and working to counteract it, or denying its existence and reconciling themselves to the new situation. According to the survey, 64% of those who were not interested in immigration to Israel said that their current situation was better than or no different than it had been five year ago. In my reading, this means that anti-Semitism did not have significant weight as a push factor for leaving Argentina for Israel.[105] We can only regret that the researchers' final report did not address the question of anti-Semitism as a factor pushing those who were favorably disposed to it to emigrate.

Yaakov Israeli referred to this survey in a letter to Shragai in September 1965.[106] He wrote that the idea for the survey was born against the background of the change in the scope of Argentinian Jewish immigration to Israel, starting in mid-1964, and evaluated the findings:

> The survey demonstrates that only 29.7% have thought about making aliya (and I emphasize: thought) and only 1.7% said they were ready to make aliya immediately. It seems that this percentage corresponds to the number of candidates who had already registered for aliya and have now in fact gone through with it. This opinion was confirmed when we followed up personally with the 28% of positive respondents, that is, people who responded in the affirmative, and we wanted to "collect on the contract"—that is, get them to turn their potential into reality and talk seriously about implementing their aliya. Their response was: "That was just idle talk, an informal conversation that carries no obligation with it." We came to the realization that the survey still does not

provide a faithful reflection of the potential for aliya and it will not be the key to our salvation.[107]

Israeli went on to write that even though there was a desire to live in Israel, not only was the traffic not increasing, there was actually a sharp decline. He told about the phenomenon of yerida, return migration by young families from all sectors and all circles, by businessmen and young members of the liberal professions, and even by those who had been brought to Israel by Youth Aliyah.[108]

The economic and political situation in Argentina did not improve. The Red scare and the fear of Peronism did not abate, and the unrest in the armed forces increased. On June 30, 1966, two years and eight months after Illia had taken office, Argentina was shaken by a new coup that installed yet another military dictatorship, the fifth since 1930.[109] According to a secret and classified document written by the Mossad in July 1966, the Onganía coup heightened tension in the Jewish community.[110] The Mossad document cites various details about the ideological background of the military junta that had seized power and the civilian circles, some of them ultranationalist and radically anti-Semitic, that stood behind it and openly preached hatred of Jews. The document goes on to offer the following assessment:

According to the information at our disposal, the principles that guide the leaders of the new regime point to their adherence to the essentials of corporatism and opposition to democracy: the disbanding of the political parties; the dissolution of Congress; the transfer of the legislative function to a corporative body; the establishment of a socioeconomic council composed of representatives of the various productive sectors.... It is still too early to tell whether the reports about the closure of Jewish stores and arrest of their owners and the banning of the DAIA point to a deliberate intention to damage the Jewish community's status and situation, in keeping with the worldview of the plotters of the coup and its ideological patrons. It may be that these steps are part of the regime's desire to silence any public body that is by nature likely to have qualms about such a regime, and, in the guise of fighting against corruption, to provide an outlet for the bitterness of the masses, at least in the first stage.[111]

It was during that tumultuous time that Avraham Bar-Kahan arrived in Argentina to replace Yaakov Israeli. In one of his reports, Bar-Kahan asserted that the "cloudy" political situation in Argentina was apt to increase the scope of immigration to Israel and even put an end to the return of disgruntled immigrants to Argentina. He went on to describe how the new military regime had made its mark on the economy and how, despite the relentless and long-entrenched inflation, prices had actually fallen as a result of the scarcity of customers, as stores were forced to sell off their stock at any price in order to pay their bills. His assessment was that the economic crisis had harmed mainly the middle class. He had spoken with wholesalers who complained that their turnover had decreased by 60% to 70% and with industrialists who were faced with the possibility of having to close their factories. "Everyone is now on the verge of despair and perhaps on the brink of shutting down, because of a lack of financing." And, Bar-Kahan added:

> There is absolutely no doubt that the situation here will set off a wave of emigration, mainly by our Jewish brothers. The conspicuous difference between today and the similar situation that prevailed in 1962 and 1963 is that back then the Jews saw Israel as a place of refuge, whereas now, in the wake of the situation in Israel and because of the yerida, which is enough by itself to sabotage our work, the community is looking at the country through a magnifying glass, in light of the items being published in Israel, which the local press reprints with the addition of its own contributions.[112]

In fact, the political events of 1966 did accelerate emigration from Argentina; there was a marked "brain drain," particularly from the universities in reaction to their violent suppression by the military dictatorship. The emigrants included many Jews, although the number of those who opted for Israel continued to decline. It has to be remembered that this was the period of the most severe recession in Israel's history, whereas Onganía's government actually managed to restore some stability to the Argentinian economy in 1967.

"There has been a decrease [Hebrew: yerida] in aliya and a rise [Hebrew: aliya] in yerida," punned Bar-Kahan in early 1967.[113] He maintained that the recession in Israel had a strong deterrent effect on immigration to Israel and discouraged potential immigrants who had heard about the sorry state of the Israeli economy. He also believed that the policy of population dispersal had contributed to return migration to Argentina. He illustrated this statement with the story of a family that had relocated to Israel three years ago, but had now gone back to Argentina because it could not make ends meet in Israel. The family had arrived with an adequate nest egg and requested housing in the center of the country, where they had relatives and where they could work in their regular occupations. But instead they were sent to Dimona and employed at the Dead Sea Works as a laborer and a cook. They had hoped that after three years they would be allowed to move to the center of the country, but when they ran into a "brick wall (the sacred principle of population dispersal!)" as Bar-Kahan put it, they packed their bags and went back to Argentina. "This, without a doubt, is a classic example of the fecklessness that prevails in the field of absorption."[114]

The Six-Day War stirred up great enthusiasm among Argentinian Jewry. The atmosphere in Argentina was electrifying, and public opinion supported Israel overwhelmingly. In late May, a Joint Emergency Committee was established in Buenos Aires, comprising the three umbrella organizations of Argentinian Jewry—the DAIA, AMIA, and OSA. The Emergency Committee's stated goal was to galvanize all Argentinian Jews to take part in Israel's battle.[115] Their anxiety on the first day of the fighting knew no bounds. That day, Jews streamed to the Ezra Jewish Hospital and other medical institutions to donate blood. The collection points run by Keren Hayesod (United Israel Appeal) reported unprecedented financial donations, some of which were very moving: the children at a Jewish orphanage who relinquished their fortnightly evening at the movies and donated their ticket money to the appeal; the residents of a Jewish old age home, who contributed a modest sum; the teachers of the Scholem Aleijem school network, who contributed a month's salary; and doctors at the Jewish hospital, who also gave up part of their salary. All these contributions came to more than $20 million.[116] But the outpouring of support went no further than this; there was no increase in Argentinian Jewish immigration to Israel in the second half of 1967, and 1968 actually saw a decline.[117]

"What drives Latin American Jews to make aliya?" asked a very detailed article published in *Davar*.[118] The reporter had interviewed Reuven Golan of the Absorption Department and the head of the Aliyah Department, Shlomo Zalman Shragai. "Every answer leads to a combination of two types of motives: the Jewish spark and the economic calculation," he ended the article.[119]

Without a doubt, in the case of Argentinian Jews there was a significant interaction that took place somewhere along the axis between the Jewish spark—the pintele yid—and the economic issue. The developments reviewed in this chapter lead to some interesting conclusions. The documents cited demonstrate a clear and strong interdependence between immigration to Israel and various circumstances in Argentina. An analysis of all the factors behind immigration shows the crucial role of the political situation as able both to spur the move and to postpone it. The political horizon turns out to be one of the most significant spurs for emigration. The economic situation in Argentina was a major push factor. Anti-Semitism may have expedited the process in certain economic and political conditions, but in and of itself was not enough to get a significant number of Jews to leave Argentina. This is clearly reflected throughout the period studied here.

Given that anti-Semitism was not one of the major push factors for Argentinian Jewish immigration to Israel, and that "the economic panic" was much more significant, we are confronted by an interesting paradox. On the one hand, it seems that the Argentinian Jewish community had a very shaky footing in a political arena that was characterized mainly by instability. Anti-Semitism, in its various forms, pervaded Argentinian society at the deepest levels. The severe anti-Semitic incidents described above had no parallel elsewhere on the continent. Many Jews certainly felt threatened and apprehensive. There was no letup in the anti-Semitic attacks in the 1960s, when the government and law-enforcement agencies, and especially the police, paid little or no attention to them. However, despite their insecurity and the rabid anti-Semitism, the Jews of Argentina lived in a heterogeneous society that granted them equal standing with other minorities and included them in the majority civil society, especially in the late 1950s. It is a fact that the decisive majority of Argentinian Jewry chose to stay in the country and take part in its socioeconomic, cultural, and political modernization.

The representatives of the Zionist-socialist establishment in Israel, such as Kitron, tended to exaggerate the dangers lurking for the Jews of Argentina. Their appraisals cannot be disconnected from their Borochovist outlook, which dominated the Labor Zionist discourse both in Argentina and in Israel. From that perspective, the Jews were an ethnic and cultural minority that was not fully integrated into the hostile majority society, living on the edge of a volcano, and the future of Argentinian Jewry was viewed in that light. Events in Argentina and the changes among its Jews proved time after time that despite the severe and frequent economic and political crises and severe anti-Semitism that marked Argentina in the period under discussion, the Borochovist perspective did not reflect the reality and was in fact very wide of the mark. Writing under the title, "Our Assessment of the Dangers and Prospects Was Overblown," the author notes that despite the manifestations of anti-Semitism in Argentina, the Jews were not running away and hiding from the pogromists. On the contrary, the anti-Semitic incidents inspired a brave and assertive response by the young Jews there. The Jews of Argentina were not sitting on their suitcases but felt deep roots and security in the country:

> They feel themselves to be citizens with equal rights. The high schools and the universities are open to them at no charge and they have full benefit of them. The country's culture and language are their culture and language, too. They do not need to be liberated from any other national, religious, or cultural burden. There are almost no inhibitions and the process of assimilation plays out in the most natural way, with no pangs of conscience. And there is absolutely no resistance by non-Jewish society.[120]

During this entire period, the DAIA's struggle was abetted by the network of connections it had developed over the years, mainly with liberal civic elements. It chalked up a number of nontrivial achievements, including the passage of laws against anti-Semitic organizations. On June 28, 1962, Jewish merchants and businesses all across Argentina staged a general strike to protest the surge in anti-Semitic violence that followed Eichmann's execution. The strike garnered tremendous support from the public at large, and many sectors of civil society seconded the Jewish protest. Later, during Illia's presidency, the DAIA managed to have the representative of the Arab League expelled on account of his anti-Semitic incitement. Even during Onganía's dictatorship, when anti-Semitic incidents were common, the military regime denied any ties to the anti-Semites and even showed sympathy for the Jews. By way of conclusion, and to illustrate this, I quote a 1964 letter by the engineer Moshe Dayan, one of the leading Revisionists in Argentina:

> I do not believe in the antisemitic character of the Argentinian people. This country has gone through and continues to experience difficult years of turmoil and confusion. After the fall of the Perón regime, democracy did not live up to the hopes people placed in it. The frequently changing governments caused the economic situation of the weaker sectors to get worse, and everything kept deteriorating at a pace in which the poor got poorer and the rich got richer. . . . It is true that Dr. Illia, the president of Argentina, avoids the use of force and is not an advocate of retributive laws. And all the more so when they would be applied against anti-Jewish activities. But in economic and social terms, most of the people are more tolerant. All of this has created fertile ground for disturbances and riots. An anti-Jewish campaign began, which included, in addition to the traditional forces from the ultranationalist sector, elements of the clergy, who were joined by immigrants

> from Europe, Nazi Fascists, and the Arab incitement. Despite the use of various weapons, explosives, tar bombs, fireballs, and more, they have had little impact when compared to the general tremors that have shaken Argentina in recent years. The murder of Dr. Stanovsky, which has never been solved, was not included "for some reason" among the anti-Jewish actions. The reaction to the strange case of Sirota, too, which had international reverberations, was weaker than to the incident at the Law School, where a devout Catholic female student was shot and killed. We cannot deny, and it is true that we must not publicize it, that in recent years many Jews have excelled in remarkable acts of fraud and forgery. And some of them have found shelter in Israel. And also that more Jews have run way on account of their debts than of antisemitism.[121]

In this chapter, we have seen that the weight of the push factors was decisive for the entire process of Argentinian Jewish immigration to Israel. In the overall balance, the economic and political crises in Argentina were more significant than the anti-Semitic attacks. This can also be deduced by tracing the variation in the annual traffic from the establishment of Israel to the present, as found in the annual publications of the Central Bureau of Statistics.[122] Despite the common assumption, throughout this period anti-Semitism never seems to have been the main reason for Argentinian Jewish immigration to Israel. This is clearly seen in the years of the "Dirty War" of the military junta, in the 1970s, and in the 1990s, when there were two bloody attacks in Buenos Aires—the bombings of the Israeli embassy in 1992 and of the AMIA building in 1994. Rather, it was economic factors that catalyzed the decision to move to Israel. This is shown must strikingly by the sharp spike in Argentinian immigration to Israel in 2002, energized by the severe economic crisis that struck Argentina that year and brought some 6,000 immigrants to Israel (similar to the number who arrived in 1963).

3

"We Do Not See the Living Individual"

The Crystallization of Israel's Immigration Policy

The Mechanism of Immigration to Israel in Service to the Ingathering of the Exiles

In the first months after Israel achieved independence, the mechanism for bringing and absorbing immigrants was devised and developed. The Aliyah Department of the Jewish Agency was the natural and indeed only institution that could take over responsibility for a domain that had previously been under the purview of the Mandatory government. The moment the country was born, the Aliyah Department's offices in the large cities were available to provide the required services at all points of entry to Israel, replacing the Mandatory Immigration Department and Border Control. These services included the routine activities of registering immigrants; granting visas; and issuing licenses, passports, travel documents, citizenship papers, and more. The department's offices abroad became the State's representatives in foreign countries, and their officials carried out the consular chores formerly handled by British diplomats, including the issuance of entry visas to Israel to immigrants of all categories.[1]

Despite the sovereign powers enjoyed by the new country, the struggle for sovereignty had in fact only just begun. Achieving it in full involved many trials and tribulations, including in the domain of immigration. The painful chapter of the detention camps on Cyprus is a good illustration of the obstacles that stood in the way of immigrants, even after the country's gates were ostensibly thrown wide open. At the time, there were some 24,000 Jewish refugees on Cyprus, but the British authorities on the island impeded their departure. At a press conference in mid-August 1948, the minister of immigration in the provisional government, Moshe Shapira, said that there were still some 12,000 would-be immigrants in Cyprus, stuck there because Britain would not allow men of military age to leave for Israel.[2]

It also proved difficult to charter ships to carry immigrants to Israel from the DP camps in Europe. Foreign companies were not willing to lease their vessels because of the ongoing hostilities. The War of Independence, until May 15 between the Yishuv and the local Arabs only, had entered the second and decisive stage after the country was invaded by the Arab regular armies, and there were bloody battles all over Israel. As a result, even though the doors had been opened to immigration by the Proclamation of Independence, during the next few months, immigrants continued to arrive more or less as they had during the period of clandestine immigration, traveling on ancient and overloaded ships, their route strewn with obstacles. They had to rely on the infrastructure of the Mossad la'Aliya Bet (the pre-State agency that handled clandestine immigration) and on covert and indirect links with countries overseas, because the regular channels of communication had been severed or disrupted by the war. Yet despite all the hardships, difficulties, and obstacles, more than 32,000 immigrants arrived in Israel between May 15 and August 1948.[3]

During the War of Independence, the topic of immigration remained firmly on the agenda. The provisional government and the Jewish Agency redoubled their efforts to increase the flow of immigrants, with the main consideration being the newcomers' potential contribution to the war effort. "Immigration is the apple of our eye," even though "we are not free to maneuver and cannot do everything we would like to," reported the newspaper *Davar* in August 1948.[4] These lines were written against the background of the second truce and in light of the peace proposal drafted by the UN mediator, Count Folke Bernadotte of Sweden, which included severe restrictions on immigration. At the start of that month, the UN truce observers also demanded that no more than 500 immigrants of military age be admitted each month. Despite the restrictions, there was a general consensus that it was essential to double the country's population, which would require immigration on an unprecedented scale.[5]

At the August 1948 press conference, Shapira shared interesting details about the immigration and absorption plan drawn up by his ministry. He reported that the monthly budget for immigrant absorption was a million and half Israeli pounds, and that the ministry was devising a plan to bring over 125,000 Jews from Europe every year. He said that the plan was based on the potential number of aliya candidates, the possibility of leaving various countries, and the combined absorption capacity of the government and the Jewish Agency. Nevertheless, the minister declared: "The gates of Israel are open! Anyone who wants to and can make aliya will make aliya!" Shapira explained that the numbers in the plan referred to immigrants for whose immigration and absorption the government would be responsible. People of means or immigrants supported by others, who would not be a burden on public institutions, could enter the country without restriction.[6] As for what was being done abroad as of that date, Shapira said that immigration officers were working out of the Israeli consulates in Munich, Berlin, Salzburg, Rome, London, Warsaw, Bucharest, Prague, Stockholm, New York, Paris, Sofia, Athens, Tunis, Amsterdam, Geneva, Budapest, Brussels, Rio de Janeiro, Buenos Aires, and elsewhere, and were authorized to issue entry visas to Israel on the basis of the instructions they received from home.[7]

Beyond the immigration minister's attempt to publicly demonstrate Israel's policy independence, it is also important to understand his remarks as part of the contest that was under way between the Zionist establishment (the Jewish Agency and World Zionist Organization) and the Israeli government regarding the division of authority between them. Shapira, like most members of the provisional government, including the prime minister, believed that the functions and powers related to immigration and absorption should be the province of the state and that it was government's job to set policy and determine numbers, rates, quotas, and so forth. This ran counter to the opinion of most members of the Zionist leadership, who preferred a division of tasks and authority between the government and the Zionist institutions and had demanded, before independence, that the responsibilities of each be defined clearly.

This demand won the backing of the Zionist General Council at its first meeting since independence, in August 1948, only a few days after Shapira unveiled his ministry's plan at the press conference. The council defined the roles and authority of the Zionist institutions in domains outside the country's sovereign functions. It was decided that the Jewish Agency Executive would continue to be the supreme arbiter in matters of aliya, as in the past, through its twelve departments—five of which dealt directly with immigration and absorption: Aliyah, Rural Settlement, Youth Aliyah, Youth and Hehalutz, and the economic department. In the new organizational structure, absorption was removed from the brief of the Aliyah Department and assigned to a new department established for this purpose.[8]

The Aliyah Department's function and the scope of its activities were redefined. They now included preparing candidates for immigration (except for agricultural training, which was transferred to Youth and Hehalutz); running the former Palestine Offices in the Diaspora; proposing immigration quotas and their breakdown by countries and categories, in coordination with the Israeli government; and handling the arrangements for the immigrants' passage to Israel. The Zionist General Council approved the continued existence of the Mossad la'Aliya as one of the main mechanisms for bringing immigrants to Israel, even though independence had been achieved, but henceforth it would operate as part of the Aliyah Department and not independently, as before. It was also decided to establish public boards for the two offices of the Mossad la'Aliya, in Israel and in Paris, and to assign it responsibility for bringing over the immigrants by sea and air, in accordance with the countries, quotas, convoys, and dates determined by the Aliyah Department.[9]

When the Jewish Agency/WZO portfolios were handed out, every party tried to get the most important ones, which included the Aliyah Department and the Absorption Department. Mapam (a left-wing socialist party) demanded the aliya portfolio on the grounds that its members had been prominent in the prestigious clandestine immigration mechanism. Minister Shapira of the religious Zionist Hapoel Mizrahi party was vehemently opposed to his party's giving up the Jewish Agency portfolio and managed to have it entrusted to Yitzhak Rafael, his party colleague. As compensation, Mapam received the Jewish Middle East Affairs section. Absorption remained the province of the ruling Mapai party.[10]

The new head of the Aliyah Department, Yitzhak Rafael, saw himself as representing his party.[11] When he took up his post, he began implementing the new arrangement that had been decided on, both in Israel and abroad. Within a few days, the department's main office was consolidated with its branches in Tel Aviv and Haifa, and all the necessary steps were taken to restore central control of the activities of the various institutions and agencies that operated in the field of immigration, in Israel and abroad, with which contact had been lost in the early months of the War of Independence. In the first communiqués issued by the reconstituted department, on September 15 and 22, 1948, it conveyed its instructions to the former Palestine Offices and the aliya emissaries in the Diaspora, renewing contact with them and clarifying its authority under the new arrangement.[12]

Once the department returned to normal operations, Rafael traveled to Europe in order to take a closer look at the immigration needs there, make progress on reorganizing the offices, and coordinate the work within and between the various countries and between them and his headquarters in Jerusalem. An office was opened in Paris to serve as the liaison with the bureaus in Europe and the aliya emissaries in North Africa. By the time Rafael returned to Israel, the mechanism for implementing immigration to the sovereign state was up and running.[13]

From then on, immigration and absorption were overseen in parallel and redundantly by the Jewish Agency and the Israeli government. The Zionist Executive, through the departments of the Jewish Agency, handled the actual work of organizing and dealing with potential immigrants and financed their move. The Jewish Agency set immigration quotas; it also selected and processed candidates until they arrived in Israel and covered the costs with funds from the United Jewish Appeal in the United States and the Joint Distribution Committee. Policy was supposed to be left to the government. However, the Zionist Executive's autonomy in the organization of immigration, reinforced by its deep pockets, gave it the whip hand in setting policy too. In light of this development, and especially the changes in the mechanisms of immigration, Shapira's Ministry of Immigration lost most of its importance and was eventually reduced to the status of the immigration and registration section of the Interior Ministry.[14]

All along, the flood tide of immigrants continued to reach Israel. From July to September, the number of immigrants averaged more than 12,000 a month. In early October, the primary task facing the officials in charge of immigration and absorption was bringing over the refugees who were still living in DP camps in Germany, Austria, Italy, Aden, and Cyprus. But they also recognized the need for continued immigration from other places as well. In particular, the authorities were concerned by the need for immediate and massive emigration from Eastern Europe. The plan drafted by the Jewish Agency Aliyah Department in late 1948 provided for the emigration of most of the 40,000 Jews of Bulgaria, as well as thousands more from Romania, Yugoslavia, and Poland. In the last quarter of that year, emigration averaged more than 20,000 persons a month. The peak was in December, when 28,000 newcomers landed in Israeli ports. This was the beginning of the "Great Aliya," which accelerated in 1949.[15]

The "Day of the Million" or "Ingathering of the Exiles Day"

In early December 1949, the Jewish population of Israel reached the one million mark. Those who were involved with immigration and absorption, in the government and Jewish Agency, saw this as a onetime opportunity and proposed to celebrate Hanukkah that year with the motto of "the first million." The Jewish Agency Aliyah Department set up a special committee, which included representatives of the Immigration Ministry and other agency departments, to plan this event. When the Jewish Agency Executive gave the go-ahead, December

19, 1949, the fourth day of Hanukkah, was proclaimed a holiday in Israel and the Diaspora—"Ingathering of the Exiles Day."[16] The details of the program were revealed at a special press conference, along with future programs related to immigration.[17] The program for the special day was summed up by the head of the Aliyah Department, Rafael, in three main points: "a summation of the first stage of mass aliya, commemoration of those who perished making aliya, and the spreading of aliya awareness among the public at large."[18] In a personal letter to mayors and local council heads, Rafael focused on the main goals of the festivities:

> This day is intended to place aliya at the center of public interest, to open hearts to help and understand, to knock down the barriers between the veterans and newcomers, to plant in the immigrants' heart the feeling that they are indeed part of the Yishuv, and to strengthen their sense that they are citizens of Israel. One of the day's objectives is to stimulate the people living in Zion to volunteer to teach, guide, and provide spiritual assistance to the immigrant masses.[19]

The Israeli press lavished attention on the event. *Hatzofeh*, *Davar*, and *Al Hamishmar* published special supplements that included surveys and statistics about aliya and how the Yishuv was flourishing. *Davar* devoted an entire page in the supplement to this topic, including a poem by Nathan Alterman—"The Day of the Million." There were lead articles about aliya and the ingathering of the exiles, under the bylines of prominent writers and journalists such as Moshe Smilansky, Yisrael Dov Frumkin, and Yaakov Amit.[20] *Hatzofeh* ran an item under the headline "The Miracle of the Ingathering of the Exiles," and *Haboker* printed the following lines:

> The day of the ingathering of the exiles is intended to remind us that we should set aside a special time in our lives for taking a moral inventory and reflecting on the amazing historical events that are taking place before our eyes, and not stand before them stunned and mute. For until a short while ago we truly did not anticipate that this miracle of the ingathering of our exiles from among the nations would take place in our day and that we would merit to see with our own eyes our brothers ascending and coming to this country from all the ends of the Earth, by all the means of transportation that exist in the world today.[21]

Over the airwaves, radio broadcasts highlighted the topic, with speeches by President Chaim Weizmann, Immigration Minister Moshe Shapira, Eliyahu Dobkin of the Jewish Agency Executive, and the head of the agency's Aliyah Department, Yitzhak Rafael.[22] On the Voice of Israel, Dr. Binyamin Zvi Gill, the statistician of the Central Bureau of Statistics, provided details about the demographics and growth of Israeli society. The broadcast opened with a speech by Rafael, in which he described the dramatic developments and provided figures on the mass immigration: Since May 1948, 333,000 Jewish immigrants, from fifty-two different countries, had entered Israel—17,000 a month.[23]

Later in his speech, Rafael proclaimed the day's motto: "From one million to the ingathering of all the exiles"; in other words, Ingathering of the Exiles Day "is merely a way station on the long road we still have to travel."[24] Immigration Minister Shapira conveyed a similar message and asserted that the main task of the next few years was the settlement of millions more in the national homeland.[25] President Weizmann continued in this spirit: "The road to the second million must be short! More than at any other time, we are now commanded to make a great leap forward."[26] Prime Minister Ben-Gurion, addressing the Knesset to mark the day, which he described as revolutionary, said that the three main tasks now incumbent on the State of Israel were defending its security, absorbing the immigrants, and molding a progressive and sovereign nation. He added that the underlying principle that guided government activity in the national and international arenas was the effort to double the country's population by its fourth birthday.[27]

The organizers achieved their goal of placing immigration and absorption at the center of public attention; all who were asked to cooperate to make the day a success responded favorably and enthusiastically. Municipalities and local councils organized eighty-three public rallies in cities, agricultural settlements, and housing developments for new immigrants, with the participation of public officials and artists.[28] Nor did the younger generation remain aloof. Regional gatherings of the youth movements, held all around the country, drew close to 10,000 teenagers. The military and agricultural settlement organizations ran most of their educational and organizational activities under the banner of the "Ingathering of the Exiles." All of them conducted aliya-related study days, seminars, conferences, and field trips during Hanukkah. The Chief Rabbinate organized a central prayer service in Jerusalem; a specially composed prayer was recited in all the synagogues, including mention of those who perished en route to the Land of Israel during the period of clandestine immigration.[29]

Ingathering of the Exiles Day culminated in a mass event sponsored by the Jewish Agency Aliyah Department and the Immigration Ministry. A large crowd assembled at the airport in Lod, including government ministers, members of the Jewish Agency Executive, members of the Knesset, members of the Zionist General Council, intellectuals, and representatives of various public organizations. They heard the roar of the planes as they landed with their loads of new immigrants; the crowd ran out to the runway, which was brilliantly illuminated. Chief Rabbi Ben-Zion Meir Hai Uziel gave the new immigrants a fervent blessing. "It was an unforgettable experience," noted Rafael in his memoirs.[30] Immigration Minister Shapira waxed poetic in his speech over radio: "The Hanukkah lights we are kindling this week will burn like a torch, illuminating the way to Zion and Jerusalem for our brothers in the Diaspora."[31]

The Diaspora, too, made preparations to celebrate the day, under the baton of the Aliyah Department. Reports about the day's festivities streamed into the department's offices in Jerusalem from every place where the Zionist movement was active. Representatives of the Zionist Executive disseminated information about aliya at press conferences in the major cities of Europe and America.[32] The day received particular attention in the eighteen transit camps that the Aliyah Department had set up near the ports of embarkation in Europe. There were even festive programs on the decks of several ships at sea, with thousands of immigrants on board—the *Kedma*, *Artza*, *Galila*, and *Atzma'ut*. "These were the closing hours of a great and protracted enterprise," is how the Aliyah Department newsletter described it.[33]

From Myth to Reality

The description of the events held on Ingathering of the Exiles Day is based on Aliyah Department documents, articles printed in its newsletter, press clippings, and personal memoirs. These sources strongly reflect the ideology that played a decisive role in molding the immigration policy of the young State of Israel: free immigration and the ingathering of the exiles. According to those same principles, the source of "the driving force that propels the people and demands that they move towards Zion, with great and expeditious speed" was the unexpected awakening of the Jewish people, which heard the ram's horn of the redemption when the State was born. Underpinning this human tide was the great and ancient vision that encompassed the yearning to return to the homeland as well as the expectation that, in the sovereign State of Israel, all the exiles would fuse into a new and reborn nation, an Israeli Zionist version of the "melting pot" concept that was prevalent in other countries of immigration. What stands out in the sources that document the events is the joint and active enlistment of the Zionist Executive, the government, and the veteran Yishuv to help realize the vision of the ingathering of the exiles. As Nathan Alterman wrote: "Let us also remember this: a million is powerful if the million stand together as a single man!"[34]

In contrast to the festive, miraculous, and ideological spirit described above, other sources quoted in the academic literature and in various primary sources produced by those who organized, implemented, and absorbed the mass immigration paint a dramatically different picture, which is at odds with the impressive myth. First, the wave of immigration was not self-starting, an automatic reaction to the tidings of redemption. Instead, it was the result of a deliberate and concentrated initiative that required extensive organizational effort. Second, and despite expectations, not everyone took part in it. Third, immigration to Israel was not completely free and unrestricted. Finally, the documents about the relations between the Israeli government and Jewish Agency do not indicate close cooperation. On the contrary, a split between them and duplication of roles and authority, with social clashes and political rivalries, would be a better account of the true situation, both in Israel and abroad.[35]

At a press conference held in Jerusalem on August 22, 1949, a year after he took up his post, Yitzhak Rafael said proudly that the bureaucracy he directed numbered "more than 500 persons, handling all stages of aliya until the immigrants board ship in the ports of embarkation."[36] Immigration flowed smoothly according to the monthly plans drawn up in accordance with the applications and prospects. The plan for 1949 foresaw 330,000 immigrants. But because of problems with absorption and housing, which were exacerbated by the increased flow of immigrants, the plan was cut back, with the approval of the Zionist Executive, to a quarter of a million newcomers. Even this soon produced an unprecedented tidal wave. The zenith was recorded in March 1949, when some 31,000 people entered the country. As the months passed there was no letup in the pressure; total immigration for the year came to roughly 240,000.[37]

The numbers were dramatic. Between the day the State was established and the end of 1949, more than 341,000 immigrants arrived in Israel. The ramifications of this influx and the meaning of these statistics were tremendous. The population of Israel grew by 50%; in other words, for every two Jews who lived in the country on May 15, 1948, a third Israeli was added during these nineteen months.[38] Given the ratio between the immigrants and the veteran population, the demographics of the former, the rapid pace of their arrival, the high costs of the enterprise, and the tensions associated with organizing and carrying out this immense project, the mass immigration and absorption of those years was one of the most challenging and difficult social experiments in the annals of Israel. At this juncture, immigration and absorption were the core process in the young country and the focus of attention for citizens and leaders alike.

The official data about the immigrants' countries of origin indicate that the largest group, 56%, were Eastern European Jews, mainly from Poland, Bulgaria, and Romania. Immigration from Asian and African countries, especially Tunisia, Libya, and Yemen, also increased and accounted for more than a third of the immigrants during this period.[39] This breakdown hints at the principle that guided immigration and absorption then. The main potential for mass immigration lay beyond the Iron Curtain in Eastern Europe, countries whose borders had been sealed by the authorities. The Jews from Muslim countries, another reservoir for Jewish immigration and estimated to number about a million, had strong roots there. Following the establishment of the State, however, most of these countries evinced strong hostility toward Israel, and the Jewish communities there found themselves in grave peril. In these circumstances, the timing of immigration, along with its dimensions and source countries, depended on Israeli initiative and on major funding and concentrated effort that required extensive organization as well as diplomatic efforts, sometimes sub rosa.[40]

In light of the huge scale of immigration in 1949, the severe problems with absorption, and the fiscal shortfall, the first signs emerged of a fierce controversy among policy makers, related to the issue of unrestricted immigration and matching its pace to the capacity for absorption. This was the background for the decision by the Jewish Agency Executive, at the end of the year, to instruct its Finance, Absorption, and Aliyah Departments to cap the immigration budget for the coming three months at fifteen million Israeli pounds. The Zionist leadership ruled that immigrants with independent means who did not need to be housed in immigrant transit camps, immigrants who could be taken in by relatives in Israel, and those sent directly to agricultural settlements would not be included in the agency's absorption budget. It was clear, however, that new planning and organization, consistent with the available budget, were essential for those whose transportation and absorption costs had to be covered by the agency (85% of the total). "There are, then, no aliya quotas, but there are funding quotas," stated the Executive.[41]

The deliberations about immigration led the government and Jewish Agency to define a formal distinction between "countries of distress" and "developed countries." Based on that distinction, immigration policy was guided by the rationale that the rate and demographics of immigration could be regulated as long as the restrictions did not pose a threat to Jewish communities in existential danger, which were referred to as "terminal communities." By contrast, limits could be set for immigration from places where the Jews were in no immediate danger. The assumption behind the uniform treatment of all the developed countries was that Jewish emigration from these countries was not propelled by "catastrophic" motives, such as severe financial distress or hostility toward Jews, but exclusively by ideology and personal reasons. According to a retrospective of two decades of immigration, published in the last issue of the Aliyah Department newsletter, *Dappei Aliyah*, in 1968, "It is clear that the scale of aliya from the developed countries should not be judged by the standards for aliya from countries of distress," because unlike the latter, where the push factor was decisive, in the former it was the pull factor that was dominant.[42]

These were broad definitions, based on generalizations, but their main problem was the impossibility of setting absolute criteria for the level of distress or urgency. Often, as I will demonstrate with regard to Argentinian Jewry, this led to vagueness, ambiguity, and inconsistency. The distinction did, however, produce a clear pattern of action: whenever and wherever Jews were felt to be in danger, immense efforts were made to bring them to Israel, with no limits on their number. This pattern was clearly reflected in the article in *Dappei Aliyah*:

> The Aliyah Department, which is the physical arm that reaches out to the Jews in the Diaspora, functions—in addition to its broad organizational roles—as a sort of seismograph, which immediately detects the traces of earthquakes and tremors in Jewish communities. Twenty years of aliya to Israel have long since proved that every change for the worse in the situation of a Jewish community and every surge in antisemitic activity, in any place whatsoever, immediately increases the number of candidates for aliya. And when the possibility of a new wave of immigration emerges, the department must translate these fluctuations into the language of action—organizing its staff and preparing for the sometimes panic-stricken knocks on the gates of aliya to Israel.[43]

The mere trickle of immigrants from the developed countries caused great disappointment in Israel, not to mention scathing criticism. The official statistics on immigration to Israel by country of origin, during the first year of independence, counted a negligible number of arrivals from the Americas, in proportion to the total. On December 9, 1949, ten days before Ingathering of the Exiles Day, the daily *Al Hamishmar*, the organ of the socialist Mapam party, published an article by Moshe Sneh, its associate editor and leader of the party's leftist faction, under the headline, "Where Is the Aliya from the West?" Sneh analyzed and assessed the meaning of the immigration figures: "The immigrants from the free countries do not make up even 1% of all olim!" Sneh noted. "The overwhelming majority of the Jewish people are standing on the sidelines and not taking an active part in the revolutionary process of the ingathering of the exiles."[44]

Despite the disappointment and criticism, we see from the documents that those who shaped Israeli immigration policy recognized that without some encouragement there would be few immigrants from developed countries. An example of this, in the South American context, is found in a report submitted by Jacob Tsur, the Israel minister to Argentina, soon after he took up his post in October 1949: "The Jews lead a fairly comfortable life and are not willing, in today's conditions, to uproot themselves from their homes and go to meet the unknown, merely out of a yearning and love for the Land of Israel."[45] As for North America, the documents indicate that the emissaries from Israel and the local community leaders adopted the role of panic mongers and doomsayers, employing comparisons and parallels intended to prove that anti-Semitism could exist in every place and every time, including America, and that the Jews there should internalize the lesson of the bitter experience of the Jewish communities of Europe.[46] "Of course they will never come because of resolutions by the Zionist Congresses, or decisions made in Jerusalem, and all the less will they come as a result of our spreading fear in the Jewish community," wrote the author and editor Hayim Greenberg, a member of the Jewish Agency Executive and head of the Education and Culture Department.[47]

It follows that the organization and encouragement of Jewish immigration to Israel did not rely only on ideological arguments—namely, that unrestricted immigration and the ingathering of exiles were essential for making the country stronger—but also on doomsday prophecies of the "crisis of the Jews" and sometimes the "crisis of Judaism," which presented the State of Israel as a safe haven for all the Jews in the world. These principles cannot be detached from the historic context of Zionist aliya policy, going back to the founding of the movement in the late nineteenth century. In fact, Israel's Proclamation of Independence did not alter policy makers' attitude toward immigration or the principles on which that policy was based after the establishment of the State.[48]

The principles of unrestricted immigration and the ingathering of the exiles were enshrined in Israel's Proclamation of Independence in 1948, which stated that "the State of Israel will be open for Jewish aliya and for the Ingathering of the Exiles." This festive declaration was given legal status by the Law of Return, passed in July 1950. It stipulated that every Jew had the right to immigrate to Israel, except for those who worked against the Jewish people or were liable to pose a threat to public health or national security.[49] Two days before the law was passed by the Knesset, Prime Minister David Ben-Gurion defined it as "the Bill of Rights of the Jewish people in the Land of Israel."[50] According to him, it was not the state that was bestowing this right; rather, this right was "innate to any person inasmuch as he is a Jew, and has its source in the historic bond, which has never been broken, between the Jewish people and its homeland."[51] The dialectical solution to this complex issue that Ben-Gurion proposed, based on the distinction between natural rights and privileges, was further sharpened by the Citizenship Law of 1952, which laid down that aliya under the Law of Return confers citizenship on any Jew who decides to settle in Israel. Only non-Jews must comply with rules for immigration and naturalization parallel to those in force in most countries.[52]

The Law of Return and the Citizenship Law gave the final stamp of approval to the national exclusivity of Jewish immigration, on the basis of ethnic and national principles, and expressed the State's commitment to unrestricted aliya and the ingathering of the exiles. On the surface, the moral commitment to aliya took precedence over economic interests and ostensibly distinguished Israel from other countries that limited immigration according to various utilitarian criteria, such as the newcomer's age, health and physical condition, and ability to work. The Law of Return created a climate in support of the principle of free and unrestricted Jewish immigration, even though that did not really exist. The law did not define the scope and rate of immigration and did not include provisions for deliberate steps to encourage it or to provide organizational and financial assistance for the immigration process.[53]

The topics mentioned above came up in the discussions of immigration policy conducted by the Israeli government and the Jewish Agency Executive, particularly from May 1950 on, following the establishment of the Coordinating Committee and its designation as the forum that set and coordinated policy related to immigration and absorption. The committee, which consisted of four government ministers and four members of the Agency Executive, was chaired by the prime minister. Its deliberations and decisions were confidential.[54] The committee decided to implement a selective approach to immigration from countries where Jews were not threatened or in danger. Immigrants from those countries would be screened on the basis of economic and cultural criteria and partisan political affiliation. Any analysis of the case of the Jews of Argentina must not be severed from the developments described above—neither the myth of "free aliya" nor the reality of selective immigration.

The Policy of Selective Immigration

The clash between declared principles and the many problems of absorption led to the formulation of a selective immigration policy. It is important to understand this decision against the background of the vast numbers who arrived in the first years of Israel's independence. Nearly 700,000 immigrants entered Israel between May 1948 and the end of 1951. The demographics of this immigration changed significantly over these months. About half of the immigrants were from Eastern Europe, most of them Holocaust survivors who had been living in DP camps; the other half came from Muslim countries. Most of the latter were airlifted to Israel in special campaigns, such as Operation Magic Carpet and Operation Ezra and Nehemiah, which brought almost all the Jews from Yemen and from Iraq, respectively, to Israel. Jews from Libya, Syria, and Lebanon, as well as about half the Jewish communities in Turkey and Iran, also came to Israel then, as did many Jews from Egypt and India. There was only a handful from Western Europe and the Americas.[55]

Most of the immigrants in those years arrived penniless and without an occupation. They included many who were elderly, infirm, and disabled and placed a heavy financial burden on the Israeli economy. The mass immigration had to be absorbed by a young state that had a shaky financial infrastructure and was not really prepared to deal with it. The huge number of immigrants had not been anticipated, and the absorption institutions had not made adequate preparations to provide them with housing, jobs, health care, education, and social assistance. The system of basic services was on the verge of collapse.[56] In this situation, the Jewish Agency and government officials who dealt with immigration and absorption formulated a new concept in late 1951, whose main points were as follows:[57]

1. Eighty percent of the immigrants will be selected from the candidates for Youth Aliyah, persons intending to join or found agricultural settlements, professionals under age thirty-five, and families in which the principal wage earner is below thirty-five.
2. With the exception of professionals and those with the means to provide their own housing, immigrants must undertake to engage in agricultural labor for a period of two years.

3. Candidate will be approved for immigration only after a thorough medical exam, supervised by an Israeli physician.
4. Up to 20% of the immigrants will be older than thirty-five, but only on condition that their family includes a breadwinner who is able to work or that they are invited and absorbed by relatives in Israel.
5. The Aliyah Department will approve immigrants invited by relatives in Israel only after the latter's ability to absorb them has been confirmed.

These criteria were designed to prevent immigration by the chronically ill, those with disabilities, and families without a breadwinner. It was decided that they would not apply to immigrants from countries defined as countries of distress or from Eastern Europe.[58] "I am happy with the decisions," Rafael said at the end of a plenary session of the Agency Executive in March 1952, which discussed the new rules of selection.[59] According to him, the decision to introduce such restrictions on immigration represented a compromise between two different approaches: the principles of increasing the number of productive immigrants and enhancing the quality of the newcomers with regard to their age and heath would be maintained, while the influx from countries where the Jews where in danger continued unabated. Relying on his own experience and available data, Rafael forecast 100,000 immigrants in 1952.[60] However, despite the expectations and assessments, the wave peaked at an annual rate of 100,000 in mid-1951, began to ebb in August of that year, and decreased drastically over the coming years: fewer than 24,000 immigrants arrived in 1952, and fewer than 10,500 in 1953.[61]

In light of this sharp decline, the issue of Jewish immigration to Israel from the West (the English-speaking countries, Western Europe, and Latin America) received increased attention in the deliberations of those responsible for immigration and absorption affairs. Immigration from those countries was the "order of the day," as Rafael put it from the podium of the Zionist General Council in November 1952. He noted that during the previous activity year, from September 1951 to September 1952, only 183 Jews had moved to Israel from the United States and forty-three from Canada, which he referred to as "a strongly Zionist country." During that same period, 569 immigrants came from Central and South America—twenty times the figure for North America, proportional to the number of Jews there, Rafael noted. During those same months, there were 1,247 immigrants from Western Europe, twenty-eight from Australia, and twenty-two from South Africa, for a grand total of 2,092 immigrants from the Free World. These data were cause for concern, because they represented a serious drop from the 4,519 immigrants who arrived from the same countries during the previous twelve months (September 1950 to September 1951).[62] Later in his talk, Rafael reviewed the complaints that reached his department about the mishandling of immigrants from the developed countries; they were "exaggerated and unjustified, but still with quite a bit of truth in them." "Perhaps they [the Jews in the West] are not the only ones to blame. It seems that we too have sinned to no small extent."[63]

First Steps to Encourage Jewish Immigration from the Developed Countries

In early 1953, in light of the plunge in immigration, the Jewish Agency and Israeli government functionaries who dealt with immigration and absorption introduced measures to encourage Jews from the developed countries to move to Israel. The Aliyah Department worked on the basis of the reports and assessments submitted by its representatives and public figures in Western Europe and Latin America. According to those reports, there was a potential for Jewish immigration by many families, if appropriate steps were taken in advance to transfer their capital and facilitate their absorption in Israel. The department's proposals, submitted to the Agency Executive and government, included the establishment of a central agency to oversee Jewish emigration from the West; allowing immigrants to purchase apartments in public housing projects on convenient terms; authorizing Israeli representatives abroad to issue licenses for the import of machinery, raw materials, and the like; setting a unified exchange rate for immigrants and investors; and exempting merchandise from the requirement of import licenses if included in the transfer of the immigrants' property to Israel, as long as its value did not exceed $10,000.[64]

One of the immediate results of these initiatives to encourage Jewish immigration to Israel from the West was the establishment, in early 1953, of the Center for the Immigrant Investor, as part of the Ministry of Industry and Trade and in cooperation with the Jewish Agency Aliyah Department and Economic Department. The center was designed to handle all stages of the process for middle-class immigrants, starting with investigating the possibilities for their settlement in Israel and issuing licenses to transfer capital and continuing through their practical arrangements and absorption. A joint committee of the government and Jewish Agency oversaw and advised the activities of the center, which functioned as an administrative unit within the Investments Center (which operated under Finance Ministry auspices). It did not actually begin work until October 1953, however; even then it was not accorded real authority, and all its decisions about the affairs of immigrant investors required ratification by the Finance Ministry. "The problem of the investor oleh, the little man with limited means, has yet to be resolved," noted the Zionist Executive's report on the period from mid-1951 to the end of 1955, drawn up for the twenty-fourth Zionist Congress in 1956.[65] The center proved short-lived; it was disbanded in August 1955 and its functions transferred to the Investments Center.[66]

Another joint initiative taken by the Aliyah and Economic Departments to encourage Jewish emigration from the West was the establishment of an Artisans' Unit. It was given a clearly defined set of tasks: organizing the immigration of craftsmen, making sure that they would be able to work in their trades in Israel, providing them with financial assistance to acquire equipment and premises, and steering them to localities where there was a need for their services. The division developed contacts with more than forty local councils throughout the country in order to amass information about the employment situation in the various regions and the possibilities for absorption there. This information, which was forwarded to the Aliyah Department offices abroad, included lists of available jobs and the possibilities for absorption in the towns and rural settlements, as well as general information about the employment prospects for the various skilled trades. The division established a company, the Workshop for the Immigrant, whose board included representatives of the Economic Department, the Absorption Department, and the Union of Skilled Tradesmen; its purpose was to facilitate the immigrants' absorption by helping them acquire tools and workshops on reasonable terms.[67]

In addition to these two units, in June 1953 the Coordinating Committee decided to establish a Council for Aliya from the West. The council, which comprised three members of the government and three members of the Jewish Agency Executive, oversaw the activities of the subcommittees that consulted with experts in the field and then drew up proposals for encouraging emigration from the West, dealing with issues such as relatives, capital transfers and customs duties, absorption, housing, and employment.[68] Speaking to the council in June 1953, Yitzhak Rafael reported on additional activities that his department had initiated to encourage aliya from the Free World. They included building a special housing project of a higher standard; establishing homes and hostels for single immigrants; expanding the office for Professional and Technical Workers' Aliya, which had previously been active only in England; creating revolving loan funds for professionals and experts; and dispatching Israeli public figures for short visits to their countries of origin or places where they had influence among local Jews.[69]

By now, the various groups that dealt with immigration and absorption understood that the selection rules needed to be revised and that the original regulations had in fact hindered the arrival of many large and healthy families. As early as February 1952, it was decided to increase the maximum age of the breadwinner to forty; during 1953, other changes and amendments effectively raised the ceiling to forty-five.[70] Significant modifications to the rules were introduced in March 1953, including the concept that the entire family unit would serve as the basis for selection. Nevertheless, the Agency Executive reaffirmed the current practice with regard to a medical certificate and decided that only the Health Ministry and its authorized representatives could rule on immigrants' physical condition. In response, in June 1953 the Coordinating Committee decided to abolish the requirement of a medical examination for the families of teenagers and young adults who were candidates for immigration.[71] The revised regulations of March 1953 empowered the Aliyah Department to determine the fitness and social situation of potential immigrants, in consultation with the Absorption Department in Israel.[72]

From these steps, which were intended to encourage immigration, we may conclude that the policy makers had come to appreciate the importance of middle-class olim and understood that their successful immigration depended on productive exploitation of the small capital at their disposal; that is, not only the transfer of their nest egg to Israel but also the absorption of the immigrants themselves and the availability of services to facilitate their striking roots in Israel and integrating into the Israeli economy. This was the basis for the Jewish Agency's request that the government establish a central authority to deal with investors, which, as noted, led to the creation of the Center for the Immigrant Investor. It was also the idea behind the Absorption Department's establishment, in early 1953, of a special unit for immigrants from Latin America.[73]

Despite all these actions to encourage immigration from the Free World, there was no change in the number of newcomers from those countries in 1953. Fewer than 10,500 immigrants came to Israel in 1953 from all countries; of these, less than 900 came from the developed countries—half of them from Argentina. It was the smallest number of immigrants in a year since the establishment of the state.[74] Rafael told the Council for Aliya that the sharp drop would continue; among the main factors he noted the closing of the gates of Eastern Europe, the end to the organized liquidation of Diaspora communities, and the policy of selective immigration.[75]

In December 1953, in the shadow of the drastic decline in immigration during the past year, the Zionist General Council met in Jerusalem. During its sessions, the new ideas to attract immigrants from the West received favorable attention. The council told the Agency Executive to ramp up its efforts to create appropriate housing for immigrants from these countries.[76] One of its resolutions was that "the quickening pace of assimilation in the Diaspora requires that we speed up the immigration of the Jewish masses."[77] At the start of its first session, Yitzhak Rafael announced his resignation as head of the Aliyah Department. "May we all merit for the great aliya to be renewed soon and to see the ingathering of the exiles continue," Rafael said in his farewell statement to the staff of his department.[78] The Zionist General Council appointed Shlomo Zalman Shragai, a leader of the Orthodox Torah va'Avodah movement that was affiliated with Rafael's Hapoel Mizrahi party, to succeed him.[79]

The Renewal of Mass Immigration

The substantial decline in the number of immigrants made it necessary to reformulate the guidelines for immigration. To this end, the Coordinating Committee set up a committee comprised of the health minister, the labor minister, and the heads of the Aliyah and Absorption Departments. They in turn convened a subcommittee of the director generals of these ministries and departments. The subcommittee proposed rules that would, it was hoped, increase the proportion of immigrants who were capable of working and could find their place, in terms of their health and social status, in the Israeli labor market, while preventing the admission of welfare cases (who could stay in their home countries). With this in mind, the guidelines were tailored to suit the various countries, with distinctions drawn among places where the Jews were in imminent danger, where the communities were terminal due to persecution, countries from which immigration was restricted, countries of distress, and developed countries. One of the underlying principles was family-based selection, meaning that families were viewed as a single unit in terms of the prospects for their settlement and absorption in Israel.[80]

Starting in early 1954, extensive new preparations to absorb large-scale immigration got under way. The selection rules were further relaxed; henceforth, people up to age fifty with an occupation they could pursue in Israel, or who could engage in farm labor after receiving a doctor's note, could be counted as breadwinners. Immigrants past forty-five and those past fifty with an occupation were categorized as "elderly"; they would be admitted, after review by the Aliyah Department, only if relatives in Israel were willing to take responsibility for them. To solve the case of those whose relatives could not bear the costs of their absorption, leniencies were granted to parents of children brought to Israel by Youth Aliyah, parents of IDF soldiers and disabled veterans, and to bereaved parents whose children had fallen in Israel's wars. Immigrants past forty-five and those past fifty with an occupation were considered to have the means to set themselves up in the country if their capital amounted to at least $7,000 (instead of $10,000 as before). These revisions did not affect the health guidelines, which remained unchanged. In addition, an "amnesty" (thus in the original text) was granted to those who had left the country but now wanted to return, after the department in Jerusalem studied their case, their reasons for leaving, and the possibilities for their absorption. As part of the "amnesty," the returnees could receive financial assistance from the absorption institutions, but they too were subject to the immigrant-selection rules and required to commit themselves to working in agriculture.[81]

The arguments in favor of promoting mass immigration cited the vital needs of national security, demographic growth, and economic development.[82] When Prime Minister David Ben-Gurion presented his new government to the Knesset in November 1955, he expressed his concern about the weapons that were flowing to enemy states, especially Egypt. He added that now in particular it was essential to emphasize that national security could not be based exclusively on the armed forces and weapons. "Israel's security means aliya and settlement," he declared, and he illustrated this point with some numbers: Egypt had a population of more than twenty-two million; Israel, only a million and a half. Hence, "aliya is not only the apple of Zionism's eye and the State's supreme historic vocation, but also a prime security need."[83] In addition to various campaigns intended to win over public opinion, steps were taken to liquidate the transit camps. The new absorption policy, which came to be called "direct from the boat to the village," steered immigrants to development areas and supported a higher rate of immigration.[84]

At this time, the Jews of North Africa were considered to be immediate candidates for immigration due to the political situation in Morocco and Tunisia, which were about to receive independence from France, and Algeria.[85] According to expert assessments, there were 450,000 Jews in North Africa—about a quarter of a million in Morocco, 100,000 in Tunisia, and 130,000 in Algeria. Given the general impression that many of the Jews in those countries felt threatened, the Jewish Agency undertook to help them get out. "This is the pioneer aliya of the last few years," said Baruch Duvdevani, the director general of the Aliyah Department, in a speech to his staff in March 1956. He added:

> These immigrants are going to Lakhish, Ta'anakh, to every out-of-the-way place, to Eilat. Here in Israel all of us—the aliya family—are working with these immigrants, helping them get organized. But here [in the department] we are involved mainly with paperwork, dealing with people's files, with words written in ink. We relate to the file and do not see the living individual.[86]

Between 1954 and 1960, more than 80,000 Jews arrived in Israel from Morocco and more than 20,000 from Tunisia, but only 3,300 from Algeria, which was still under French colonial administration.[87] "We knew then that the process of independence in these countries would lead to changes, but we could not have imagined such a dramatic development," noted Duvdevani, adding that the situation was particularly gloomy in the backcountry villages there.[88] In 1956, he estimated the potential for immigration from North Africa at 150,000. However, the aliya offices there were forced to put a damper on registration: "We are slowing down deliberately because we have no choice." "For us, aliya has become selective and we no longer bring people to Israel according to the vision of the prophet, 'the blind and the lame among them, the woman with child and her who is in labor.' "[89]

Following the Sinai Campaign and the Egyptian authorities' persecution of the local Jews, the conditions were ripe for an organized operation to bring that community to Israel. "One fine day we were confronted by the exodus from Egypt," quipped Duvdevani in May 1957.[90] The Aliyah Department, as it had learned to do, geared up quickly. It opened a special office in Greece, organized planes and ships, and made contact with the Red Cross through the Foreign Ministry. Within a few days, the Jews of Egypt were informed that as soon as they reached Greece, Italy, or France they would be sheltered and provided for and, if they wished, transported to Israel.[91] Of the 20,000 Jews still in Egypt, more than 15,000 came to Israel between late 1956 and the end of that decade, including 13,000 in 1957 alone.[92]

It was impossible to forecast the number of immigrants who could be expected from Eastern Europe, inasmuch as it depended on the Communist countries' unlocking the exit gates. According to assessments at the time, there were roughly four million Jews in Eastern Europe: more than three million in Russia, 250,000 in Romania, 80,000 in Hungary, 70,000 in Poland, 20,000 in Czechoslovakia, and several thousand in Bulgaria.[93] "The gates of two countries have been opened," announced Duvdevani at a meeting of Aliyah Department staff in May 1957, without identifying them, because of the discretion required by the confidential nature of the issue.[94] In fact, he was referring to events in Poland and Hungary in October 1956, at roughly the same time as the Sinai Campaign. From then until the end of the 1950s, almost 39,000 immigrants came to Israel from Poland, as well as 9,000 from Hungary.[95] Jewish immigration from Romania was renewed in August 1958. At a press conference in early 1959, Shragai announced that the Romanian government had bowed to international pressure and agreed to permit unlimited Jewish emigration.[96] By the end of that decade, 19,000 had relocated to Israel.[97]

More than a quarter of a million immigrants arrived in Israel between 1954 and 1960. Over half of them came from Africa—mainly from Morocco, Tunisia, Egypt, and Algeria; 35% from Europe—mainly from Poland, Romania, and Hungary; close to 10% from Asia—mainly Turkey, Iran, and India; and slightly more than 3% came from the Americas—about 40% of them from Argentina.[98] Although the arguments employed to spur immigration drew heavily on personal security, the phenomenon was described in truly messianic terms, as by Shragai in early 1959:

> Wondrous are the ways of aliya. When we follow the sequence of events in the domain of aliya, we see the hand of Providence. When Morocco shut its gates, two and a half years ago, the gates of Poland opened at once. When aliya from Poland ebbed and almost reached its end, aliya from Romania began. . . . Today the bulk of the immigrants are from Eastern Europe, but they continue to arrive from other countries as well, albeit on a smaller scale, because we have been forced to slow down the rate of immigration from other countries. Nonetheless, Jews did make aliya from 42 countries during the period in question—from Europe, Asia, Africa, the United States, and South America.[99]

The documents at my disposal show that during the peak years of immigration, the question of immigrants from the developed countries was neglected, even as the Jews there continued to be subjected to scathing criticism for their failure to move to Israel. In Shragai's address to the Zionist Congress, on May 24, 1956, he warned that there had to be a major change in all matters related to Jewish immigration from the West. "We never stop fuming at the Jews from the Free World and asking why they are not making aliya, and hang all the blame for this on them." Shragai reported that many of those Jews had a strong desire to come settle in Israel, but the essential conditions for their absorption had to be created:

> Everyone talks constantly about this aliya and calls loudly for it, but they hardly lift a finger to make it possible. Had we done something, I believe we could have brought tens of thousands of people on aliya, about 2,000 families. And if they are absorbed smoothly, they will serve as the wedge for a large and growing tide of aliya from the West. But let us confess the truth, even if it is galling—and we must not be offended by or angry at this bitter truth: We want aliya from the West but there is no desire to make any effort to help Western immigrants.[100]

The dominant view in Israeli society was that as long as the country's revenues were based on taxes, immigrants should not enjoy the benefit of affirmative action that cost money. In the Zionist Executive's summary report on its activities from 1956 to 1960, the economic decision makers and business leaders in Israel recognized the importance of middle-class immigration, but they failed to stimulate comprehensive government planning for the absorption of productive elements.[101] The report makes it clear that even at the start of the 1960s, no solution had been found for transferring the assets of middle-class immigrants to Israel, which was made particularly troublesome by the decision to impose customs levies on equipment imports and to allow the importation of capital only. This forced immigrants to liquidate their property abroad, but converting it to cash entailed losses that could exceed its value.[102] This issue raised another problem, related to the exchange rate, which, as we will see, was particularly severe in the case of Argentina.

The Liberalization of the Immigration and Absorption System in the 1960s

In the early 1960s, the approach toward immigration from developed countries changed markedly. This change was the start of a liberalization of immigration and absorption procedures, even though centralization under government direction continued to shape policy. The documents show that, for the first time since independence, policy makers drafted concrete absorption plans with defined absorption tracks tailored to newcomers from the developed world. With these plans in hand, special emissaries were posted there, where they visited potential immigrants in their homes and clarified details and possible problems with members of the family, in coordination with the Absorption Department.[103]

A number of circumstances led to this fundamental change of approach and perspective. To begin with, the Israeli economy experienced rapid growth in the first half of the 1960s, as accelerated industrialization led to a substantial rise in production and exports.[104] Second, immigrants were being absorbed in more comfortable circumstances, without the makeshift solutions that had characterized the process in the 1950s. The economic burden that immigration imposed on the country in the 1960s was small in comparison to that created by the waves of immigrants in the 1950s. Third, the newcomers' sociodemographic and economic characteristics were different.[105]

The significant rise in immigration from the developed countries in the early 1960s illustrates the importance of pull factors. Of the 15,000 immigrants from the United States in the first two decades of Israeli independence, about 65% arrived between 1961 and 1967.[106] The available documents show that this bulge was catalyzed by the improvement in the economy, but especially by the significant change in how the absorption agencies in Israel dealt with Western olim.

Official documents indicate that 1964 was the watershed year for immigration from the Free World.[107] From then until 1967, the average influx from these countries exceeded 7,000 a year and accounted for a quarter of all new arrivals.[108] At this stage, the basic idea that certain steps should and could be taken to encourage immigration, even if they infringed on the principle of fair and equal treatment, came to be accepted. For example, in order to resolve the severe problem of their having to liquidate assets at a loss, immigrants were granted a number of fiscal leniencies and assistance. They were exempt from the special travel tax on tickets abroad for their first three years in the country; they received a customs exemption on their personal possessions and work tools; they enjoyed an income tax rebate; and so forth.[109] These measures reflected a view that all of the complex problems related to absorption could be solved through legislation and regulations. This view can be heard in a speech delivered by Prime Minister Levi Eshkol to a gathering of 120 leaders of Diaspora Jewish communities and representatives of Jewish and non-Zionist organizations from forty-eight countries, who attended the dedication of the new Knesset building in August 1966: "I can promise you that we will make sure that the leniencies we are able to grant in matters of aliya and absorption will be given generously, with an open heart and with a maximum curtailment of bureaucracy and administrative heavy-handedness."[110]

In addition to the leniencies noted above, the organizational infrastructure for the absorption of immigrants from the developed countries was expanded. One manifestation of this was the establishment of a special unit for immigration from the developed world, housed in the Aliyah Department offices in Israel, and tasked with assisting individual immigrants by helping with their advance arrangements, in coordination with the Absorption and other Jewish Agency departments, employers, and others.[111] In 1964, the unit broke new ground by publishing a "Guide for the New Immigrant" in English, Spanish, and French, with the basic information required by potential immigrants, from their initial contact with the Aliyah Department through housing and job arrangements in Israel. The guide led the immigrants step by step until they landed in Israel and settled down in the country.[112]

One of the most prominent phenomena related to immigration from the developed countries was the sharp rise in the 1960s in the number of those with temporary-resident and tourist visas who decided to stay in the country. Some 65% of the newcomers from South Africa, a wealthy country, arrived with this status. The figures among immigrants from North America were almost as high—58% from the United States and 53% from Canada; even 40% of these "potential immigrants" from England first registered as long-term tourists or temporary residents. The phenomenon was less common among those from Latin America: about 15% from Argentina and 19% from Brazil.[113] Avraham Cygel, the head of the Jewish Agency Absorption Department, explained this phenomenon as follows:

> Many Jews from the developed countries come to Israel for an undefined period with the status of "temporary residents." What is the purpose of their visits and why they define themselves as temporary residents—that is not clear. What is clear is that the goal of their visit is much more than just a visit. Otherwise, they would call themselves by the appropriate and standard name: "tourist." If they do not do so, but also adopt the concept of "citizens," without the addition of "temporary," this hints at their plans and inclination to bind their fate to that of Israel. Nearly 9,000 "temporary residents" like these come to us every year; and even if when they go back to their country of origin they do no more than share their impressions of the country with people there, that too is a form of service to Israel. The fact that the lion's share return to their home country after a stay of indeterminate length leaves room for explanations and

> assumptions that the reason is that the "temporary resident" was still unable to find opportunities to integrate in Israel. So he may visit again and again, until he finds the appropriate situation. We see support for this in the reports of the heads of the units for the absorption of Jews from the developed countries, who say that "it takes an average of at least three visits for a Jew from the Free World to be absorbed in Israel."[114]

This phenomenon was not common among immigrants from "countries of distress" (many of whom could not go back where they came from even if they wanted to). From Romania, which trailed only Morocco as a source of immigrants in these years, only 321 tourists and three temporary residents settled in Israel—about 0.1% of the total number of immigrants from that country. Fewer than 1% of the immigrants from Poland opted for one of these two statuses. The phenomenon was only slightly more prevalent among those from Asia: only about half a percent of the immigrants from Iraq came as tourists; only two of them asked for a temporary resident's visa. There were six "tourists" from Yemen and no temporary residents. The figure was higher for Turkey; 6% of immigrants from this country registered as long-term tourists and temporary residents.[115]

In late January 1967, the Coordinating Committee decided to establish the Joint Authority for Immigration and Absorption. It comprised five government ministers and five members of the Jewish Agency Executive; the Agency chairman was its presiding officer, with the minister of labor as his deputy.[116] The authority outlined immigration and absorption policy and oversaw the implementation of the restructuring of the various departments that dealt with immigrants. On March 16, 1967, the Executive gave its final approval to the new structure, in which the Aliyah Department, the Absorption Department, and the Economic Department were merged into the United Department for Aliyah and Absorption. It was headed by three members of the Executive, Shlomo Zalman Shragai, Leon (Arye) Dulczin, and Avraham Cygel, who assumed joint direction of the department and served as the highest authority in the Jewish Agency on all matters related to immigration and absorption. The reorganization was designed to resolve the old issue of coordinating the work of the Jewish Agency departments to streamline their handling of immigration, make it easier to deal with potential immigrants, and prevent duplication and waste of time and resources.[117] Shragai, however, had a different take on the matter:

> In my humble opinion, this decision has nothing to do with merger or efficiency, but will be a factor that creates new divisions. I take special

> exception to the decision that the united Aliya, Absorption, and Economic Department will have three heads, which is in utter contradiction to the idea and decisions to put an end to the division and duplication in the handling of aliya affairs abroad and of absorption affairs in Israel. In my opinion, not only will this decision fail to make the aliya operation more efficient, it will also interfere with aliya matters and lead to further complications and foot-dragging for aliya abroad and absorption in Israel. The merged staff, too, will find itself trapped in the thicket of contradictory instructions and clarification of authority. What will be created is a climate of dual loyalty, gossip, and intrigues.[118]

It stands to reason that it was not only the matter of centralization and coordination that bothered Shragai, but also the religious issue (the Aliyah Department, and before that the Immigration Ministry, had always been headed by a representative of the religious Zionists [Hapoel Mizrahi and its successor, the National Religious Party]). "It is hard to imagine what will happen if the planned reorganization of the Jewish Agency is in fact implemented and the Aliyah Department is no longer headed by an observant person," noted one of the department's overseas emissaries.[119] But the merger was carried out in the end, and the combined operation began in September 1967.[120] The new department had three divisions: one to organize, encourage, and implement immigration by all social classes and from all countries; one for activities in Israel, in the fields of housing, employment, welfare, health care, Hebrew-language instruction, hostels, and education; and one to deal with industry, crafts, commerce, and services, financial arrangements for the self-employed, including those in the liberal professions, funds to subsidize enterprises that contributed to the national economy, and a consulting bureau for tourist investors. Each unit fell in the purview of one of the three members of the Executive in the department troika.[121]

Historians of contemporary Jewry view the Six-Day War as a sort of watershed or turning point, both for Israeli society and for Jewish life abroad.[122] Documents from the period emphasize the changes it effected in Israel's international standing and its relations with the Diaspora. They describe the response by Diaspora Jewry during the weeks leading up to the war and after the victory as deeper and broader than anyone could have predicted, as if the wave of enthusiasm and voluntarism took even them by surprise: "They rediscovered the full meaning of their identification with Judaism and realized that there is no sense to Jewish identity without an identification with the State of Israel."[123] During the fighting, the Israeli press published reports about the growing stream of volunteers arriving from abroad, along with many stories about young people who came from every direction to help the country in its time of need.[124]

In the domain of immigration, by contrast, no change was felt. When the war was over, the issue of immigration from the developed countries resurfaced in full force. "How can we fill up the liberated land with Jews?" asked the Zionist Executive's summary report for 1964–67.[125] It noted regretfully that throughout the history of the state, the Jews of the developed countries had never shown any real desire to come settle in Israel, and that not many had done so—fewer than 7% of all immigrants. "They apparently did not feel an emotional need to be redeemed as individuals and to enhance their Jewishness by making aliya."[126] Even the Six-Day War, an event that triggered an astonishing resurgence of identification by Diaspora Jews with their people and with Zion, was not a strong enough motivation for them to do so. "No political success and no decision or declaration can make the liberated territories Jewish, other than populating and settling them with Jews."[127] In fact, the pace of immigration from the developed countries in late 1967 and throughout 1968 fell relative to the first half of the decade.[128]

4

Politicization, Selection, and Bureaucratization

The Organization of Argentinian Jewish Immigration to Israel

The Politics of Immigration: The Establishment of the Bureaucracy in Buenos Aires

Two days before the fateful UN General Assembly vote, on November 29, 1947, to partition Palestine and create a Jewish state, there was a major restructuring of the Buenos Aires offices of the Jewish Agency, which involved the establishment of a regional office for all of South America. The new unit had been authorized by the Zionist General Council in August 1947; its direction was confided to Arieh Eshel (Scheel), a Mapai man who had been Moshe Shertok's (Sharett) secretary in the Political Department of the Jewish Agency.[1]

Eshel's arrival and the establishment of the regional office meant splitting up the Jewish Agency's activities in Latin America. Until then, the Latin American Department of the Jewish Agency, headquartered in New York, had a branch office in Buenos Aires. The liaison person there was Dr. Abraham Mibashan. His office coordinated Zionist propaganda and public relations operations and worked in close collaboration with the Higher Zionist Council (the Zionist umbrella organization in Argentina). Aliya was included in Mibashan's brief, particularly right after World War II, when there was a surge in applications for immigration certificates to Palestine. According to Mibashan, his answer that "there are no certificates [the equivalent of immigrant visas under the Mandate] and the few that exist are essential for bringing refugees from Europe" did not satisfy the applicants.[2]

After the establishment of Eshel's office in Buenos Aires, and pursuant to the new division of authority, from that time on the former Latin American Department of the Jewish Agency in New York functioned as the Organization Department's regional office for Central America. The same department's office in Buenos Aires was assigned responsibility for all matters related to the Zionist organizations in South America, except for political issues, which remained the province of the office in the United States.[3] The agency's operations in Argentina were split between Mibashan's and Eshel's offices. This two-headed arrangement is illustrated in a report preserved in the files of the Aliyah Department in Jerusalem:

> In 1946, the comrade Moshe Tov was summoned from Argentina to New York to run a Latin American Department for the American branch of the Jewish Agency Executive, with special emphasis on the political and public information aspect. This department did not receive authority to act on behalf of any Agency department in Jerusalem. In 1947, the Organization Department in Jerusalem dispatched a special envoy [Eshel] to Argentina to establish a South American regional office there. He, too, was authorized only by that department, but generally acted as if he held power of attorney to represent all departments of the Agency. Accordingly, he called his unit the Regional Office of the Jewish Agency for South America. This led to a sharp quarrel between the offices in New York and Buenos Aires.[4]

So, starting in November 1947, Eshel was in charge of emigration from Argentina and other South American countries. According to the report that the Zionist Executive submitted to the twenty-fourth Zionist Congress, his office, with the active assistance of the Higher Zionist Council, was responsible for encouraging and organizing the immigration process until Israel became independent in May 1948.[5] The report emphasized the work by the office and the council during the War of Independence, when postal communications between Israel and the Diaspora were disrupted, and in particular their efforts to recruit South Americans to serve in Mahal, the Foreign Volunteers group established in 1948. Eventually this produced 450 volunteers from thirteen countries in Latin America—about half of them from Argentina.[6]

In the first period after the establishment of Israel, the Jewish Agency's regional office in Buenos Aires served as the official representative of both the Zionist movement and the Israeli government; Eshel was accorded diplomatic status. Evidence of the severing of contact with Jerusalem, because of the disruption in mail service during the War of Independence, is found in a letter written by Eshel in late 1948 and addressed to the Jewish Agency Aliyah Department in Jerusalem. According to that letter, the Proclamation of Independence had spurred many Argentinian Jews to think seriously about relocating to Israel now, and many others were planning to do so when the war was over. "But things are very unclear for those who want to come on aliya immediately, despite the state of emergency in Israel." Eshel added:

> The Zionist movements in the various countries have yet to come up with a solution for organizing the aliya process. The only thing they are aware of is the need to establish "Israel Offices"; but there are no clear ideas about how they should be set up and no explicit instructions from the Agency Executive. It is not clear what powers the Israel Offices possess. Nor is there a formal division of labor between the office and the aliya officer representing the State of Israel. The latter has received instructions from the Immigration Ministry of the Israeli government, which authorize him to issue visas to specific categories of candidates: those with capital, halutzim, and certain technical experts. But we do not have a definition of the terms "halutz" and "capitalist." Does the Israel Office have to approve every applicant who is physically and mentally suitable, even if he is not a member of a youth movement that sends its graduates to an agricultural training farm? All of this requires immediate clarification.[7]

Concealed behind Eshel's frank request for updated information, given the awakening of an interest in immigration right after the state was declared, was a desire for a clear definition of the powers of the several agents in the field, and especially Dr. Mibashan. Lacking explicit definitions, the duplication of effort continued. What is more, Argentina did not extend official recognition to the State of Israel until February 1949, so its representatives had to conduct most of their activities from Uruguay. It was not until late July of that year that Jacob Tsur and the staff of the Israeli legation moved from Montevideo to Buenos Aires.[8] They took up residence in a large building in the center of the diplomatic quarter, which had been purchased by a group of wealthy Argentinian Jews.[9] When he reached Buenos Aires, Tsur added Eshel to the legation staff as first secretary. In his memoirs, Tsur recounted how, until then, Eshel had operated a sort of temporary consulate, where he worked on behalf of the Israeli legation and issued visas, even though no one knew how to stamp visas or what the procedure entailed.[10]

Additional evidence of Eshel's irregular consular activities appeared in a small notice in *Davar* in May 1949, after Argentina officially recognized Israel but before the legation opened. It reported that the aliya office of the Israel mission in Buenos Aires had been temporarily shut down by the local authorities, on the grounds that it was exercising various consular functions without having officially informed the Argentinian government and before consular relations between the two countries had been formalized.[11]

The legation became an important address for Argentinian Jews from the day it opened; this included issues of immigration, "which is vital to the future of our work," as Jacob Tsur phrased it in one of his first reports to the Foreign Ministry and the Jewish Agency Aliyah Department.[12] Like Mibashan and Eshel before him, Tsur too noted the lack of readily available information for potential immigrants: "It is all a riddle for the medium-sized and small investor. And we too, the government's representatives here, cannot offer him the required explanation because we ourselves still lack the necessary information."[13] This situation led to several cases of unproductive and overpriced investments, which alienated and repelled potential immigrants. "I must say candidly," Tsur confessed, "that when such a Jew comes to ask us for help, we do not encourage him, because we are afraid that he will pull up stakes here and move to Israel, where he will be trapped in the net of unsubstantiated proposals."[14]

Tsur made a number of suggestions to stimulate Jewish immigration to Israel from South America, but none of his ideas was implemented at the time. In the short term, the only change, which was not based on his proposals, came in December 1949, when the first emissary of the Jewish Agency Aliyah Department, Shlomo Garner, a member of Hapoel Hamizrahi, left Israel for Buenos Aires to set up its regional office for all of South America. After its official opening in April 1950, the office coordinated all immigration-related activities in accordance with the instructions issued by the Aliyah Department in Jerusalem.[15]

The establishment of the Immigration Ministry exacerbated the redundancy that already existed. The Zionist groups in Argentina longed to cut the strings with Jerusalem. This desire was encouraged by both Mapai and the General Zionists. In one of his reports, Garner indicated that the legation also had a hand in the matter: "The Israeli legation here is an active element in Zionist life, to the point of substantial intervention; and as is known, not a few Mapai members work in the Foreign Ministry."[16] So even in distant Argentina, too, tens of thousands of kilometers from the thicket of Israeli politics, party politics ruled the roost.

Politicization and Selection: The Activity of the Aliyah Department in Argentina in the 1950s

The immigration bureaucracy in Argentina became even more convoluted in the early 1950s. The Jewish Agency Economic Department sent its own representative to Buenos Aires in June 1953, to assist potential immigrants who had capital to invest, as well as tourists.[17] A month later, the first representative of the Professional and Technical Workers Association (PATWA) found a desk in the Jewish Agency offices in Buenos Aires, where he interfaced with skilled tradesmen and technicians, liberal professionals, and university students.[18] PATWA fell under the Youth and Hehalutz Department, which had been the first agency unit to set up shop in Argentina, and promoted and organized the immigration of young adults to agricultural settlements, with and without a prior stint on a training farm.[19] The agency worked out of the building of the Higher Zionist Council, located in the Once district, the economic center of the Jewish community in Buenos Aires.

The expansion of the aliya bureaucracy in Buenos Aires should be understood against the background of the sharp drop in immigration in 1952. The relevant Jewish Agency and government officials began taking steps to encourage immigration from the developed countries. With regard to Latin America, this change was exemplified by the establishment within the Absorption Department, in early 1953, of a special unit for immigrants from Latin America. The office handled all matters related to the absorption system—greeting the immigrants when they arrived, finding them housing, enrolling them in Hebrew-language study programs, and providing economic guidance for those with means. The department, headed by Ephraim Avigur (Gorman), a lawyer by profession and native of Entre Ríos in Argentina, who had made aliya in 1950, opened branches in Jerusalem, Tel Aviv, and Haifa.[20] In the introduction to the information bulletin published by Avigur's office, starting in June 1953, he enumerated the reasons for the establishment of his unit:

> After the decline in mass aliya, those involved with aliya and absorption focused their attention on aliya from the Western countries and their specific needs. In the first stage, a unit was established to deal with the olim from the English-speaking world and to encourage and absorb aliya from those countries. Representatives of the Latin American

> immigrants in Israel, including the Union of Latin American Olim in Israel [OLEI], requested that the Jewish Agency Absorption Department gear up for similar activities, according to the same principles, for olim from Latin America. This initiative led to the formation of the special office for Latin American immigrants. The Absorption Department works in close cooperation with the immigrants' associations. In addition, the Council for Aliya from the West, with representatives of the olim from Latin America, was established.[21]

We should note the major influence that the immigrants themselves and their voluntary activities exerted on policy making. OLEI (Organización Latinoamericana en Israel) is a voluntary organization, founded while the War of Independence was still in progress, that focuses on the social and cultural absorption of Latin American immigrants in Israel. It is true that the "melting pot" paradigm allows no place for immigrant associations, because such organizations, based on the Landsmannschaft principle, are theoretically incompatible with the vision of the ingathering and fusion of the exiles. In practice, however, their central role in the social absorption of immigrants made them vitally important. They won official recognition and were co-opted into various frameworks by both the Zionist Executive and the government.[22]

The documents that record the relationship between prominent local players in Argentina and the representatives of the Jewish Agency departments, as well as their internal friction, reflect the troubled work patterns that impeded the organization of Jewish emigration from Argentina to Israel.[23] Squabbles over authority were nothing new in the politics of immigration, but the issue resurfaced after the twenty-fourth Zionist Congress in 1956. In keeping with its decisions, the Higher Zionist Council in Argentina set to work implementing a new mission—the establishment of a countrywide Zionist organization. This move was made in November 1956, when the Higher Zionist Council became the Argentine Zionist Organization (Organización Sionista Argentina or OSA). Henceforth, the Jewish Agency offices in Argentina were to be subordinated to the OSA, working within its structure and under its authority.[24]

The power struggle that ensued and the split it caused in Jewish Agency activities in Argentina are faithfully reflected in a letter written by Dr. Isaac Goldenberg, the chairman of the Higher Zionist Council in Argentina, to the head of the Aliyah Department in Jerusalem, just a few days before the council was transformed into the OSA. From this letter, we learn that the Israelis' main complaint against the locals related to the latter's lack of the capacity and moral force to call for aliya when they themselves were not setting a personal example. With regard to this argument, Dr. Goldenberg noted that they did have this moral power, derived from the fact that "we are sending our children to kibbutzim." He added that what was impeding Argentinian Jewish immigration to Israel was the "wretched [party] key that drives a wedge between the various departments in Israel."[25]

According to Dr. Goldenberg, Zionist circles in Argentina tended to the view that the only emissaries who were truly essential were the counselors dispatched by the youth movements. Those sent out by the other departments were the object of scathing criticism by Argentinian Zionists:

> We see them as parasites. If they receive their salaries in dollars, they live a life of luxury, which does not win respect for the State and Zionism. As Jews and responsible Zionists, we see it as our obligation to make sure that the movement's good name and moral character are not besmirched by people with no talent who are sent to us because they cannot hold a job in Israel, but happen to belong to the political parties that run departments with budgets larger than their needs, which they consequently invest in overseas missions for which there is no necessity. You even know of emissaries who decided not to return to Israel.[26]

Documents from Israeli sources, too, highlight deficiencies in the operations of the immigration apparatus in Buenos Aires. In the late 1950s, at the end of his two-year overseas assignment to run the Aliyah Department office there, Moshe Armon summarized his mission in a report he drew up for department headquarters in Jerusalem. With a candor unusual in such reports, Armon emphasized that, except for the representatives of the Zionist youth movements, none of the emissaries deserved any real credit for influencing people to come settle in Israel.[27] On another opportunity, Armon recounted that within six months of his arrival in Argentina he had written that the element that did the most harm to the prospect of increased emigration from the Western countries was the "politicization of the Jewish Agency departments."[28] The papers of Ephraim Avigur of the Absorption Department, too, indicate that the politicization of the agency departments, along with the resulting duplication, competition, and fragmentation, did significant damage to the efforts to encourage and organize Jewish immigration from Argentina.[29]

The documents left behind by the Aliyah Department also illustrate its expectations of Argentinian Jews.[30] On October 20, 1950, Shlomo Garner received an internal memorandum from Yehuda Kashtan, the secretary of the

Aliyah Department in Jerusalem, with a detailed description of the plan it had set for South America for the next sixth months:

> In the aliya plan we have defined, in consultation with the Coordinating Committee, for the winter months, October 1950 to March 1951, aliya from South America has been counted as follows: 50 olim a month from Argentina, 30 olim a month from Brazil, and 40 olim a month from the other countries. In consideration of absorption conditions in the winter, all of them must be young people under 25, with adequate means so that they do not require assistance from the Jewish Agency—and all within the compass of these numbers. You must make sure that aliya from the South American countries during these six months is in accordance with the aforesaid, except for cases where you find absolute justification for treating them as an exception from the line stated above, in an extraordinary manner.[31]

On the surface, the plan for emigration from South America was based on the figures for those countries since the establishment of the State. A 1951 report by the Zionist Executive notes that a thousand immigrants had arrived each year from fifteen countries in Central and South America since May 1948, whereas "before then, these countries were allotted no more than a handful of certificates."[32] The interesting detail in this document, with regard to immigration policy, is that independence did not alter the decision-makers' attitude. Both before and after the establishment of the State, emigration from Argentina was subject to the principles of selection devised in Jerusalem.

The directives about candidates for immigration were clear and specific. The office in Buenos Aires was authorized to approve people who met the selection criteria, and no one else. Others could make the move only with special permission from Israel, whether they were coming with their own resources or dependent on Jewish Agency funding, whether they were planning to live on a kibbutz, join relatives already in the country, or any other arrangement. Potential immigrants who did not satisfy the criteria could be considered at the request of a relative in Israel and subject to an investigation of their social status, or in response to a notice from Buenos Aires that specified where they would be absorbed, and subject to approval by the Aliyah Department in Jerusalem.[33]

In addition to these official rules, there were also local rules in Argentina. As a precondition for processing the file of a potential immigrant or tourist, the office required documentation that applicants had paid their pledge to the United

Jewish Appeal.[34] Everyone who contacted the Jewish Agency departments had to fill out a form and enclose a curriculum vitae, which included information essential for investigating opportunities for their absorption in Israel and a declaration of their disposable capital. After registration, the candidates were sent for a series of medical examinations by the physician attached to the consulate in Argentina. One of his tasks was to verify that the male applicants were circumcised. It was also stipulated that the consulate would issue an Israeli visa only at the recommendation of the Aliyah Department. Immigration by people who were separated or divorced required a notarized waiver by the former spouse. All the information was sent to the Aliyah Department in Jerusalem and the Absorption Department in Tel Aviv for final approval.[35]

One day each month was fixed for departure. The immigrants oriented their preparations and affairs toward that date. The department also handled the negotiations with the steamship companies in order to reduce the cost of passage and helped middle-class immigrants who found it difficult to pay their fare. In the case of the latter, the office in Buenos Aires forwarded their personal details to Jerusalem in advance of their immigration to request funding of their travel expenses. Immigrants who received a subvention had to undertake to repay the full sum if they subsequently left Israel. To make decisions about funding, the office relied on information received from the Buenos Aires community, or from the Council of Communities for candidates from the provinces. It was further decided that those who came to Israel on tourist visas would not enjoy financial assistance from the Jewish Agency, even if they had spent time on a training farm and were headed for a kibbutz, and certainly not those who had never had agricultural training.[36]

The selection procedure and individual processing created bureaucratic red tape that interfered with and delayed emigration from Argentina and reduced the number of emigrants. Many documents support this conclusion. A memorandum sent by the Aliya Office in Buenos Aires to the department in Jerusalem, in October 1956, noted that, under the current procedure, several months passed from when the department's representative in Buenos Aires forwarded an application to Jerusalem until the day of departure: "As [a] result, poor families sometimes have to wait until the allocation for their aliya arrives. In the meantime, they must spend all their meager resources on living expenses."[37] At the end of that year, the OSA sent another letter to the Aliyah Department in Jerusalem:

> The process is very slow and causes unnecessary delays. You doubtless know that almost all of the olim from Argentina have very limited means. After disposing of their small businesses and selling their homes

> they are left with no way to make a living. It is very difficult to coordinate the date when they liquidate their business with when they receive the aliya subvention. Moreover, three months usually pass after the day we receive your notification about the subvention. It frequently happens that we have not received the funds and have to take out loans, which are not easy to obtain. On the other hand, it is impossible to defer the olim's departure, because that would cause them serious harm.[38]

The selection and foot-dragging that characterized the bureaucracy in Buenos Aires forced the emissaries to spend much of their time on routine office work. This, too, is reflected in many documents. When he arrived in Argentina in January 1955, the new representative of the Economic Department in Buenos Aires reported that the Jewish Agency functionaries there were prisoners in their offices and spent most of their time dealing with the public and corresponding with the department in Israel.[39] Ephraim Avigur, too, observed that the bureaucratic overhead of processing immigration candidates contributed to the inefficiency of his office.[40] The selection method and bureaucratic snail's pace it entailed set off waves in Israel as well. In a letter published in *Yedioth Ahronoth* in June 1956, under the heading, "Are We Breaking the Law of Return?" the writer confessed that he was stunned to discover that a Jew who wanted to settle in Israel had to submit a letter of invitation from relatives already in the country, as in the following instance:

> We have a relative in Argentina, a woman with higher education and a rich Zionist past. Her children were raised in a Zionist environment and her daughter, a member of Nitzanim, was captured by the Egyptians during the War of Independence. When she requested an entry visa from the Israeli consul in Buenos Aires, he insisted that she show him an invitation from her relatives in Israel. With no other choice, we filed a request with the Jewish Agency a few months ago, but as of today there has not been any progress on the matter.[41]

The Organization and Encouragement of Argentinian Jewish Immigration in the 1960s

In the early 1960s, the policy makers introduced a major change in their approach to Jewish immigration to Israel from the developed countries. The earliest plans specifically for South American Jews dated to the late 1950s. Now, for the first time since independence, the Jewish Agency devised a program for immigration by families, on the basis of absorption plans prepared in advance.[42] These schemes were meant to encourage immigration by middle-class Jews of limited means; candidates with resources equivalent to $4,000 were eligible for a loan of 70% of their capital, provided by the Jewish Agency and the Israeli government, in order to acquire housing and a store or workshop. In addition, the candidates could choose where they would settle in Israel.[43]

The action plan drawn up by the aliya offices in Buenos Aires on the basis of the new scheme rested on the assumption that comprehensive absorption plans were not enough to encourage Argentinian Jews to relocate to Israel; it was also necessary to expand the work of the office in Buenos Aires to cover the suburbs and main provincial towns. This included a change in work methods: instead of its exclusive reliance on the OSA and political parties, the office would henceforth reach out to a broader spectrum of organizations and institutions that could help promote immigration.[44] According to the new plan, the efforts to encourage immigration should be based on "constant information about the experiences in Israel of immigrants from South America who had already settled in successfully."[45]

An important change in the bureaucracy in Buenos Aires was introduced after Israel became aware of the unrest in Argentina in June 1962. The economic crisis, political instability, and anti-Semitic incidents that struck Argentina that year set off a wave of visitors to the offices of the Jewish Agency. The primary sources reflect the changed climate among local Jews. At the time, the Aliyah Department representative in Buenos Aires was Yaakov Israeli. He and his Argentinian secretary, David Estrich, were processing potential immigrants on an individual basis. At the end of July, Israeli informed his supervisor in Jerusalem about the heavy pressure on the agency offices in Buenos Aires and expressed his fear that they would not be able to deal with the "tidal wave of aliya, which is growing day by day."[46]

The number of Argentinian Jews suddenly interested in relocating to Israel in mid-1962 brought the officials responsible for immigration and absorption face to face with a challenge of a new kind—mass immigration from a developed country. To cope with it, a joint government–Jewish Agency committee was established, under Finance Minister Levi Eshkol, with Shlomo Zalman Shragai of the agency as his deputy. Within a short time, the World Zionist Organization sent a delegation to Argentina.[47]

The WZO delegation to Argentina brought with it an absorption plan for hundreds of families, mainly those whose breadwinners were skilled craftsmen—such as carpenters, plumbers, metalworkers, lathe operators—or members of the liberal professions. According to Cygel, these plans showed potential immigrants that Israel could absorb them, but that they would have to "roll up their sleeves and work in various jobs." He added: "If they do not have sufficient funds, they will not be able to work in commerce or business, and not even in small factories."[48] Regarding liberal professionals, especially young doctors and engineers, "we have shown them that there are places for them in Israel, not only in Tel Aviv but also in the Negev and in the North."[49] But even these plans remained selective, with clear directives about who was eligible to immigrate:

> First and foremost, those who are physically and mentally fit, who have suitable occupations, young people willing to learn a trade, families that are suitable for kibbutzim and moshavim, young people for various courses, and so forth, and generally people whose absorption, in our opinion, will not pose a special problem. . . . Approvals based on these directives will be forwarded to the Aliyah Department, which is responsible for implementing them.[50]

The reports and memoranda written by members of the delegation during their time in Argentina expose the many problems they discovered in the aliya bureaucracy in Buenos Aires. Because of the large number of applicants, many months passed from initial registration at the local offices and the transfer of files to Jerusalem until applicants received a final answer. The arrangements in advance of immigration, including liquidation of assets, also took a long time. "The olim set in motion by the first tremor will not reach Israel for seven or eight months," wrote Menachem Gelerter in one of his reports.[51] The members of the delegation agreed that there was a vital need to organize and coordinate the work of the various Jewish Agency departments, particularly in those stormy times.[52] "We must simplify and streamline the clerical work by reducing the correspondence with the various departments in Israel, because by the time they reply, the candidates' desire is gone," notes one document.[53]

The visitors' recommendations were heard and accepted, and help was soon on the way: the staff of emissaries was expanded in October and November, and it was decided to dispatch Moshe Kitron to assume a new position of overall coordinator.[54] In a letter from Shragai to Yaakov Israeli in Buenos Aires, dated October 24, 1962, he explained the background of the decision to send Kitron to South America.[55] Shragai wrote that when the first reports of the events of Argentina came in, the Zionist movement and Israeli government saw themselves as obligated to make a special effort to encourage the Jews there to move to Israel and set out to create special conditions to ease their absorption in Israel:

> We saw coordination as a prime condition for the success of our work, particularly when we realized that our success depends not only on the programs and on coordination among the emissaries, but also on creating a climate for aliya and a movement of aliya among the public—which, as things stand today, must be done without any noise, but must be done. This is why the department turned to Mr. Kitron, who is a public figure, the chair of the Association of Latin American olim, and himself from South America. We are confident that he is the best man for the job.[56]

Part of Kitron's assignment was to represent the Jewish Agency to other groups in Argentina, including the OSA, the main Jewish institutions in the country, the Israel embassy in Buenos Aires, and, if necessary, the Argentinian government. He was also given the job of coordinating the work of the emissaries of the various agency departments. His letter of appointment, issued by the Aliyah Department and signed by Shragai, stated that he must comply with the department's regulations, whose programmatic provisions would be issued on behalf of the subcommittee of the Joint Coordinating Committee as well. Shragai then went on to enumerate Kitron's main tasks as representative of the department: creation of a favorable climate for immigration, in full coordination with the Israel embassy; coordination of the emissaries' work; and actual implementation of the immigration process.[57]

When he reached Buenos Aires, Kitron came to the conclusion that the system there was riddled with problems, mainly due to the burden of technical and bureaucratic matters. The staff in Buenos Aires was able to process several dozen immigrants each month—a few hundred a year; but in the second half of 1962 it was confronted by a "vast torrent, relative to the concepts and dimensions of the aliya from developed countries."[58] Kitron concluded that the physical conditions in the offices and the technical and bureaucratic restrictions interfered with the ongoing work. On various occasions, he described the red tape and delays in processing immigrants. In one document, he illustrated this by the effort associated with the required physical exam: a prospective immigrant had to run around among three different places—a doctor certified by the consulate, blood tests at the Jewish hospital or a health clinic, and a chest X-ray at the League for the War against Tuberculosis.[59]

Kitron thought that unifying operations and reception hours was essential. The Aliyah Department had to be in the center, making the decisions and wielding final authority on every matter. But it, too, had to coordinate with the rest of the agencies; if not, "the representatives of the other departments and leaders of the OSA will revolt and not accept the verdict," as he wrote to Shragai.[60] One of the first operative decisions he made was to purchase a new building for the OSA in the Once district of central Buenos Aires. The staff was beefed up, new positions were defined, and technical arrangements were installed in order to promote coordination among all the departments handling immigration, such as a common questionnaire for all of them, a single venue for the required lab tests and X-rays, using the emissaries of the Zionist youth movements to greet applicants and conduct the initial interview with them, dispatching the emissaries on short tours of the provincial towns, and establishing an aliya committee to visit Jewish institutions in greater Buenos Aires.[61]

The problem of coordination was not resolved during 1963—the year that saw a record number of immigrants from Argentina. Kitron's dispatches from Buenos Aires make it clear that every department saw the immigrant as its own "client" and was annoyed by and cold to the procedures to amalgamate and speed up the process.[62] In June of that year, the unresolved and exhausting problem of coordination came to the surface again. This time, Kitron wrote that despite the decisions by the Agency Executive that all matters be coordinated by the Aliyah Department, the other departments had continued to be in direct contact with their representatives, had sent out contradictory instructions, and had dealt with candidates independently. Kitron added that every time he tried to get involved in this issue, he was bombarded by protests and comments by the department heads in Israel.[63]

The financing of passage to Israel was another issue that impeded immigration. As the crisis continued and deepened, an increasing number of people asked the local offices to cover their travel expenses. The funding problem worsened in early 1963, when the Argentinian government raised the fee for a passport to 5,000 pesos ($40); this represented a serious outlay for large families in which everyone needed a new passport.[64] This amount was roughly half of Kitron's monthly salary, which was considered to be relatively large and was paid in dollars. The Jewish community in Buenos Aires, which contributed significant sums to immigrants, also cut its support drastically.[65] Here is Israeli's description of the situation in the offices early that year:

> If a family comes to us to ask for help in preserving its capital, which comes to $10,000, as the basis for its economic future in Israel, we are placed in an uncomfortable situation. With this sum, they have to build their entire future lives: $2,500 for an apartment and furnishing it, $500–$600 for a pinched existence during the initial period for a family of four, and $1,200 for the trip—so you have to deduct $4,000 or more from

> their initial assets. We do our utmost to collect what we can, but we must also encourage this aliya, which is no "worse" than that from Algeria and Morocco, for which we can find fantastic sums.... We are facing immense pressure by people who are struggling with their bitter fate, which came upon them so suddenly that they do not know what world they are living in. It simply makes no sense that on the one hand, we are screaming that we need this aliya and want to invest large sums in the programs, but on the other hand are trying to put a spoke in the wheels.[66]

Kitron admitted that many candidates for immigration were taking advantage of the Jewish Agency's willingness to cover their travel expenses. Such actions engendered public hostility toward the whole idea of aliya, particularly because the potential immigrants included people who had filed for bankruptcy or were mired in debt. Kitron also warned that the Jewish press in Argentina had started to complain that Israel was turning into a "city of refuge." In light of all these problems, a joint committee of the Argentinian Jewish community, the credit unions, and representatives of the Aliyah Department was established to screen applicants.[67] In November 1963, Yaakov Israeli asked the Finance and Aliyah Departments for permission to hire a social worker to conduct financial and social inquiries before applicants were granted an immigrant's visa. Israeli's request was approved only twelve days after it was submitted.[68] It seems that everyone was happy to put the brakes on immigration and multiply the complicated bureaucratic procedures.

The database constructed for my research indicates that 93% of the 4,178 immigrants and temporary and returning residents listed for 1963 received funding from the Jewish Agency; only 297 immigrants paid their own way.[69] The local institutions provided substantial support. Although it is not possible to estimate the breakdown of the funds from the various sources, it is clear that the surge in immigration in 1963 was made possible by the joint effort of local groups and the Jewish Agency. The issue of funding and its ramifications, including the impression it made on the public, had an immediate impact on the nature and scope of immigration and slowed its pace.

Organized Emigration from Argentina: Operation Shalhevet

The reports and surveys composed by Jewish Agency representatives demonstrate that immigration depended on a number of factors linked not to the month but to the season, such as the end of the school year in Argentina and in the Hebrew-language institutes in Israel, and to a number of variables, such as how many berths the Aliyah Department could reserve on ships at various times of the year. Throughout the period under discussion here, the person who was most deeply involved in the technical arrangements and who was the hands-on expert at organizing Argentinian Jewish immigration to Israel was Yaakov Israeli. When the number of those registering for immigration at the Jewish Agency offices in Buenos Aires increased, officials in the Aliyah Department began weighing the idea of chartering a ship for a special voyage from South America. This was the main reason for the meeting in Europe, in early October 1962, between Israeli and Yehuda Dominitz, the secretary of the Aliyah Department in Jerusalem. In practical terms, the idea was to ease the "traffic jam" of immigrants from Argentina and reduce their travel expenses.[70]

While in Europe, Israeli and Dominitz reached an agreement to charter the MS *Flaminia*. The ship was leased from its owners by Zim Shipping Lines, and the Aliyah Department undertook to use the vessel to carry more than a thousand immigrants from Argentina.[71] In a document written in late December 1962, David Estrich reported that the first thing Israeli did upon his return to Buenos Aires was to convene a committee, with representatives of the major institutions, to organize a special sailing. The declared goal of the committee was "to set off a broad (but quiet . . .) echo that would encourage aliya." Everything, of course, would be done in "consultation with the embassy in Buenos Aires, to define what was permitted and what was forbidden."[72] At the end of the document, Estrich emphasized that "given the situation, we will have to restrain our desire to publicize this matter widely" and lauded the planned sailing as a historic event for South American Jewry.[73]

Despite the secrecy, the preparations for the *Flaminia*'s sailing indeed set off waves after Israeli's trip, which came "suddenly and at the last minute," as Kitron noted in a letter to Shragai.[74] In fact it was this secrecy, the very attempt "to set off a broad (but quiet . . .) echo" of an organized rescue mission, as a strategy to encourage Jewish immigration to Israel in the midst of the prevailing economic and political crisis in Argentina, that generated antagonism about the enterprise, among both Jews and the Argentinian public. The demand for explanations soon landed on Shragai's desk in Jerusalem. Nevertheless, "I think it was a miracle that we made this decision," Shragai wrote to another member of the Executive, L. A. Pincus, in January 1963. "Otherwise, we would not have been able to transport the immigrants in an orderly manner and we would have failed in our first steps on that continent."[75] He told Pincus that the decision had been made after consultation with the ambassador in Buenos Aires, who approved the plan and even encouraged it. As for the arguments against the operation, Shragai countered them as follows:

> Among other things, the argument has been made that the arrival of the special ship for olim is supposedly liable to cause problems for local Jewry, and of course nothing is easier than sowing such fears among the sensitive community there. I have no way to investigate these reports thoroughly. On the other hand, I have no basis for doubting the reliability of the sources from which we received these reports. So I will not be surprised to receive one day a letter or telegram of protest from some community bigwig, railing against the arrival of the *Flaminia*.[76]

Protests by community leaders also reached Moshe Kitron. In a February 1963 letter to Shragai he went into detail about the issue and its ramifications. In advance of the *Flaminia*'s sailing, Kitron convened a press conference to ask the representatives of the Jewish media to act responsibly and to give serious thought to what to publish and how. Two of the papers did more or less as he requested, but a third (*Di Presse*) ran details he had asked be kept under wraps. Kitron noted that pressure had been exerted on him not to distribute information about immigration to Israel to local outlets; at the same time, though, items were appearing in newspapers in Israel, including wide-ranging conversations with the staff of Jewish Agency departments, details about the Higher Committee for Aliya from Argentina, the special plans for absorption in various domains, including the transfer of assets, the establishment of factories, and so forth. He had in mind locals who opposed the "aliya panic" but supported aliya itself, including Dr. Isaac Goldenberg, the president of DAIA, the umbrella organization of Argentinian Jewry "whose Jewish and Zionists standing does not require confirmation by any committee." Kitron added:

> Claims have been voiced that I cannot accept, because the rising tide of aliya cannot be hidden; but also arguments that require an answer: that we must not flaunt openly what is liable to be exploited by antisemitic groups and by antisemitic elements in government circles. In any case, there is talk about the smuggling of the millions and even billions that the Jews have amassed in this country; of young people who were born in Argentina and are evading military service; and so on. The fact that the Italians and Spanish are leaving Argentina in much larger numbers than the Jews are does not alter the risk, which we have known as long

> as there has been a "Jewish problem" in the world. And I will allow myself to add: the emotional and festive clarifications and responses that reach (and sometimes originate with) the governing institutions do not always contribute to the resolution of the problems that arise for real live people who are working and troubled.[77]

It is important to understand that the policy of secrecy was totally at variance with the strategy followed by DAIA in its battle against anti-Semitism, which relied on an open campaign meant to mobilize favorable public opinion in society at large and registered a significant number of achievements. For example, on June 20, 1962, at the peak of the anti-Semitic violence, DAIA called a general strike of Jewish stores and businesses throughout Argentina, which garnered tremendous sympathy in public opinion; large sectors of civil society supported the Jewish protest.[78] This was reflected in the coverage of the *Flaminia* affair by the Jewish periodical *La Luz*. Two weeks before the ship sailed, its editor published a lengthy article about its planned voyage.[79] "We do not understand why all the activities related to aliya are being kept confidential, as though this was Morocco, Romania, or Algeria." He added:

> On various occasion[s] we approached the authorized agencies to request information, but we have been rebuffed every time, on the grounds that it is confidential. So we have decided to give up on these sources and track down the information ourselves. Our starting point is the assumption that the activities of the Zionist movement are lawful and legitimate and must be conducted by light of day and in full view. Moreover, we do not live in a country where the circumstances impose secrecy. But it is a fact that certain players have decided to charter a ship exclusively for aliya. Perhaps this is to create an atmosphere of an exodus from Argentina? Such an atmosphere of strained romance—600 olim on a special ship—or of a makeshift operation could set off an upheaval about aliya among Argentinian Jewry, which is liable to generate needless panic and ultimately to damage both the aliya process and Argentinian Jewry. Patterns that are appropriate, for example, for the Jews of Algeria must not be adopted for these Jews. Those responsible for carrying out the policy must take into account the different circumstances at play here, work calmly and responsibly, and refrain from patterns that are inappropriate here and even liable to harm us.[80]

This extract from *La Luz* is representative of the general tenor, because the paper was considered to be Zionist, right wing, and conservative; it generally hewed to the Israeli perspective on aliya and the ingathering of the exiles, while being critical of the local leadership. This example clearly highlights the gap between the Israeli agencies that dealt with immigration and the locals. For the Israelis, "the time has come to save the Jews who are facing spiritual danger," intoned Shragai at a plenary session of the Zionist General Council in March 1963, "especially those who are facing the danger of willful assimilation, but who could save themselves because there is nothing to prevent their leaving their exile and making aliya."[81] The Israelis found it difficult to understand a Jewish community that had national and Zionist sentiments and a secular Jewish identity, but wished to integrate into the host society while preserving its Jewish and Zionist character as part of its Argentinian identity.

The organization and encouragement of Jewish emigration from Argentina were based on the arguments about an impending catastrophe, spread by interested parties that depicted Israel as a safe haven for all Jews. The documents examined here present those who worked to organize and encourage the process as heralds of crisis and salvation who paint every aliya as a headlong flight from disaster. The representatives of the Aliyah Department evinced a deep and sincere desire for it to succeed, sometimes in the form of plaintive calls for rescue from the despair, economic misery, and anti-Semitic persecution. In their reports, they tended to exaggerate the dangers lurking for the Jews of Argentina. In October 1964, the director general of the Jewish Agency Aliyah Department, Baruch Duvdevani, received a very interesting letter from engineer Moshe Dayan, a prominent Revisionist in Argentina:

> I do not believe that one needs to appeal to the Jews of Argentina in 1964 in a style similar to what should have been employed for the Jews of Poland in 1938. One would have to be an ungifted and shallow disciple of Jabotinsky's to want to repeat, without a proper assessment of the situation, his call of 25 years ago. In his warnings Jabotinsky, too, distinguished between the Jews of Poland and the Jews of South Africa and the United States. The antisemitic threat used to be effective, but is no longer a sufficient basis for encouraging aliya from Argentina.[82]

Beyond the interest aroused by Dayan's letter itself, the most interesting point is that even to a Revisionist it seemed that the attempt by the Aliyah Department emissaries to employ the threat of anti-Semitism as a strategy to encourage Argentinian Jews to immigrate to Israel was overdone and absurd. Time after time, the developments in Argentina and the changes among its Jews proved that, despite the severe and frequent economic and political crises and manifestations of anti-Semitism that were endemic to Argentina, the methods employed to motivate the Jews to leave the country for Israel did not reflect the true situation and proved to be unrealistic and exaggerated.

The documents reviewed in this chapter show that the aliya system in Argentina failed to take advantage of the latent potential of the Jewish community. What is more, its flaws, such as the lack of coordination, complex bureaucracy, and redundant officials actually slowed, delayed, and reduced emigration from that country. The Aliyah Department files are in great disarray. The ideological differences and influence of officials' party affiliation stand out. The political considerations that tipped the balance in various decisions overflowed onto the Jewish street and caused significant harm to the very idea of aliya emissaries and Argentinian Jews' image of the Jewish Agency.

Starting in 1948, Argentinian Jewish immigration to Israel was subject to controls and limits, mainly because of the quotas set under the selective policy in force in those years. I believe that the individual and selective processing had a deleterious effect on immigration and decreased the number of immigrants at a time of growing interest in the idea among broad circles of Argentinian Jewry. Despite this inclination, immigration was organized and promoted on the basis of doomsday arguments about "the distressing situation of the Jews" and sometimes the "distressed condition of Judaism," which portrayed the State of Israel as the refuge for all Jews. All the representatives of the Aliyah Department, both in Israel and in Argentina, were people with a religious worldview, affiliated with the Religious Zionist movement that controlled the department after independence. The documents reveal them to have been prophets of doom and salvation. For them, aliya was always an escape from existential distress.

5

"Marginal Immigrants"

The Sociodemographics of the Argentinian Jewish Immigration to Israel

The Scale of Immigration

There are abundant quantitative and qualitative sources that document the overall scale of immigration to Israel, and from Argentina in particular, during the first two decades after independence. Statistics are available in the records kept by two different bodies: the Central Bureau of Statistics (CBS) and the Jewish Agency Aliyah Department.

In July 1948, while the War of Independence was still in progress, the CBS was created by the merger of two statistics departments that operated under the Mandate, those of the Mandatory government and of the Jewish Agency. The new CBS proceeded to lay the basis for professional statistical work on most aspects of Israeli social, economic, and demographic life, including immigration and absorption. The data were collected, arranged, and processed by the CBS for publication in its annual *Statistical Abstract of Israel*, as well as the monthly *Bulletin of Statistics*, the *Statistical News*, and various special publications.[1]

The statistics on migration are based on the register of people who entered and left the State of Israel: olim, departing and returning residents, and tourists. The border control stations recorded all those who entered or left the country and issued a daily report—with a copy to the CBS. In addition to these reports, the border posts also sent the CBS the registration forms filled out by immigrants, which listed, inter alia, "country of birth," "citizenship," and, beginning in 1950, "last country of residence." The CBS acquired the questionnaires completed by tourists who changed their status to immigrant ("settling tourists") from the district aliya offices and the files of the Interior Ministry.[2] All these inputs support the statistical processing of immigration and absorption and make it possible to study the scope of Jewish immigration to Israel from different countries.

The Jewish Agency Aliyah Department collected parallel data. At independence, the Aliyah Department supplanted the Immigration Department of the Mandatory government. In addition to the standard tasks of keeping records, issuing permits and visas, and so on, the Statistics Office within the department also processed and published data about immigrants to the country—a job it inherited from the Jewish Agency's Statistics Department that operated during the Mandate. The data gathered by the Aliyah Department was based on each immigrant's "individual record," which it kept on file.[3]

The Aliyah Department published copious information in its bulletin, *Dappei Aliyah*, first issued in April 1949. Initially published on a monthly basis, but later only every two or three months, it contained surveys related to immigration to Israel, news from the department and its offices abroad, statistical summaries of immigration, and authoritative reports on customs duties, imports, and other topics of interest to immigrants and potential immigrants, along with special sections on how aliya was portrayed in the press and Knesset debates.[4] The Aliyah Department used the bulletin as the framework for a series of special publications, including a little-known study by CBS statistician Dr. Binyamin Zvi Gill on thirty years of immigration to the country (1919–49).[5] Demographer Jacob Lestschinsky, the "father of Jewish statistics," viewed *Dappei Aliyah* as a "wonderful scientific publication."[6]

There are some small disparities in the data aggregated by the Jewish Agency and by the CBS, due mainly to the differences in the units' methods of registering immigrants. The CBS data distinguish Jews from non-Jews, whereas the Jewish Agency figures include non-Jewish immigrants only from 1957 on. As for the "settling tourists," until 1965 the agency counted only Jews. Furthermore, the CBS data omit temporary residents: only those who changed their status to immigrant were recorded (as settling tourists). The discrepancies are trivial, because more than 99% of all immigrants in these years were Jewish.[7]

The available data indicate that between May 14, 1948, and the end of 1967, close to 1.29 million immigrants—including more than 28,000 settling tourists—arrived in Israel. The impact of immigration on the country's Jewish population and growth rate makes the Israeli case a historical anomaly in the modern era of international migration. On the eve of independence, around 650,000 Jews lived

Figure 5: Jewish immigration to Israel, 1948–67

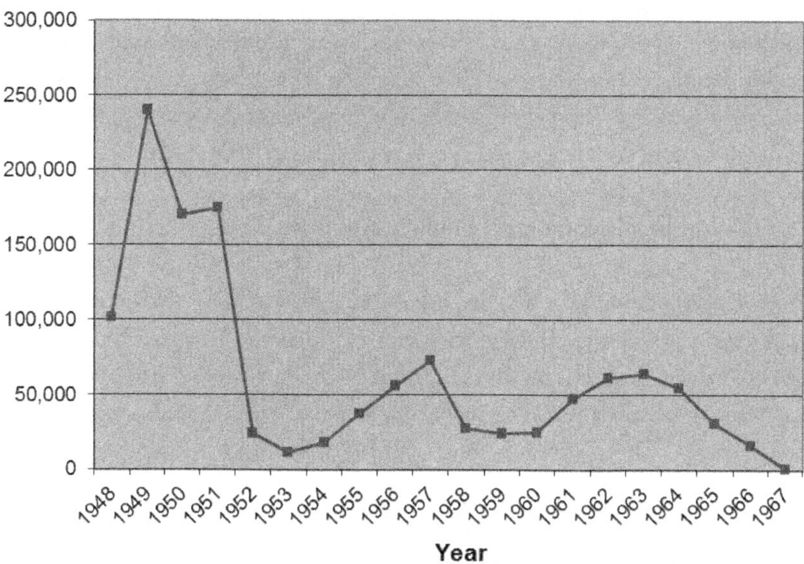

Source: Central Bureau of Statistics, *Immigration to Israel 1948–1972*, Part A. Annual data (Jerusalem, 1973).

in its future territory. During the next three years, the almost 700,000 newcomer immigrants doubled its Jewish population.[8]

By the end of 1967, Israel's Jewish population exceeded 2.38 million. Immigration is estimated to have accounted for 64% of this phenomenal growth, with the remaining 36% coming from natural increase. Furthermore, immigration led to a significant increase in the percentage of world Jewry living in Israel, from about 6% at independence to 18% two decades later.[9]

The immigrants who arrived in the country in that period hailed from more than a hundred countries. About 39% came from Eastern Europe, mainly Romania and Poland; Western Europe—mostly Germany, France, Austria, and Britain—contributed 4%. Africa provided 29%, with immigrants from Morocco predominating, followed by those from Tunisia, Libya, and Egypt. Another 24% came from Middle Eastern countries, especially Iraq, Iran, Turkey, and Yemen. Latin American immigrants, half of them from Argentina, accounted for 2%; only 1% came from North America. Oceania also contributed a small number of immigrants.[10]

Fully 94% of the immigrants came from "countries of distress," motivated by social, political, or economic difficulties. At the beginning of the period studied, about 40% of world Jewry lived in such countries; by its end, the figure had fallen to 33%. Only 6% of the immigrants came from the "wealthy countries" that were home to the bulk of world Jewry.[11] The assumption behind lumping all the "wealthy countries" together was that these immigrants were propelled by ideological and personal reasons rather than by impending catastrophe. The immigrants from Latin American countries were classified as from "wealthy countries."

Argentinian Immigrants and Immigrants from Argentina

Another methodological difficulty interferes with assessing the magnitude of immigration by country. The agencies that recorded and analyzed immigration registered several related items: "country of birth," "country of citizenship," and "last country of residence." But in many cases these do not indicate an immigrant's "origin." This problem is most acute with regard to attempts to estimate the number of immigrants who arrived in Israel from wealthy countries, especially those in the New World. In some cases, none of the categories listed here can specify where an immigrant from there "really" came from.

During the British Mandate, government agencies registered 452,158 immigrants, of whom only 259 were listed as being from Argentina. At that time, the records noted only country of birth and country of citizenship.[12] Many Jews in Argentina had not been born in that country and had yet to be naturalized there. This reflected the fact that in the interwar period and again after World War II, many Jews—especially European Jews—wandered from country to country, in both Europe and the Americas, including Argentina.[13]

Consequently, Mandatory officials registered many Polish-by-birth immigrants as Polish, even though some other country was their last port of call. For example, 23% of the Jews who arrived from Germany between 1935 and 1942 held Polish citizenship or were stateless. Another 14% indicated that they had not been born in Germany.[14] In other words, many "Polish immigrants" were in fact Polish born but immigrated from elsewhere, including Argentina. So, it is certain that the number of immigrants who arrived from Argentina during the Mandate period exceeded the 259 listed in the official statistics.

The distinction between "country of birth" and "country of citizenship" continued after independence and throughout 1949, while some 341,000 immigrants from fifty-two different countries were arriving in Israel. They included 377 Jews whose country of birth was Argentina.[15] For the reasons noted above, there is no way to extract from the available data the number of immigrants who arrived from Argentina but were neither Argentinian born nor Argentinian nationals.

However, a cross-check of the primary sources can help us arrive at an estimate. First, Dr. Binyamin Zvi Gill's statistical study of immigration between 1919 and 1949 addressed this issue.[16] His findings can be checked against the CBS data, which, starting in 1949, list both the immigrant's last country of residence and country of birth.[17]

About 1,800 immigrants are recorded as arriving in Israel from the New World between independence and the end of 1949. This number refers only to those born there, and not the larger number who had been living there before coming to Israel. To derive the latter figure, Gill compared two items related to the immigrants who arrived between May and December of 1949: their country of birth and their last country of residence. He found that 1,012 immigrants born in the Americas arrived in Israel during that period, but America was the last place of residence for more than twice as many—2,120. Gill contended that a similar ratio existed in the first twenty months after independence and inferred that there were twice as many immigrants who left the New World as were born there; that is, more than 3,500 immigrants. Gill also estimated that roughly 800 immigrants arrived in Israel from Argentina in the last seven months of 1949; but only 257 of them were native-born.[18]

At the beginning of 1950, the CBS added "last country of residence" to its immigration database; from then on, we can directly distinguish immigrants' last country of residence from their country of birth. The data for that year reflect the work of the aliya organizations in different countries, and the immigrant's "country of origin" actually indicates the land from which he or she arrived and not necessarily the country of birth. An anecdote illustrating the change in registration method ran in *Hatzofeh* in April 1950, under the headline "First Oleh from Trinidad":

> Yesterday there arrived in Israel the first Jew—and for now the only one—from the state [*sic*] of Trinidad. Even the Jewish Agency aliya officials in Jerusalem and Haifa, experts in the map of countries from which Jews immigrate to Israel, were perplexed. This Trinidad—where is it? . . . The oleh explained that it is an island; it was determined that he comes from the island of Trinidad in the Caribbean, near Venezuela in South America. From now on, another country is added to from which Jews make aliya—the 53rd on the list.[19]

The change that took effect at the beginning of 1950 was essential for regulating immigration. The immigrants' place of birth reflects their origins to a certain

Figure 6: Jewish immigrants from Argentina, by country of birth and last country of residence, 1948–67

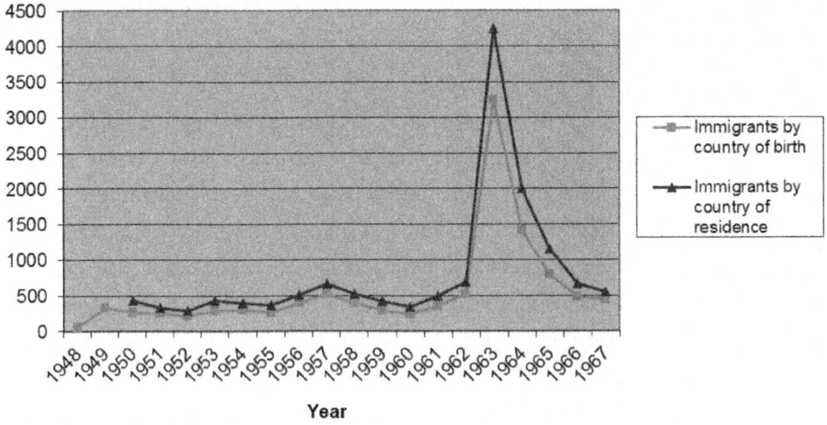

Source: Central Bureau of Statistics, *Immigration to Israel, 1948–1972*, Part A. Annual data (Jerusalem, 1973).

extent, but from the economic perspective, their last country of residence was more important. It was needed to determine the number of Jews who remained in those countries, an essential datum in that period of mass immigration.

Between 1948 and 1960, 3,792 natives of Argentina immigrated to Israel (including 3,404 from 1950 to 1960)—or 73% of the 4,681 whose last country of residence was Argentina. For the period 1961–67, the comparable figures were 7,250 of 9,806, or 74% native-born.[20] Figure 6 portrays the regular pattern and suggests that Gill's estimate of a two-to-one ratio was too high.

According to the CBS data, more than 15,000 immigrants arrived from Argentina between independence and the end of 1967, of whom about 1,200 were settling tourists.[21] Another 1,044 immigrants who registered as temporary residents between 1963 and 1967 were not included in the CBS data.[22] Most of the immigrants from Argentina (around 68%) reached Israel between 1961 and 1967, almost half of them in the tidal wave of 1963. Argentinian immigrants accounted for 1.1% of total direct immigration, 4.3% of settling tourists, and 6.8% of temporary residents after 1963.[23]

Interestingly, the breakdown of Argentinian immigration to Israel resembles that from North America. Of the nearly 15,000 immigrants from the United States from 1948 to the end of 1967, about 65% were native-born; of the 1,800 immigrants from Canada, the figure was about 70%. In contrast to the Argentinian case, most of the immigrants from the United States and Canada registered as settling tourists or temporary residents: 58% of those from the United States and 53% from Canada. Here too, most of the immigrants arrived between 1961 and 1967: roughly 65% of the US total and 60% of the Canadians.[24]

When analyzing the data for immigration from Argentina, we must consider both overall immigration to Israel and the variations in the Jewish population of Argentina. As we saw in chapter 1, Argentina's Jewish population grew steadily until the 1960s. It reached 310,000 in 1960 but declined to 286,000 by 1970. The sharp decrease reflects the demographic contraction of that decade, which was the result of a low birth rate, a drop in immigration to Argentina, and Argentina's transformation into a country of net Jewish emigration.[25]

These data reflect the marked shift that occurred in Jewish migration to and from Argentina in the late 1950s and early 1960s. The literature on general migration from Argentina shows that in those years the country became a source of out-migration, particularly to the rest of Latin America but also to the United States. This immigration increased significantly between 1960 and 1970.[26] The same pattern applied to the Jews. Although there are no statistics on the immigration of Argentinian Jews to destinations other than Israel, this is a reasonable inference from the primary sources I collected.

Yehoshua Wolberg, a senior official of the Aliyah Department in Jerusalem and head of its Latin American desk, prepared a comprehensive report when he returned from a visit to Argentina in October 1963. He pointed out the trend to emigration by the general population, similar to that of the Jews. An average of 2,000 Argentinian citizens were applying for US visas each month, and about 1,200 were receiving them. Slightly less than a third of them (that is, around 350) were Jews. Regarding the latter, Wolberg added: "I assume that among the migrants they are the strongest elements [of Argentinian Jewry]."[27]

Two points raised by Wolberg warrant further discussion: the numbers involved and the presumed composition of those who opted for Israel. During Israel's first two decades, around 5% of the community moved to Israel—a significant proportion in comparison to other wealthy countries. If the primary sources accurately reflect the process, only half of the Jewish emigrants from Argentina in the 1960s relocated to Israel. The second aspect relates to the composition of those who did come to Israel. Wolberg's words suggest that the Argentinian Jews who did so were not "the strongest."

Does this mean that moving to Israel was a solution for the margins of Argentinian Jewry? It is hard to ignore this question. We can answer it only by reconstructing the socioeconomic composition of the Argentinian Jewish immigrants and checking the data against the profile of the community as a whole and of all immigrants to Israel—a task to which we now turn.

Argentinian Immigrants by Origins and Age

The aforementioned CBS distinction between "country of birth" and "last country of residence" reveals an interesting pattern with regard to the Argentinian immigrants. In 1960, 63% of all Argentinian Jews were native-born.[28] By contrast, about 75% of those who settled in Israel had been born there. This discrepancy is illuminated by a comparison of the age composition of Argentina-born Jews with that of the Argentinian immigrants: more than 95% of Argentinian Jews through age thirty were native-born. According to the database constructed for this volume, more than 60% of the immigrants belonged to that age group. In other words, the relative youth of the immigrants from Argentina accounts for the greater percentage of the native-born. As the table shows, almost a quarter were younger than fifteen. Given the likelihood that these children immigrated with their parents, the Argentinian immigration to Israel was clearly young and family based.

Table 2: Argentinian Jewish population, Argentinian and all immigrants to Israel, by age (percentage)

Age Cohort	Argentinian Jewish Population in 1960	Immigrants from Argentina, 1954–67	All Immigrants, 1948–68
0–4	5.5	6.6	11.5
5–9	7.2	7.4	9.8
10–14	7.8	8.4	10.1
15–19	7.5	13.9	9.8
20–24	6.8	16.7	8.8
25–29	7.0	7.8	7.8
30–39	15.1	12.6	13.4
40–49	14.2	9.8	12.2
50–59	15.2	10.4	9.0
60–69	9.1	5.1	5.1
70+	4.6	1.3	2.5
Total	100.0	100.0	100.0

Sources: Uziel Schmelz and Sergio DellaPergola, *The Structure of Latin American Jewry* (Tel Aviv, 1974), 8; Sebastian Klor, "Database 10,487"; CBS, *Immigration to Israel*, Special Publications Series N-308 (Jerusalem, 1969), 16.

The foregoing data allow me to contrast the selective immigration policy promulgated by Israel after 1951 with the composition of the immigrants who reached Israel.[29] A comparison of the age composition of Argentinian immigrants and all immigrants affirms my assumption that the selective policy influenced both, but especially the former. We can trace the predominance of young people in both groups to the selection rules that effectively barred the elderly. In fact, the Argentinian immigration was even more selective. The figures for the 15–29 age group support this conclusion; including the next cohorts, up to age 49—elucidates it further. It emerges that 60% of Argentinian immigrants—as opposed to 52% of all immigrants—were of prime working age.

More surprising, though, is that there were more older "non-natives" among the Argentinian immigrants than among all immigrants. About 17% of the former were fifty or older. The historical sources indicate that they tended to be relatives, friends, neighbors, and particularly parents of those who had already immigrated to Israel.[30] (The selective policy allowed immigration by close relatives even if they did meet the criteria.)

"Family members" were a significant component of the immigration from Argentina throughout the period studied here. Mordechai Kaufman, the director of the Aliya Office in Buenos Aires, implied as much at a 1949 press conference announcing an agreement between the Jewish Agency and World ORT to institute accelerated vocational courses for prospective immigrants.[31] Kaufman distinguished several categories of Argentinian immigrants: "pioneers, refugees, members of the middle-class, and family members."[32] Four years later, Kaufman presented data on the Argentinian immigrants of those early years: more than 40% were "pioneers" (members of Zionist youth movements who had received agricultural training in Argentina); about 16% were parents of these pioneers, who followed their children; and the rest were young adults, professionals, and middle-class families.[33]

Unfortunately, for the period studied here there are no statistics on birthplace of the non-native immigrants (25% of the total). However, David Horowitz and Moshe Kitron, when they served as emissaries in Argentina, did collect applicants' place-of-birth data. Of the 1,187 who registered in the first half of 1964, about 69% were natives of Argentina. Of the non-natives, more than 85% had been born in Eastern Europe (mainly Poland); fewer than 3% were natives of Central and Western Europe, and 5% of Asia and Africa—including a handful who had been born in Palestine. The rest were born in other countries in South America, mainly Uruguay.[34]

"Our impression is that the percentage of olim born in eastern countries [that is, Asia and North Africa] and Central Europe lags behind Polish-born olim if we compare the local populations of the former and the latter," Horowitz wrote, with the qualification that "we are relying on estimates in the absence of statistics on the matter."[35] Horowitz reasoned that more Eastern Europeans relocated to Israel because "Eastern European Jews have deeper roots and received a more intense Zionist education than those from the eastern countries and Central Europe."[36] Horowitz's thesis needs to be verified, but his assessment seems to be true: 20% of Argentinian Jewry were immigrants from Central and Western Europe or Sephardim (from the Balkans, North Africa, and Asia).[37]

Kitron wrote about the origins of the Argentinian immigrants in an early 1963 article. He noted that a small number of the Argentina-born olim were young people from Sephardi immigrant families or whose parents came from Central and Western Europe. Meanwhile, adults and the elderly (the latter accounted for 20% of Argentinian Jews) were hardly represented at all.[38] In another document, written in May 1965, Kitron returned to this issue: surveys he conducted in Buenos Aires during his special mission, as well as later analyses, revealed the "regrettable fact" that there were few German-speaking and Sephardi immigrants relative to their weight in the total Jewish population of Argentina.[39]

In light of this information, we may conclude that an overwhelming majority of the immigrants from Argentina were of Eastern European origin. In other words, the immigrants did not reflect the composition of Argentinian Jewry with regard to country of origin. Still, despite the disproportionate representation of Eastern European Jews, the community's ethnic diversity was clearly recognizable among its immigrants.

The Argentinian Immigrants by Gender, Age, and Marital Status

Although the numbers of Jewish men and women in Argentina were roughly equal, fewer women immigrated to Israel; the gender breakdown was close to that of all immigration to Israel (see table 3).[40] But compared to international migration in general, the proportion of women among the immigrants (all immigrants and from Argentina in particular)—was high by any standard, supporting the theory that Jewish immigration to Israel was family based. In his research about Jewish immigration to Palestine in the early twentieth century, Gur Alroey established that Jewish migrants have always included a relatively high proportion of women.[41] The importance of this fact is the implication that the immigrants were planning to settle permanently. The situation of immigration

Table 3: Argentinian and all immigrants to Israel and the Argentinian Jewish population, by gender (percentage)

	Argentinian Jews in 1960	Argentinian immigrants, 1954–67	All immigrants, 1948–67
Women	50.2	48.8	49.9
Men	49.8	51.2	50.1
Total	100.0	100.0	100.0

Sources: Uziel Schmelz and Sergio DellaPergola, *The Structure of Latin American Jewry* (Tel Aviv, 1974), 77; Klor, "Database 10,487"; "20 years of Immigration in Numbers," *Dappei Aliyah* 69 (1968).

Table 4: Argentinian and all immigrants, by gender and marital status (age 15+)

Marital Status	Argentinian immigrants, 1954–67	All immigrants, 1948–68
Widowers	0.8	1.5
Widows	3.8	7.8
Divorced men	0.1	0.3
Divorced women	0.9	0.9
Married men	27.7	30.1
Married women	28.4	30.2
Single men	22.1	16.6
Single women	16.2	11.3
Unknown	-	1.3
Total	100.0	100.0

Sources: Klor, "Database 10,487"; CBS, *Immigration to Israel*, Special Publications Series N-308 (Jerusalem, 1969), 22.

to Israel during its first two decades confirms Alroey's findings for that period as well.

The distribution by marital status corroborates the family-based character of the Argentinian Jewish immigration to Israel:[42] 43% of the immigrants were married, 4% were widowed or divorced, and 53% (a figure that includes all the children, of course) were single.

The data indicate that singles and the divorced were more likely to migrate than were married couples; among the widowed and divorced, women were more inclined to do so than were men—a pattern common to every migration movement. We can attribute this phenomenon to the women's hopes of starting a new

Table 5: Argentinian Jews and immigrants from Argentina (15+), by gender and marital status

Gender	Single	Married	Separated	Divorced	Widowed	Total
All Argentinian Jews						
Men	29.0	67.2	0.4	0.2	3.2	100.0
Women	22.7	66.1	0.6	0.2	10.4	100.0
Immigrants from Argentina						
Men	41.6	56.4	-	0.3	1.7	100.0
Women	32.1	58.2	-	1.9	7.8	100.0

Sources: Uziel Schmelz and Sergio DellaPergola, *The Structure of Latin American Jewry* (Tel Aviv, 1974), 77; Klor, "Database 10,487."

chapter in their lives. Men, on the other hand, allegedly find female partners more easily in their country of origin.[43] And widows tend to be younger than widowers.

But the most important inference from the data on the distribution of immigrants by marital status, gender, and age is that emigration from Argentina to Israel was a movement of families and young people. This can be illustrated by the data (from my database) on the tidal wave of 1963, which brought more than 4,500 Argentinian Jews to Israel.

As table 6 shows, 84% of the families who left Argentina for Israel in 1963 comprised two to four people, with an average family size of 3.3. In 1960, according to Schmelz and DellaPergola, around 70% of Jewish households in Argentina numbered between two and four people, with an average size of 3.5.[44] For comparison's sake, note the average size of immigrant families in the period 1948–68: immigrants from Europe, 3.1 people; from the Americas, 3.2; from Asia, 4.5; and from Africa, 5.0.[45]

To a certain extent, the demographics of the Argentinian immigrants in 1963 resemble those for the entire period studied here. Slightly more than 70% of the Argentinian immigrants that year were thirty-five or younger (see table 7). The percentage of children through age eighteen was particularly large then as compared to other time periods, thanks to the preponderance of adults age nineteen to thirty-five. The relatively low percentage of immigrants past fifty in 1963 (and especially among the passengers on the *Flaminia*, which sailed that year) supports my assertion that the selective policy decisively influenced the composition of immigrants, and even more so in the large wave of 1963.

Table 6: Argentinian immigrants and all immigrants, by family composition

Persons in Family	Argentinian Immigrants, 1963	All Immigrants, 1948–68
2	33.5	34.4
3	22.5	26.1
4	27.7	17.1
5	12.5	8.6
6	2.4	13.8
7+	0.6	
Unknown	0.8	-
Total	100.0	100.0

Klor, "Database 10,487"; CBS, *Immigration to Israel*, Special Publications Series N-308 (Jerusalem, 1969), 32.

Table 7: Argentinian immigrants, by age and period of immigration

Age Cohort	1954–60	1960–61	1963	Passengers on the SS *Flaminia*	1964–67
0–16	25.7	22.2	30.0	35.2	24.2
16–18	6.3	7.0	8.8	8.5	7.5
19–35	26.6	38.6	31.5	30.6	29.8
36–50	17.9	13.8	18.2	18.1	16.9
50 plus	23.5	18.4	11.5	7.6	21.6
Total	100.0	100.0	100.0	100.0	100.0

Source: Klor, "Database 10,487."

The Argentinian Immigrants by Occupation

The Jewish Agency's departments did not begin systematic work in Argentina until 1954. Before then, the aliya staff in Buenos Aires has not left us with adequate documentation, and their correspondence with the departments in Israel was irregular and disorganized. Nevertheless, figures on the occupational distribution of the pre-1954 immigrants can be extracted from a critical examination of primary sources. These sources show that a majority of them were self-employed—artisans and a few skilled tradesmen, and business owners. Many of them had specialized training, but others did not.[46]

There was also a significant group of liberal professionals—generally young adults at the start of their career. Those most likely to move to Israel were the members of the lower middle class who—unlike most of the community—were not upwardly mobile.[47] As Kitron wrote at the end of 1951, "anyone acquainted with the history of contemporary migration will readily understand why most of these candidates were not from the wealthier or more well-established strata in the New World."[48]

My database provides a clear picture of the immigrants' occupational breakdown. Roughly 26% identified themselves as manual laborers and blue-collar workers, along with a few farmers. Liberal professionals accounted for 13%, clerical workers for 8%, and merchants and industrialists for 7% (see table 8). Much like the data on age, gender, and marital status, the high proportion of school students and housewives supports my thesis that the Argentinian immigration was family based.

We can further divide each occupational group by specific field, age, gender, and marital status. Among the artisans and skilled craftsmen, 27% were tailors, 15% needleworkers, 12% carpenters, 6% weavers, 6% engravers, and 5% jewelers. The remainder came from twenty-six different occupations, including watchmakers, upholsterers, furriers, shoemakers, locksmiths, and bakers (13%

Table 8: Occupational distribution of Argentinian immigrants, 1954–67

Occupational category	N	%
Artisans	988	10.8
Unclassified (including day laborers and those aged 18+ and still in school)	800	8.8
Skilled tradesmen	441	4.8
Farmers	97	1.1
Merchants and Industrialists	630	6.9
Liberal professionals (including teachers and bookkeepers)	1,211	13.2
Clerical workers	737	8.0
University students	311	3.4
Elementary and secondary school pupils	2,306	25.2
Housewives	1,597	17.4
Pensioners	38	0.4
Total	9,156	100.0

Source: Klor, "Database 10,487."

altogether). Other trades listed include glaziers, blacksmiths, tinsmiths, butchers, welders, slaughterers, and plumbers. As for their ages, 43% of those in this group were 15–35, 31% were 36–50, and 26% were past 50. The married outnumbered the unmarried (65% to 28%); 7% were widowed or divorced. A decisive majority were men—85% of the married and 77% of the unmarried.

Among the liberal professionals we find teachers (34%), physicians (17%), bookkeepers (13%), engineers (6%), chemists and biochemists (4%), and pharmacists (3%). The remaining 23% listed thirty-three other professions, notably accountants, architects, psychologists, social workers, journalists, and lawyers. A slight majority (56%) were married; 40% were unmarried and 4% widowed or divorced. Remarkably, women accounted for 68% of the unmarried professionals, suggesting that educated young women were more likely to immigrate to Israel than their male counterparts (or that educated woman found it harder to snag a husband in that day and age). Women also made up 85% of the widowed and divorced. However, the most prominent trait of the immigrant professionals was their age. Most were young and newly embarked on their careers. Nearly three-quarters of the professional class were 35 or younger; 19% were 36–50, and only 7% past 50.

A similar age structure prevailed among skilled laborers, including technicians of various sorts (37%), electricians (20%), and mechanics (25%). Nearly three-quarters (73%) of them were 35 or younger; 19% were between 36 and 50, and only 8% past 50. More than half (53%) were married. Unlike the liberal professionals, the married electricians, technicians, and mechanics were, as might be expected, almost all men (97%), and so too the unmarried (96%).

The office workers, too, were also young: 88% of them in the 35 and under bracket, with only 9% between 36 and 50 and 3% past 50. Of this group, 30% were married and 69% were single; men accounted for 65% of the former group and women for 52% of the latter. Most of the laborers and unclassified workers were unmarried (87%), a decisive majority of them (86%) were men. Men also dominated the married remainder (92%). Nearly 70% were 35 or below; 17% were 36–50, and 14% past 50.

The pattern among merchants and industrialists was very different. Here less than half (45%) were below 35; 30% were between 36 and 50 and a full quarter in the 50-plus age bracket. The vast majority of the merchants were married (88%), 97% of whom were men; among the 7% who had never married, 93% were men (5% were widowed or divorced). This is the only category in which widowers outnumber widows: 67% of the widowed merchants were men. Divorced merchants were not likely to relocate to Israel—only 0.4% of the total.

Table 9: Occupational breakdown of Argentinian Jews and immigrants (age 14+), selected occupations

	Argentinian Jewish Community, 1960		Argentinian Immigrants 1954–67	
Occupation	N	%	N	%
Chemists, biochemists, and pharmacists	1,386	1.2	91	1.3
Physicians and dentists	3,198	2.7	207	2.9
Architects and engineers	1,572	1.3	77	1.1
Teachers	3,228	2.7	397	5.7
Farmers	2,372	2.0	97	1.4
Clerks and bookkeepers	12,607	10.6	892	12.7
Tailors and dressmakers	7,541	6.3	441	6.3
Merchants	40,922	34.4	630	9.0
Total Labor Force	119,061			

Sources: Uziel Schmelz and Sergio DellaPergola, *The Structure of Latin American Jewry* (Tel Aviv, 1974), 112, 119–20; Klor, "Database 10,487."

To better understand the professional stratification of the immigrants from Argentina, we should compare it to the Argentinian Jewish community as a whole. During the 1960s, two-thirds of the country's Jewish workers held white-collar jobs: merchants, industrialists, office workers, and liberal professionals. In stark contrast, most of the immigrants were from the working class. Table 9 reveals the paucity of merchants and industrialists among the immigrants. The relatively high figure for liberal professionals, on the other hand, corresponds to their weight in the community (10%). However, as mentioned above, the prominent characteristic of this group was its youth, with most of its members—especially among the physicians and engineers—at the start of their careers.

Israeli press accounts of the immigrants from Argentina evoke impressions of the Polish immigrants in the pre-State era. The comparison is not unfounded; the two groups had similar sociodemographics and traits.[49] According to an article about the *Flaminia*'s arrival in Haifa, "this group's arrival recalled the times of the large aliya from Poland and Europe before the Holocaust."[50]

Another item asserts that those who came to Haifa port on the day the *Flaminia* anchored found themselves "totally immersed in the ambience of the Jewish people: Jews from the small towns of Poland and Lithuania, Romania and Hungary, speaking a Yiddish seasoned with many words of Spanish":

> Dozens and dozens of them, carpenters and weavers, shoemakers and tailors, housepainters and plasterers, shopkeepers, and government and municipal clerks; ready and willing to recount their wanderings, their eyes asking the question: What will it be like tomorrow and the next day here in Israel? Where will they be housed? Are there jobs there? How will they support themselves and their families? How far is it from Ofaqim or Sederot, for example, where they are settling, to Tel Aviv? And so on. Questions about everyday life in their new home. They speak to you at length, going into great detail, while they are actually talking out loud to themselves. . . . Will they be happy in this country?[51]

The Argentinian Immigrants by Type, Place, and District of Absorption

On the eve of independence, the Jewish population was concentrated in the coastal plain and Jerusalem, with a few settlements in the Galilee and the northern Negev. According to data for late 1949, 78% of the urban Jewish population lived on the coast between Tel Aviv and Haifa, 13% in Jerusalem, and close to 5% in the Judean foothills. Less than 4% lived in the rest of the country.[52] In the name of population dispersal, absorption policy makers directed new immigrants away from the metropolitan centers and to developing areas. Government resources were deployed to achieve this national goal.[53] In the words of historian Anita Shapira,

> In Israel the absorption process was tempered by the national ethos, which wanted and welcomed the immigrants. The state was responsible both for encouraging the immigrants to come and for directing and regulating them once they arrived. It is hard to think of another country that has invested so much in its immigrants. Therefore, the country wore both the coronet of its successes and the crown of thorns of its failures. The attempts to force upon the immigrants the task of settling the outlying areas—a mission the veteran population would not undertake—had some success, but led to a great deal of bitterness and hurt.[54]

More than 400 new agricultural settlements and thirty "development towns" were founded all over the country between 1948 and 1967.[55] Because the veteran residents were loath to move to outlying areas, the only way to disperse the population was to settle immigrants there. As late as 1967, only 2% of veteran Israelis lived in the periphery.[56]

My database corroborates the assumption that the primary settlement pattern of the Argentinian immigration coincided with this government policy. Nearly two-thirds of them made their first homes in Israel in kibbutzim and development zones; only a third settled in the big cities or center of the country. The prevalence of kibbutz absorption was an exceptional feature of the Argentinian immigrants.

According to Reuven Golan, an Absorption Department official, the immigrants from Latin America in general, and from Argentina in particular, embodied the ideal social composition—what he called "the optimal aliya."[57] "A more socially balanced aliya would be impossible, taking into account the internal equilibrium and the willingness to accept the dictate of population dispersal and settlement outside the urban areas of the coastal plain."[58] According to his analysis of the Latin American immigrants, 10% were liberal professionals and a similar proportion were skilled technical workers, and 20% were artisans; another 20% had been brought over by Youth Aliyah or were headed to agricultural settlements, including kibbutzim. A full quarter of the Latin American immigrants who arrived between 1961 and 1965 lived in development towns, and 20% in agricultural settlements. "What could be better than that?" And, Golan added, "Whoever wants to know aliya from the wealthy countries at its best should go see the olim from Latin America, especially those from Argentina."[59]

Conclusions: A Marginal Immigration

When Yehoshua Wolberg returned from a mission to South America in October 1963 he prepared a comprehensive report that included a reference to the composition of the Argentinian immigration.[60] He wrote that before his departure, Argentinian friends living in Israel had told him that the current batch of immigrants did not represent the Argentinian Jewry they had known. "I could not understand my veteran friends' meaning; their hesitations about the recent immigrants struck me as rather strange," Wolberg noted.[61] After he reached Argentina, he found that Jewish public figures made similar comments, such as: "You mustn't think that the aliya of Argentinian Jews has begun"; and "special absorption conditions are needed for them to make aliya"[62] Wolberg felt these reactions contained the key for understanding both the immigration from Argentina and the situation of the Jews there. When he returned to Israel, after about a month, he was convinced that he had found the solution for getting Argentinian Jews to move to Israel.

In Wolberg's opinion, one had to begin with the "organic aliya" from Argentina, which predated Israel and was still taking place. This category encompassed "pioneers," their parents, and their close relatives—immigrants whose motives had nothing to do with crises, disasters, or emergencies in their home country. Young immigrants pursuing their desire—or their parents'—to ensure the continuity of Jewish existence, as well as recently wed couples, also fell into this category. In Wolberg's view, the hallmark of organic aliya was simply the desire for a future in Israel.[63]

Wolberg identified four other categories of immigrants whose move was provoked by conditions in the country of origin. The first were young families in a spiritual crisis caused by Argentina's economic, political, public, and moral troubles. In other words, this group aspired to settle in Israel in order to solve current problems. Another group consisted of immigrants to Argentina who had not found their niche in its Jewish community (often because they had not lived there long enough). These Jews "did not 'find their America' in Argentina. They are still sitting on the suitcases they brought from Eastern Europe and were never able to unpack."[64] Wolberg's third group consisted of families who had been pushed to the margins of Jewish society by the economic crisis. In addition to the economic hardship, they were troubled by their loss of social status.

As for the last group—high school and university students and young professionals—Wolberg found their situation more difficult to explain. Most of them were second- and third-generation immigrants, born and educated in Argentina. Socially and culturally assimilated, they viewed themselves primarily as Argentinians rather than Jews. For them, the rampant anti-Semitism of the early 1960s was a major factor in their disappointment with Argentina.

Wolberg identified the common denominator of all five groups: with regard to their social situation and status, all of them were on the margins of Argentinian Jewish society:

> Young people are naturally on the fringes of society everywhere. Families not yet assimilated in Argentina remained on the outskirts of society. Families affected by the economic and political crisis have been pushed to the margins of society. All of them share the natural aspiration of the marginalized to fit in or to belong to society, to win or recover the confidence weakened by their social estrangement. This is the confidence they wanted to achieve by means of immigration to Israel, where they hoped to be welcomed by society with open arms and to be equals among equals.[65]

In his report, Wolberg also questioned the contention—prevalent in both Israeli and Argentinian Jewish public opinion—that the Argentinian immigrants were the product of a strong Zionist education, as opposed to the Jews fleeing Cuba and Algeria, most of whom were choosing other destinations.[66] In Wolberg's opinion, most of the potential immigrants could not migrate to another country and expect to be absorbed there as they would be in Israel.[67] As mentioned above, in the 1960s Jewish emigration from Argentina to other destinations, mainly the United States, increased and came to exceed relocation to Israel. Wolberg believed that those who went to the United States were the "the strongest elements" of Argentinian Jewry.

Wolberg's findings were repeated by demographer Sergio DellaPergola in a recent article that deals in part with this question, from the wider perspective of Jewish immigration to Israel and other countries.[68] DellaPergola asserts that the migrant's socioeconomic and demographic profile affects the choice of the destination country. He found that, as compared with other countries that absorbed Jewish immigrants in the 1960s, Israel received lower percentages of liberal professionals, managers, and clerks and higher percentages of the working class (industry, service, agricultural, and uncategorized workers, as well as the unemployed).[69]

The composition of the Argentinian Jewish immigration to Israel supports Wolberg's statement and DellaPergola's findings. These immigrants were mainly young people and families. Their distribution by age, origin, marital status, family size, and occupation, particularly as compared to the overall composition of Argentina's Jewish population, suggests a migration spurred by economic circumstances and Israel's selective immigration policy. More than 60% of the immigrants were at their peak working capacity. They were mainly from the lower middle class and, unlike the majority of the community, not moving up the social ladder. In stark contrast to the two-thirds of Argentina's Jews who held white-collar positions, most of the immigrants belonged to the blue-collar class.

These social and professional patterns aligned perfectly with the goals of Israeli absorption policy, as confirmed by the places where the immigrants were settled. The findings suggest that economic factors, too, played a major role in the decision to move to Israel. The composition of the Argentinian immigration to Israel—its distribution by age, origin, family size, and occupation—recalled in many ways the Polish immigration during the Mandate era. But despite the similarities, this was an immigration "made in Argentina," with unique characteristics anchored in the Judeo-Argentinian reality.

6

Halutzim, Capitalists, and Those Somewhere in the Middle

The Beginning of the Organized Aliya of Halutzim from Argentina

The organized aliya of halutzim ("pioneers"—immigrants whose destination was rural settlements, and principally kibbutzim) from Argentina begins with ten young graduates of Zionist youth movements. In October 1945, they used the first ten immigration certificates allocated to South American Jews by the Jewish Agency after World War II and served as the opening shot of organized aliya by their movement comrades.[1] The literature on Jewish immigration to Israel from Latin America in general and from Argentina in particular takes their adventure as a seminal event that marks the emerging awareness of the new role played by Argentinian Jews and Zionists after the Holocaust and of the beginning of organized aliya from Latin America.

From the very start, these ten young people's act carried symbolic and collective meaning. For both the international and the local Argentinian Zionist establishment, their decision was an indication that contributing money and material goods was not enough for the Zionists of Latin America; they also wanted to realize the dream themselves.[2] Their departure "symbolized the dawn of the era of practical Zionism," in the words of *Yugent-avangard*, the organ of the Zionist youth movement Dror.[3] The timing of the trip—the first such by young Argentinian Jews since the outbreak of World War II—was also significant. The ten were seen as trailblazing pioneers, the first swallows of the renewed aliya from Argentina.

The group's aliya sparked a fierce debate among Argentinian Jewry. For the entire Jewish world, the most pressing need at the time was to bring Holocaust survivors from Europe to Palestine. The Zionist establishment rallied around this mission, which became a linchpin of the conflict with the British and especially of the fight against their obstinate refusal to open the gates of Palestine to the displaced Jews. In the Jewish world, the general opinion at the time was that every certificate given to a Holocaust survivor "saved a human life."[4] Some went further and said that, in these circumstances, it was almost criminal for others to make use of the small number of certificates available.[5] Against this background, the episode of the "ten certificates" set off a harsh controversy among Argentinian Jews, whose feelings on the matter were decidedly mixed.

The documents related to this incident lay bare a long saga of partisan friction and ideological conflict among the various Zionist youth movements and a protracted series of technical snags that forced the group to split up and turned the months of their preparations into a nerve-wracking waiting period for all those involved. The actual trip, which, because of a bureaucratic snag, lasted four months, was replete with incidents typical of the stories of many other young and adventurous halutzim of the early waves of Jewish immigration to Palestine.[6]

Some accounts of the band's aliya include instructive details about those young people and their motives. "We had come from four countries and spoke four languages, until we met in the American diaspora, where we could all take up the nomad's staff, but this time with a defined goal," wrote Menachem Katzovitz in a sort of farewell letter published in his movement's organ:

> One was born in Turkey, a country that has not written glorious pages in our chronicles—the same Turkey that was long involved, historically and geographically, with the eternal Land of Israel. In this Turkey, he was born as a Turk, even though he wasn't one. He was supposed to be conscripted into the military in Constantinople, but what he wanted to do was to defend the fields of our land. He reached Argentina and is now on his way to the Land of Israel. The second was born in "mother Lithuania," in a town that no doubt contributed, like all the others, to the Jewish heritage. He is a fellow who remained Lithuanian in his soul, but had become South American in his body—a broad-shouldered talmudic genius, both modest and tall. He too had emigrated to Argentina and was now making aliya. The third did not have to come by boat. The Jewish destiny. She was born in a Jewish neighborhood in turbulent Buenos Aires. For fourteen years, she was ashamed

> to admit that she belonged (God have mercy) to the race that had rejected Jesus . . . and now she was making Aliya. . . . The fourth was born—officially, at least—in Poland, though it is impossible to know for certain whether his birthplace belongs to Poland, Lithuania, or Russia. His ear was attuned to the sounds of Polish, Russian, Yiddish, and Hebrew. . . . The last of these penetrated deep into his soul—perhaps a sign of things to come? Perhaps he would one day reach the shores of the Promised Land? Four countries and one people. Four paths and one road. Four passports and one goal.[7]

In a June 1995 interview, some fifty years after his aliya, Eliyahu Toba said that when he started to assemble the documents he needed for his trip, he ran into problems because he had been born in Poland and come to Argentina with his parents as a baby, listed in his father's passport. He didn't have the courage to ask his father for that passport. "I was only 19 years old, remember," he told the interviewer. So he took his father's passport on the sly and went to the Polish

Table 10: The ten halutzim[8]

Name	Age	Marital status	Passport	Type of Certificate	Youth movement
Bernardo (Baruch) Firstein	21	Single	Not Argentinian (born in Turkey)	Halutz	Dror
Matthias (Matityahu) Dresnin	20	Single	Lithuanian	Halutz	Dror
Menachem Katzovitz	24	Married	Polish	Halutz	Dror
Natalia (Nechama) Fishelson	20	Married	Argentinian	Halutz	Dror
Mordecai (Motl) Weinerman	24	Single	Polish	Halutz	Hashomer Hatza'ir
Jaime (Hayyim) Kopeloff	26	Single	Argentinian	Halutz	Hashomer Hatza'ir
Arie Slutzky	22	Single	Polish	Halutz	Hashomer Hatza'ir
Elias (Eliyahu) Toba	19	Single	Polish	Halutz	Hanoar Hatziyyoni
Ernesto (Yakov Kroch)	22	Single	Not Argentinian (born in Germany)	Student	Hanoar Hatziyyoni
Daniel Gigi	21	Single	Panama	Halutz	Hanoar Hatziyyoni

consulate.[9] Toba and his youth movement comrade, Yakov Kroch, had already been looking for a way to reach Palestine. Kroch, the student in the group, was born in Germany in 1923. When he was fifteen, his family fled Germany for the Netherlands. After the Nazis occupied that country, the Krochs continued their flight, arriving in Argentina in 1942.[10]

Some of the group had been born in Argentina, whereas others had been "Argentinized"—the term employed by Jacobo Paltitzky, an active member of the Zionist socialist Po'alei Zion party, in an article published in August 1945.[11] This "Argentinization" was not reflected in the official statistics; because these were based on an immigrant's country of birth, only two of them were listed there as Argentinian. But this first group was extremely important for subsequent aliya from Argentina by members of Zionist youth movements. As the firstcomers, they effectively laid the ground for reports on the situation that went back to Buenos Aires and created new possibilities for aliya by other members of their movements. After they arrived in Palestine, the young people split up in accordance with their organizational affiliation. After an initial stay in the commune run by the Kibbutz Hame'uhad federation in Tel Aviv, the four members of Dror went to Kibbutz Gvat. The three who belonged to Hashomer Hatza'ir spent a month on Kibbutz Mishmar Ha'emeq and then settled temporarily on Kibbutz Negba. The others, members of Hanoar Hatziyyoni, joined Kibbutz Nitzanim.[12]

The personal contacts that these pioneering halutzim maintained with their comrades back in Argentina, through the kibbutz movements' liaison bureaus, created the first link in the "chain migration" of young men and women from Argentina and other countries in Latin America, chains that kept growing longer within the framework of their ideological movements. These early settlers were joined by other young people from Latin America who managed to reach Palestine as clandestine immigrants during these fraught years after the war. These were the years when the stream of refugees from Europe to Palestine reached tidal-wave proportions, especially in 1947, which came to be known as the year of "the exodus from Europe." But there was also a trickle from Argentina and other countries in Latin America of young immigrants who joined the halutzim on Gvat, Negba, and Nitzanim.

In late 1947, around sixty young Jews from Latin America (Argentina, Chile, Mexico, Brazil, Paraguay, and Uruguay) settled in Negba, Gvat, and Nitzanim.[13] In November of that year, the cadre in Gvat expanded: "We received the first reinforcements—fifteen comrades who arrived 'by the back way,'" wrote Menachem Katzovitz (later Carmi), one of the original ten.[14] The Nitzanim cadre, too, was reinforced by fifteen new members in 1947. "We knew what was happening on the kibbutz from the letters that Yakov [Kroch—one of the first ten] sent to the movement," one of them recalled half a century later.[15] Another five arrived by independence in mid-May.[16]

The war drew the Latin Americans to the frontlines: the cadre from Dror fought at Deganya Bet and Kefar Hahoresh and at various locations in the Jordan Valley. The Negba settlers took part in the battle to defend the kibbutz against the Egyptian attack that was launched as soon as independence was declared. Those who fell there included Mordechai Weinerman, who had come to the country with one of the first ten certificates. The members of Hanoar Hatziyyoni on Nitzanim also bore the brunt of the war. Three of them were killed during the Egyptian assault, including Yakov Kroch. The rest were taken as POWs along with the other members of the kibbutz.[17]

Despite the War for Independence and its victims, the stream of youth movement members from Latin America continued and even grew. The roster of the Negba cadre for August 1948 lists sixty-three young men and women from Latin America: thirty-seven from Argentina, thirteen from Chile, ten from Mexico, and three from Brazil;[18] by the end of that year, the cadre numbered one hundred.[19]

The Borochov Jugend and Aliya

Following the establishment of Israel, the stream of pioneer aliya from Argentina expanded to other Zionist youth movements. For example, the first band of young people from the Borochov Jugend, which was affiliated with Left Po'alei Zion, arrived in July 1948 and settled on Kibbutz Mishmar Hanegev. This initial cadre of five young men and three young women had coalesced as part of the youth movement, founded seven years earlier. What the members of this movement had in common was their education through TZVISHO, the umbrella organization of the Scholem Aleijem school network, founded by members of the parent party at the start of 1934.

In 1941, in light of the persecution of the Jews and the war in Europe, and the ferment they generated among Jewish youth, members of Left Po'alei Zion and the teachers at the Scholem Aleijem schools[20] resolved to establish a new youth movement to guide their charges. Most members of the various youth movements grew up in the same neighborhoods, attended the same schools, and were nurtured by the same Jewish proletarian milieu. In the case of the Borochov Jugend, their Jewish education played a formative role, shaping their ethical values, political and ideological worldview, and national identity, as expressed in the movement and its activities. The lost world of Eastern Europe, with its array of organizations for different age groups, was taken as the model: the Polish Borochov Jugend, Yung Bor, Tzugreytung, and Hovenetkurs (a night school for young laborers) were copied and adapted to life in Argentina, where the social reality and cultural environment were quite different from those of interwar Poland.[21]

We can learn about the motives behind the movement's establishment and its initial composition from a lecture delivered by Eliyahu Bleiweiss, one of its founders, at the second National Conference of the Borochov Jugend in Argentina. He described the mixture of anxiety and excitement that struck most Jews in that country in 1941. Outside Europe, at this stage no one was aware of the danger of imminent extermination, but the crisis was certainly felt by the Jews of Argentina. In his lecture, Bleiweiss recalled the first meeting held by several members of the Borochov Jugend, most of them graduates of the Scholem Aleijem school, at the party headquarters in the Villa Crespo neighborhood of Buenos Aires in early June 1941. Adult members of the party also took part; the main topic of conversation was the urgent need to take steps to protect the Jews and their dignity and to combat anti-Semitic manifestations.[22]

The biography of Leibel Roizman (later Dr. Arieh Vardi), one of the founders of the Borochov Jugend and its first secretary, can also teach us about the motives behind the establishment of this youth movement and the identity of its members.[23] Roizman was born in Lodz, Poland, in 1921. After his parents immigrated to Argentina in 1923, he spent his childhood in Boca Barracas, a proletarian district of Buenos Aires with no strong Jewish presence. He quickly integrated into the working-class community, the only Jew among children of Spanish and Italian ancestry. Attending high school in the turbulent 1930s, he identified and preferred to bond with his non-Jewish peers, who were also the children of immigrants. It was the early days of the Nazis in Germany and of the civil war in Spain, which was the main topic of controversy in the public high school he attended.[24]

The events in Europe agitated the boy, especially after the outbreak of World War II, by which time he was studying medicine at the National University of Buenos Aires. Roizman found himself unable to shake off the heavy burden of these dramatic events. He had barely completed his second year at university when he first considered dropping out in order to fight against the Nazis. He went to the embassy of the Polish government-in-exile to look into the possibility of volunteering for military service, but was told that he could not be accepted because he had taken Argentinian citizenship. A few days later,

Roizman tried his luck with the Comité De Gaulle, which represented the Free French forces (but was turned away as too young).[25]

Trying to keep his son at home, Roizman's father decided to consult with two leaders of Left Po'alei Zion, Jaime Finkelstein and Alter Lustigman. During their meeting, Finkelstein tried to harness the young man's energy on behalf of Argentinian Jewry's struggle against the rising local tide of nationalism and anti-Semitism by organizing the teenagers affiliated with the party. Roizman accepted the proposal, left the university, and devoted himself totally to his new mission. He was supplied with the names of candidates, all of them from families that identified with the party and most of them students at the TZVISHO schools.[26]

The first meeting of recruits for the new youth movement was held in early June 1941 at party headquarters in Villa Crespo, with Alter Lustigman in attendance. He presented the Left Po'alei Zion platform to the group and suggested that the new movement be named for Borochov. The youngsters decided that their first goal was attracting additional members. Leibel Roizman was appointed secretary of the movement; he and Eliyahu Bleiweiss began drafting the basic principles of the Borochov Jugend.[27] In his writings of those years, Roizman gave vent to the need to cope with the questions that troubled his soul and that led the group to organize as a formal youth movement:

> We see with sorrow the confusion that reigns among the young people, both Jewish and non-Jewish. This is why we want to propose and disseminate among them our position on the current problems that trouble and upset us. We identify ourselves as Jews; we have reached maturity at a time when the world is fighting to annihilate Nazi Fascism.... During our conversations on June 4, 1941, about establishing our movement, we said that the present war would effect a change in the international social order.... As socialist Zionists, we are at war the Axis, and consequently call for the establishment of a Jewish army so that we can take part in the struggle as a nation. In the meantime, alongside this struggle, we face other problems whose solution depends on the war—the social, political, and economic problems of Argentina and of the Jewish laboring masses there, as part of the Jewish people.... The Ber Borochov youth movement calls on the Jewish proletarian youth and on those with proletarian sentiments to join its ranks and take part in our struggle.[28]

The ideological principles and goals that underlay the initiative to establish the youth movement were also reflected in a notice, published in *Di Presse* on July 21, 1941, which announced the founding of the Ber Borochov youth movement in Buenos Aires and outlined its principles and goals: "At the initiative of a group of young people and adult members of Left Po'alei Zion, the Ber Borochov youth organization, affiliated with that party, has been established in Buenos Aires." The text added:

> Ber Borochov was the ideologue who devised the theoretical basis of the Po'alei Zion movement. This is why, in their practical and educational endeavors, the young members of the movement will lead the Jewish youth of Argentina along the path of Borochovism. The aim of the Borochov Jugend is to spread socialism among Jewish youth in Argentina, with the goal of inspiring them with the ideals of socialist Zionism; to give them a clear picture of all the national and social problems that beset the Jewish people; to develop extensive Jewish cultural activities among the youth; to interest the youth in practical efforts on behalf of the Land of Israel; to encourage a link to the youth organizations that are similar to Po'alei Zion in Palestine and Jewish communities throughout the world; and, finally, to make contact with socialist and democratic youth organizations in America in order to take part in the democratic front against fascism.[29]

The ideology and practices of the Borochov Jugend took shape over time. The core of its ideology was the aspiration to reconstruct society along socialist lines, the demand for Jewish territorial autonomy in Palestine as part of the nation's social and national liberation, and the desire to better the cultural, economic, and social condition of the Jewish proletariat in Argentina through education. The commitment to the Jews in Argentina was a hallmark of the movement's regular work, even after it had defined its goal as aliya by its members. The movement's leaders saw no contradiction between their Zionist allegiance and loyalty to the Jewish homeland, on the one hand, and devotion to their people in the Diaspora. "We wanted to be a political and educational organization, so we took part in both Jewish and non-Jewish life," observed one of its young members at the celebrations to mark the movement's tenth anniversary.[30]

The connection between Mishmar Hanegev and the movement in Argentina resulted from Jaime Finkelstein's visit to the kibbutz in early 1947, on his way home from the twenty-second Zionist Congress in Basel in December

1946. His impressions of this visit had a strong impact on high school students and on the members of the Borochov Jugend. The story of the thirty-six comrades who founded Mishmar Hanegev as part of the operation that established eleven new Jewish settlements in the Negev in a single night (October 6, 1946), which Finkelstein brought back, was a seminal incident for the Borochov Jugend and the start of the relationship between the movement and the kibbutz.[31] "We aspire to expand our circle of contacts to other places in the world, which is why we want to strengthen our ties with the Borochov Jugend in Argentina," wrote a member of the kibbutz to the movement's secretariat in Buenos Aires in July 1947.[32]

The movement experienced a significant turning point and expanded after the United Nations adopted the Partition Resolution in November 1947. "Hundreds joined the Zionist youth movements. We too experienced these moments with great satisfaction; we too saw how our ranks were growing," noted one of its members.[33] A notice published in the movement's house organ, *Di Fraye Yugent*, in November 1947, reported that in response to a call by members of the Borochov Jugend already in Palestine, it had been decided to establish a training farm for the movement in Argentina. A joint committee of the party and the movement, convened to discuss the burning issues of the training farm, aliya, and settlement, had decided to take the necessary steps to open the training farm in early 1948.[34]

The Kibbutz Ber Borochov Training Farm officially began operations in early March 1948 in Colonia Julio Levin, in Buenos Aires Province.[35] Its members produced the first settlement cadre of eight young men and women: Shalom Irlicht, Guillermo Galker, Reuben Cohen, Dov Hassin, Berl Friedman, Susanna Lesnik, Jaika Katz, and Rosa (Mona) Romano. Coming to the training farm was a decisive stage in their aliya process.[36] In later years they waxed nostalgic about that period and recounted many anecdotes from it. They had fond memories of their instructor in agricultural labor, a local farmer of Italian descent named Luccini. The first emissary sent by the Kibbutz Me'uhad organization, Gershon Hazanovitch, did not arrive in Argentina until late in 1949, so it was Luccini who guided the young people and got them ready for kibbutz life.[37] A special moment in the annals of the training farm took place with the proclamation of independent Israel. When the news arrived at midnight of May 14/15, the young people jumped out of their beds and began singing the Zionist anthem *Hatikvah* at the top of their lungs. The shocked Luccini broke into their room armed with a rifle. Many of those interviewed recalled that day as a unique and unforgettable moment of joy.[38]

After that, the preparations for their departure proceeded rapidly. By late July they were en route for France. After a short stay in the transit camp in Marseilles, the young people sailed for Israel on a ship acquired by the Mossad la'Aliya Bet. The Argentinians were the first to board; as soon as they came on deck they were treated to a detailed explanation of their assignment during the trip. About 2,000 people were about to board, most of them Holocaust survivors who had been smuggled into France. Because the ship had only a skeleton crew, the Argentinians were expected to fill the role of stewards and maintain order. The trip to Haifa took a week, in conditions almost identical to those of the clandestine immigration operations of years past. This encounter left a strong impression on the eight pioneers. The ship docked in Haifa in early September, during the second truce in the War of Independence.

A few days after they arrived, they traveled to Tel Aviv to check in with the secretariat of Left Po'alei Zion. They also visited the offices of Hakibbutz Hame'uhad, where an attempt was made to persuade them to join a cadre of the Dror movement from Germany (the Buchenwald group) and settle on Kibbutz Netzer Sereni. The young Argentinians dug in their heels: "We made aliya to go to Mishmar Hanegev and we are not going to retreat," they countered, and their request was honored. After one failed attempt, they managed to cross the Egyptian lines in a military convoy and reach their destination. Their adventure getting there is documented in a letter written by Reuben Cohen on September 26, 1948, just a few days after their arrival on the kibbutz, and published in *Die Fraye Yugent* that November. He noted, among other things, that "at Negba we met many of the 100 South Americans who live in the region."[39]

As might be expected, the first band of Argentinians who joined Mishmar Hanegev anchored the subsequent chain migration of their young compatriots who were energized by the movement's ideology. After they reached the kibbutz, there were direct contacts between the halutzim and their fellow Borochov Jugend members back in Argentina, particularly through the Overseas Affairs Committee of the Kibbutz Me'uhad central office. *Die Fraye Yugent* was another effective channel for reinforcing the ties between the olim in Israel and potential immigrants back in Argentina. Its pages allow us to track the groups that joined the kibbutz. Its eighth issue reported the arrival at Mishmar Hanegev of the second Borochov Jugend cadre on March 14, 1949,[40] bringing the total number of Argentinians there to twenty. And, it continued,

> This number is only the beginning. We are certain that the Borochov Jugend in Argentina will soon provide a significant number of members

> who are ready to join the first group. . . . The Borochov Jugend is developing as a pioneer organization, but it is not insular. On the contrary, it is strengthening its bonds with the proletarian masses from which it comes and on whose behalf it struggles. Through our group on Mishmar Hanegev we encourage the close and cordial contacts between the Borochov Jugend and Left Po'alei Zion, as part of Hakibbutz Hame'uhad. From here, a long chain will emerge and unite our young people with the Zionist-socialist enterprise that is being realized by the efforts of the kibbutz movements, under the direction of Mapam, the United Workers' Party. . . . The Argentinian members of Mishmar Hanegev are only the vanguard, which will soon by followed by many more of us.[41]

Jaime Finkelstein visited his former youth-movement charges, students, and friends at Mishmar Hanegev in early 1950. "I am on my way to Mishmar Hanegev and constantly thinking about our members who are on the kibbutz," Finkelstein observed. "The feeling is that I am going home."[42] Those who greeted Finkelstein included Yossel Katz, who, along with his wife, had come to Israel to join their daughter Jaika on the kibbutz.[43] Finkelstein wrote that he had not conversed with all 140 members of the kibbutz, but did manage to speak with all the Argentinians there:

> Dozens of our comrades are on Mishmar Hanegev now. . . . I look to see if they have changed, if Eretz Israel has changed them. But these are the same faces. . . . From Irlicht I hear the voice of a halutz, confident, never hesitating; he has no doubt that the forest will grow. He does not speak about the kibbutz in ideological and theoretical slogans. For him, the kibbutz is a fait accompli that means a livelihood, labor, love of the land, loyalty, friendship, idealism, and socialism. . . . I have learned a lot from my visit to Mishmar Hanegev. I have seen how the Borochov Jugend from Argentina are building a home for hundreds or perhaps thousands.[44]

The chain migration inaugurated by these first olim grew over time. It was not only members of other movement cadres who followed their comrades; in some cases, parents and acquaintances, like Yossel and Rosa Katz, also moved to Israel in the wake of family members. The early cadres sent by the other movements also expanded. Young people from Dror established Kibbutz Mefalsim on June 11, 1949. Next, members of Hanoar Hatziyyoni founded Kibbutz Ein Hasheloshah, named in memory of three comrades who fell in the War of Independence. Later, members of Hashomer Hatza'ir established Kibbutz Gaash. An article in *Davar* reported on the groundbreaking ceremony for Kibbutz Mefalsim, the first Latin American kibbutz, which was founded by member of the first cadre on Gvat:

> Mefalsim is a new link in the chain of settlements that surround the coastal strip [the Gaza District] that remains in Egyptian hands. . . . Transportation is convenient; the main road to the Negev passes right by the settlement. Dozens of the kibbutz members are still in training camps in South America and will make aliya this year. The members' average age is 23. There are fifteen families, and four children have already been born. Many of the members are children of wealthy parents who chose the clandestine pioneer route, frequently despite their parents' opposition to their leaving university. Many came after them as part of the Overseas Volunteers program (Mahal). About two months ago, they were discharged from active military service and began preparing to break ground for the settlement. The kibbutz has affiliated with Hakibbutz Hame'uhad and its members belong to Mapai. Mefalsim is the first. Three more South American cadres of Hashomer Hatza'ir and one cadre of Hanoar Hatziyyoni are training in Israel and will establish new settlements in the coming months.[45]

Recruitment in Argentina for Mahal (the Overseas Volunteers Program)

Volunteers from the Free World began streaming to the Middle East in early 1948, during the first months of the war, when the institutions of the "state in the making" authorized the recruitment of those who had expressed a desire to take part in the struggle to establish a Jewish state.[46] In most places, they signed up under the supervision and organization of the military procurement missions, mainly in the United States, Canada, and South Africa. In Western Europe, the delegations recruited hundreds of volunteers in France, Britain, Switzerland, Scandinavia, Belgium, and the Netherlands.[47] The volunteer spirit appeared in Latin America as well; in Argentina, it was organized by the Buenos Aires office of the Jewish Agency, in concert with the Higher Zionist Council and its active members.[48]

The precise size of the Mahal overseas volunteers' organization is unknown, for several reasons. First, although many of the volunteers stayed and settled in Israel after the war was over, modifying their status to new immigrants, many others went back home. Second, Mahal volunteers tended to keep the reason for their trip under wraps, fearing that their home countries, especially the United States, would see it as grounds for revoking their citizenship.[49] The general consensus is that there were around 3,500 Mahal volunteers, from forty-three countries;[50] four hundred of them came from thirteen countries in Latin America: Argentina, Brazil, Chile, Colombia, Costa Rica, Cuba, Ecuador, Mexico, Nicaragua, Panama, Peru, Uruguay, and Venezuela.[51] Most of them came in the second stage of the war, after the Arab states' invasion of newly independent Israel on May 15, 1948.

According to the sources at my disposal, most of the volunteers from Latin America went to fight alongside their comrades on kibbutzim, chiefly Gvat and Negba. Quite a few served in the Palmach, while others found their way to Brigade 9 (the Oded Brigade), as part of the 91st and 92nd battalions, which were composed of Spanish-speaking volunteers.[52] The volunteers in these two battalions came to Israel in separate groups. The first, which left Argentina in late May 1948 and arrived in Israel in early July, comprised forty-five volunteers: twenty-seven from Argentina, sixteen from Uruguay, and two from Brazil. Another group of twenty volunteers from Chile left Santiago in late June and reached Haifa on July 23. A third group, which left Argentina in late June, included several volunteers from Argentina, Uruguay, and Brazil.[53]

Among the second set of volunteers from Argentina was twenty-four-year-old José Itzigsohn, born in Concordia (Entre Ríos province), who had completed his fifth year of medical studies at the National University in the city of La Plata and then served ten months in the Argentinian army, from which he was discharged as a reserve second lieutenant. While in Israel as a Mahal volunteer, Itzigsohn kept a record of his time with a Spanish-speaking battalion in the Oded Brigade. Two decades later, Dr. Itzigsohn composed an informal autobiography in which he documented, among other things, his experiences as a soldier in the Israel Defense Forces (IDF) during the early days of the state. Itzigsohn supplemented his description of events with thoughts about his Jewish roots. I filled in the missing biographical elements and checked them against various primary sources, as well as from my interview with Dr. Itzigsohn in his Jerusalem home in October 2009.[54]

José Itzigsohn's parents immigrated to Argentina in 1910. His father, born and raised in Bessarabia, in the Pale of Settlement, received a traditional education but then attended a Russian public high school in Odessa. When he graduated, he went to Switzerland to study engineering. In Zurich, Itzigsohn met and married a medical student from Ukraine, the daughter of an assimilated Bundist family. When he finished his studies, they followed his parents, who had already immigrated to Argentina.[55] The couple settled in Concordia, a typical urban center that was beginning to attract Jews from rural districts, and soon integrated into the professional, intellectual, and political elite in the city. José, born in Concordia in 1924, was their third and youngest son. Even as a child, José heard revolutionary sagas from his parents, including accounts of the repression and social injustice, particularly the pogroms that had been the lot of Russian Jews. "The pogroms were part of my worldview at a very early age," Dr. Itzigsohn wrote in his memoirs.[56]

His chief memory of his years in a public high school was the hostile anti-Semitic environment. One event that was deeply engraved in his mind and symbolized his entire high school experience took place on May 25, Argentina's National Day. During the celebrations in the city's central plaza, each student received an Argentinian flag to wave. But the teacher refused to give flags to José and his Jewish classmate on the grounds that they were Jews: "This was not the only time that I was denied my Argentinian nationality, but it was certainly the first time." He continued:

> Members of my generation, born between the two world wars, had to confront decisive events from a very young age. These were difficult years in the world. The rise of Nazism was felt among us as well, among many young people of the middle class and the oligarchy who displayed mixed and confused anti-imperialist and antisemitic sentiments. It was in this climate, and against the background of the general retreat of democracy in Argentina, that I began high school and, at the same time, the existential conflict with my condition as a Jew.[57]

Dr. Itzigsohn's words reflect the place that international and domestic events of the 1930s occupied in the growth and development of many of his contemporaries. Manifestations of anti-Semitism escalated both in Europe and Argentina. Itzigsohn began medical school in 1942 in La Plata (Buenos Aires Province). Soon after, the first reports of the extermination of European Jewry began to reach Argentina. He particularly remembered how one speaker at a 1944 ceremony held by the Jewish community in Concordia requested a moment of silence in memory of the Jewish victims in Transylvania, the strictly Orthodox communities annihilated by the Nazis and their henchmen. The Holocaust became an important and significant element of his Jewish identity. "It would be wrong to disconnect from it," he wrote.[58]

In 1947, José was called up for ten months of military service to fulfill his civic duty as an advanced medical student. "I performed my military service in Argentina knowing that I was getting ready for the conflict in Palestine. I already knew by this stage that I wanted to fight and take part in the national struggle of the Jewish people," Dr. Itzigsohn told me. It was a year of decision in the Middle East. Early in 1947, Britain referred the Palestine issue to the United Nations; in November, the General Assembly voted for partition. The Palestinian Arabs and their leaders rejected the UN resolution. The day after the vote, they launched hostilities to thwart it. This was the beginning of the War of Independence.

With this dramatic development in the background, in early 1948 José Itzigsohn decided to volunteer to defend the embattled Jews of Palestine. Equipped with five years of medical school, ten months in the Argentinian army, a fair command of Hebrew, and a creed that blended national elements with personal aspirations, he sailed for Israel in late June 1948, along with other volunteers from Argentina, Uruguay, and Brazil. He described the group's members and their motives for joining it as follows:

> The members of my group came from various and diverse places: some of them belonged to youth groups that had trained them to settle on kibbutzim, and that's where they went. Others, like me, had been involved with the Jewish problem for years. There were also those who answered a romantic or emotional call; for others, it was an inner need for adventure. Ours was a heterogeneous group; tracking down their subsequent lives would be a fascinating topic for a book.[59]

When their ship reached Le Havre, the South American group was met by an emissary from Israel, who escorted them to Paris and then to Marseilles. At the time, southern France was the assembly point for thousands of displaced Jews who had escaped Central Europe, survivors of the concentration camps, persons who had spent years in hiding, Romanian and Hungarian Jews, and Jews from eastern Poland who had managed, in various ways, to escape the Nazi extermination machine. In Marseilles, they all lived in a temporary camp called Grand Arénas. This was the South Americans' first encounter with the victims of the war. Dr. Itzigsohn described it as follows:

> The meeting weighed heavily on us. On the one hand, because of the ceaseless repetition of boundless suffering; seeing the numbers tattooed on their skin; hearing the descriptions of humiliation and loss—hearing, for example, from one of the survivors how all seven of his sons were murdered in Auschwitz. . . . Familiar stories that repeat themselves until they lose their original horror, to a certain extent. On the other hand, many of the refugees had cast loose their bonds to normal life—they were undisciplined, repulsed human contact, and, in some cases, totally destroyed. Our ideal image of the Jewish people, with which we had grown up, was subjected to a new test, almost unbearable. I think that we were not ready and mature enough to be fair and honest judges of the blemishes that were revealed to our eyes.[60]

While they were waiting at Grand Arénas to sail for Israel, the South American group received military training. On the long-awaited day, they were taken to a harbor near Marseilles, where they then boarded the *Kibbutz Galuyot* for the voyage to Israel. The volunteers from South America, along with a few English-speaking volunteers, functioned as stewards. They had to tell the passengers, most of them Holocaust survivors, to find themselves places on the narrow bunks. The crowding and noise reminded the refugees of their experiences in the camps; they shrieked and demanded to leave the suffocating place, Itzigsohn recalled. "This was the human material that was soon to urgently fill the ranks of the Israeli army and the builders of the State."[61]

On board, there were clearly two classes: the Israelis, who were the organizers and commanders, and the newcomers, who all but swamped the boat. The volunteers occupied a sort of intermediate and undefined status. They received unexpected emotional support from the ship's small crew, which included Spanish Republican exiles. Their language and worldview united them. One crew member, who came from a non-Jewish family in Catalonia, bonded strongly with the volunteers, joined them, and enlisted in the IDF. When the war was over, he married a young female immigrant from Argentina and settled with her on a kibbutz.[62]

As the ship approached the Israeli coast, the fear of Egyptian bombers increased but proved to be unfounded. After seven days at sea, the South American volunteers reached Israel in the middle of August 1948. They were taken at once to a camp near Haifa for a few days of rest. After that brief interlude, they were shipped from camp to camp and began to get to know the country's landscapes and people. Their first encounter with Israelis proved problematic, because, according to Itzigsohn, the volunteers were anticipating an abstemious and frugal lifestyle of asceticism and deprivation, which still existed only on some of the kibbutzim. In fact, they found a more comfortable situation than they expected, and this posed "a huge spiritual contradiction" for them. Here is Itzigsohn's description of his impression of the Israelis he met then:

> For the veteran settlers, whose roots here went back a generation or two, the changes that had taken place before their eyes went deeper. Independence had indeed finally arrived, and the state was stronger and more secure. But in a certain way all this came at the expense of their old world. They used to talk about the golden age when they could take walks in Tel Aviv without locking their doors, and the loss of the quiet and attractive corners in a city that was now filled with the shacks for immigrants. . . . The veteran residents experienced both the joy of growth and development and the inevitable agitation of change, which on occasion made them ill-mannered and suspicious towards those who were willing to sacrifice their past lives in order to come to the country. All the same, the olim felt a mixture of relief, on the one hand, because of their new-found security, and frustration, on the other hand, because of the discrimination they experienced in their early years in a state they thought of as their own.[63]

At the end of this brief respite, some of the volunteers, especially those with a military background, including Itzigsohn, were sent to a course for NCOs: "When you are an immigrant, you lose one or more ranks," joked the former lieutenant in our interview. After the course, the South Americans joined the Spanish-speaking battalions 91 and 92 of Brigade 9 (the Oded Brigade). The military authorities assumed that mustering the volunteers into the same unit would make their integration in the army easier, solve most of their social and linguistic problems, and permit better attention to their specific difficulties. With this in mind, a special office was established to deal with the volunteers. A letter dated October 14, 1948, addressed to Lee Harris, the civilian advisor to this office, which had been established a month earlier, estimated that there were around sixty South American volunteers in the two battalions.[64]

The battalions were rather heterogeneous. In addition to the Spanish- and Portuguese-speaking volunteers from Latin America, there were also Ladino speakers from Bulgaria and Turkey and, maintaining the general linguistic principle, a few Moroccan Jews who spoke French and some non-Jewish volunteers from Spain. Most of the officers were native-born Israelis. Itzigsohn was sent to Battalion 92, where he commanded a platoon of ten young refugees from Turkey who came from the poorest stratum of the Jewish community in Izmir. "In this case," Itzigsohn wrote, "there was more division in the linguistic community than unity." They managed to communicate despite the language problem. The real problem was the cultural gap.[65]

One of the most colorful figures in the battalion was its commander, a Hungarian Jew named László Pataky, who came to Israel from Nicaragua to fight in the War of Independence. Born in Budapest in 1917, at age eighteen he moved to Managua, the capital of Nicaragua, in the wake of his father and uncle, who had prospered there in the textile business. In 1941, he made his way to England to join the Free French. Pataky fought and was injured twice in the decisive battles in North Africa in 1942.[66] He reached Israel right after independence and received an officer's commission because of his military background and experience, but mainly as thanks for the service he rendered the young state by arriving with a shipload of weapons at a critical juncture in the war.[67] "For us, he was completely foreign: his relations and contacts with the Spanish-speaking world were grounded in circumstances quite different from ours," Itzigsohn recalled.[68]

In September 1948, as a result of an initiative by the volunteers themselves, the IDF established a special office for them in the Manpower Branch of the General Staff. It was led by Akiva Skidell, a member of Kibbutz Kefar Blum, who had served in the US Army in World War II; Lee Harris, a volunteer from the United States, who came to Israel to manage the Mortgage Bank; and Gideon Baratz of Kibbutz Deganya Aleph, a British Army veteran. Harris served as a civilian advisor; his office saw to the publication of pamphlets and information materials in various languages, welfare activities, the distribution of pocket money to volunteers, the resolution of personal problems, and so forth. The department even established a clubhouse on Hayarkon Street in Tel Aviv, where the volunteers could congregate when on leave.[69] The new unit, Mitnadvei Hutz La'aretz (Hebrew for "Overseas Volunteers"), better known by the acronym Mahal, consisted of all those who came to Israel to enlist in the IDF and help found the State while the fighting continued, but with the intention of returning home at the end of the war.[70]

And that is what most of the volunteers did after the armistice agreements were signed and they were demobilized. Itzigsohn remembered that at this point, many of the volunteers were torn between an inclination to stay in the country for which they had fought and the desire to return to their homes and families.

"For many, it was easier to fight for the state than to settle in it," he wrote, adding that he, too, had been of two minds:

> I remember walking around in Tel Aviv on the day of the parade to celebrate the first Independence Day. During those moments, I was witness to a glorious event for which I had yearned deeply, but I could not become part of or identify with what was happening around me. I chose to return to [Argentina], where my studies, family, and dear ones were waiting for me, a framework in which I could feel truly important, and, finally, the roots that bound me to my native country. During those days, the Peronist regime was speaking out publicly and vehemently against antisemitism and it was possible to believe, particularly if you wanted to, that after the fall of fascism and birth of Israel, the most aggressive forms of antisemitism would be left behind.[71]

Dealing with the volunteers required keeping meticulous records of their personal details. A document preserved in the Central Zionist Archives, "The Settlement of Mahal Fighters in Israel," estimates that there were 3,500 volunteers, of whom 1,500 expressed a desire to settle in Israel. Their average tour of duty had been nine months. The authors of the document conjectured that between 200 and 300 of the volunteers who went back home would eventually return to settle in Israel. Of the 1,500 volunteers who expressed a desire to stay on after demobilization, about 600 were directed to border settlements.[72] Mahal documents put the number of volunteers from Latin America at around 400, a figure that includes both those who came to the country as part of the pioneer youth movements and the volunteers who were not members of any movement. The assessment was that 200 to 250 of them wanted to settle in Israel as "volunteer olim."[73]

The young people affiliated with the pioneer youth movements who arrived during the war were lumped together with those who came to join Mahal, as the various cadres expanded. The Mahal chapter is important not only because of its contribution to the growth of the pioneer movements in Israel, but also because the volunteering impulse expanded the potential for immigration to Israel to include other young adults who were not members of Zionist youth groups. Evidence of this survives in files from the Prime Minister's Office now in the State Archives. In February 1950, Arieh Eshel, who was by then first secretary and consul at the Israeli legation in Argentina, wrote a letter to Prime Minister David Ben-Gurion about the Mahal chapter and its ramifications:

> This mobilization, even though it set off stormy arguments in the pioneer camp, which was afraid that the recruitment of people who had not gone through all the lengthy stages of ideological and occupational training would pull the rug out from under its feet, brought hundreds of young men and women to the country. At least 80% of them found their place in Israel; many joined the agricultural settlements of immigrants from South America, while others remained in various units of the Army, Navy, and Air Force. It is also clear that none of them would have made aliya were it not for the possibility offered by the special enlistment apparatus. These young people did not belong to the frameworks—too narrow, alas!—of the organized pioneer movement.[74]

Working from the materials left behind by the Mahal section, I was able to compose a list of ninety-six volunteers whom it processed and assigned to urban settlements near Tel Aviv (Hadar Yosef), Haifa (Qiryat Yam), and Jerusalem (Bayit Vegan). The list of candidates for urban settlements includes their first and last names, country of origin, marital status, and occupation as well as whether they had relatives in Israel. Unfortunately, their age is not stated. The breakdown by countries of origin shows that about half of the volunteers from Latin America came from Argentina.[75] More than 60% of them were single; the majority were working class, mainly artisans and craftsmen. A quarter reported that they had relatives already living in the country.[76]

Immigration by Members of the Zionist Youth Movements in the 1950s

In the early 1950s, the Zionist youth movements in Argentina and the rest of Latin America had a solid organizational infrastructure and registered notable achievements in sending their members to kibbutzim in Israel. This was the heyday of Zionist pioneering and the finest hour of these movements in Argentina.[77] They represented the main potential for aliya by organized Jewish youth, with more than 10,000 members in Argentina, Brazil, Uruguay, and Chile alone (about 7,000 of them in Argentina); about 500 of them prepared for aliya on fourteen training farms.[78]

Seven Zionist youth movements were active in Argentina. All but one were identified with political parties in Israel.[79] During these years, the "movement rule" that prescribed aliya right out of high school left its mark on most of these movements. It produced a stream of immigration by halutzim, but also reduced the ranks of the movements, because many members left for Israel and others dropped out after they failed to do so. A solution to the problematic situation of the latter was found in the early 1950s, when young adults, mainly university students who had not moved to Israel, set up their own groups ("brigades"). They too coalesced around a partisan identity centered on Israeli politics.[80]

According to one study, these new groups were never very large, with no more than 150 active members in each, plus a periphery of up to 300 more.[81] In addition to the brigades, there was also the Federation of Zionist University Centers for nonpartisan student organizations. One document estimates that the federation numbered about 2,000 students in 1958, with an active nucleus of around 250.[82] The young-adult brigades, too, embodied great potential for immigration to Israel. But the data suggest that their membership was negligible in proportion to the Jewish student population—no more than 5% of the 12,000–16,000 Jews on Argentinian campuses in the 1950s and 1960s.[83]

In 1957, the Jewish Agency published Moshe Joselevich's *Jornadas pioneras* (roughly "Pioneers' Progress"), which was the first attempt to describe the role played by the immigrants from Latin America in settling the kibbutzim.[84] He focused on the 2,000 halutzim from Latin America, more than half of them from Argentina, who had made their home on more than thirty rural settlements all over Israel.[85] He relied mainly on the impressions of his visit to Israel in 1956 and on data collected before and during the trip. The timing of the visit was not coincidental, but was scheduled to mark the end of the first decade of pioneer aliya from Latin America, whose start Joselevich dated to February 1946 and the arrival in Palestine of the first ten pioneers from Argentina. Joselevich profiled the Latin American halutzim and their accomplishments. One of their hallmarks was their strong predilection for the communal life of the kibbutz; they had founded only one semicollective village (moshav shitufi)—Mevo Betar.[86]

The story of Devorah (Dora) Schachner (née Graukop), as recounted in her literary autobiography *A Political Girl*, is a paradigmatic case that can be taken to reflect the experiences of thousands of young Argentinian Jews who belonged to the Zionist youth movements in the 1950s.[87] The memories, accounts, and letters included in her book create a document of extraordinary historical value. Schachner's passionate and wholehearted devotion to realization of the Zionist idea coalesced in Hashomer Hatza'ir. She portrays the ideal and vision as the main force that shaped her comrades' lives and identities, but her parents' home and the political and economic situation in Argentina also had a significant impact on the course of her life. Like many Jews who immigrated to Argentina, her father, Osher Graukop, originally from Bialystok, prospered in the textile industry in the early years of the Perón regime. He was active in Jewish community organizations in Buenos Aires, particularly the Left Po'alei Zion party. Unlike the parents of many young members of the youth movements, Osher Graukop did not oppose his daughter's decision to settle in Israel. On the contrary, he encouraged his daughter's practical Zionist education, as emerges from this description of the decisive moment in her decision to make aliya, taken from a letter she wrote to a friend in early 1951:

> A few days ago, we organized a movement ceremony in Villa Lynch. Hundreds of people were present—all the workers at my father's Modern Textiles factory were there (Jews and non-Jews: the proletariat turned out!). I spoke at the ceremony (almost like Evita [Eva Perón]). I allowed myself to say every word in Hebrew that came to mind. Of course you know that there is a law that says that speeches can be made only in the language of Cervantes. But my father has significant influence in Villa Lynch. The police officer who was present at the ceremony was upset because he didn't understand what the words meant, but Berele (that traitorous Jew from OIA [the Organización Israelita Argentina, a pro-Peronist Jewish organization]) translated for him: kibbutz, aliya, settlement, army, comrades, peace. And then rousing applause; the audience was enthusiastic. Osher Graukop and his partners were proud. My mother, a woman with an extremely sharp eye, asked me: what's happening to you, Dorita? What can I tell her? It's only because of them, because of my parents' admiring look, that will I make aliya to Gazit.[88]

Devorah was in Israel from July 1949 to August 1950 as part of the first class at the Institute for Overseas Counselors in Jerusalem. It was a year of formative experiences, but also of disappointments: "What I looked for and didn't find was 'the new man' who had so preoccupied us," she wrote in the same letter. During her time in Israel, Devorah discovered that Israeli society, including the kibbutzim, was not really different from the mixed society of Jews and non-Jews she had come from in Buenos Aires: "Trivial details of daily life, stupid fights, the quest for positions of control, jealousy." But she had not yet made it to her future home, Kibbutz Gazit, where she placed all her hopes the moment she made her decision to leave Argentina permanently in September 1952, hoping that at Gazit "we will perhaps have the opportunity to begin working to create 'the new man' (and the new woman)."[89]

Devorah Schachner's life story, like those of many other young men and women who belonged to the Zionist movements and relocated to Israel, reveals the element that propelled the ideological immigrants from Argentina: the ambition to return to the new and renewing homeland and take part in the Zionist revolution by creating a new man and a new and just society. This deep motivation produced the chain migration of members of the Zionist youth movements, which expanded over the years in keeping with the policies of the settlement movements. In addition to the movement members and the cadres who came in the wake of their friends, sometimes parents and acquaintances followed their relatives to Israel. The future of Kibbutz Gazit, for example, where Devorah Schachner settled, was guaranteed when Hashomer Hatza'ir cadres and their parents moved there from Argentina. Of its 132 members in 1960, eighty-two were young adults from Argentina, along with sixteen of their parents.[90] These figures highlight the decisive importance of chain migration on the process.

The data in table 11, extracted from the database I assembled, reflect to some extent the composition of the total Jewish immigration to Israel in the 1950s and the share that the halutzim played in it. The Aliyah Department of the Jewish Agency dealt mainly with immigrants who lacked financial resources. The Economic Department processed candidates with capital, whose immigration was usually associated with an investment plan devised in advance. Two corporations founded by Argentinian Jews, Zemorot and Maris, organized the immigration of members of the solid middle class, while the CAIRA joint stock company focused on bringing lower-middle-class immigrants to Kefar Argentina. The PATWA Center dealt mainly with liberal professionals

Table 11: Immigration from Argentina to Israel by supervising agency, 1954–60

Agency	Number of immigrants	Percentage
Aliyah Department	903	34.3
Economic Department	46	1.7
PATWA	289	11.0
Youth and Hehalutz Department	1,184	45.0
Youth Aliyah	72	2.7
CAIRA	120	4.5
Zemorot	20	0.8
Maris	2	-
Total	2,636	100.0

Source: Klor, "10,487 Database."

and students. The Youth and Hehalutz Department oversaw the pioneer aliya that included the cadres of the Zionist youth movements and members of the young-adult brigades, by ideological key. The former received pioneer visas; the latter, untrained pioneer visas. Children through age sixteen fell into the province of Youth Aliyah.

As noted, the line in the table that refers to the Youth and Hehalutz Department includes graduates of the Zionist youth movements and the young-adult brigades. But it also covers a certain number of children through age of sixteen (processed by Youth Aliyah but not included in the Youth Aliya line in the table) and adults with immigrant visas—the parents, siblings, and other relatives of the halutzim.[91] So to gain a truer picture of the composition of the Argentinian Jewish immigrants, we need to check these data against the type of visa. Correlating the official data from the Aliyah Department with the identity of the agency that dealt with the immigrant and the type of visa allows us to conclude, as a very close approximation, that about 40% of all immigrants from Argentina in the 1950s belonged to the pioneer category. The database confirms the kibbutz profile of this sector: in the 1950s, the pioneer immigrants from Argentina settled on thirty-six kibbutzim and two collective moshavim.

According to my database, an overwhelming majority of the halutzim were young men and women age 18–24, of whom 80% were unmarried males—proportions typical of pioneer aliya over the decades. Most of them came from lower-middle-class families of the petite bourgeoisie, along with a sprinkling of better-off merchants and tradesmen. The artisans and skilled tradesmen among them (about 80% of the total) included tailors, lathe operators, weavers, carpenters, and silversmiths. Registered under the rubric of "miscellaneous occupations" were 180 university students, along with mechanics, drivers, metalworkers, and construction workers. Technicians of various kinds and electricians were prominent among the skilled tradesmen.

These data debunk the widespread assumption about the composition and profile of the halutzim in general and of those from Latin America in particular. A cursory glance at the memoir literature and the few academic studies yields the impression that most of the halutzim were the children of well-to-do families and university students whose material needs were provided for in abundance. But the data I collected clearly refute this assumption. A large proportion of them were young adults from the less-well-off classes of the Argentinian Jewish community. Devorah Schachner was one of the exceptions, not the rule. Wealthy people simply did not tend to move to Israel, whether as halutzim or otherwise.

The Capitalists: Immigration to Israel by Wealthy Argentinian Jews

Wealthy Jews were rarely inclined to leave Argentina and resettle in Israel. However, they did look for opportunities to invest in Israel after independence (and before as well) and transferred some of their capital there. The most important initiatives were associated with ARPALSA, the Argentina-Palestine Economic Corporation, established by Argentinian Jewish investors in 1946.[92] In 1949, ARPALSA established a subsidiary in Tel Aviv, called Isar (Israel-Argentina), which financed construction and the purchase of lots in Haifa, Ramat Gan, Petah Tiqva, and Rishon LeZion. ARPALSA also get involved in import-export deals, especially after the two countries signed a trade pact in April 1950.[93] A finance company, Arg-Il, was also established that year and made a substantial investment in a luxury beachfront hotel in Herzliyya, the Accadia.[94] The Inca company, established in 1951, collaborated with the Jewish Agency on immigration and absorption projects and made construction loans to the Israeli government.[95] Another initiative by Argentinian capitalists was the establishment of the Mefalsim Company, which provided direct and indirect assistance to Kibbutz Mefalsim; most of its investors were parents of members of the kibbutz.[96]

At a Tel Aviv press conference in June 1952, Dr. Isaac Nissenson, the president of the Argentine Zionist Federation, a lawyer by profession who had spent forty-eight years in Argentina, announced the establishment of the Israel-Argentina Development Company, Ltd.[97] Nissenson related that thousands of families in Argentina were looking for ways to move to Israel and invest there. The plan was to set up two parallel companies, one in Israel and one in Argentina, to serve as a channel to link people and enterprises in Argentina with plants and institutions in Israel. The two companies would work with individuals and groups and advise potential immigrants on issues such as transferring assets and factories. They would also serve as their liaison with enterprises in Israel to help the enterprises expand and supply them with raw materials thanks to investments by immigrants from Argentina:

> Until now, Israel has received either Jews or money. We want to provide Jews along with their money. We will not work with Jews who want to invest but do not plan to make aliya. But we will help guarantee financing options for Jews of limited means, so that they can get established in Israel. The main thing is for the oleh to be able to find something waiting for him when he arrives and to be protected against the failure

caused by ignorance of the conditions and the possibilities there. With this in mind, the management of the Israeli company includes persons active in all branches of the Israeli economy: farmers, industrialists, financiers, factory workers. If people receive the proper treatment, we hope that, over time, not just two thousand families but tens of thousands, or even more, will make aliya in this manner.[98]

Nissenson added that he himself was planning to settle in Israel, and that if the new company succeeded, he would expand its activities to the entire South American continent. The managers of the Israeli company—Gad Machnes (formerly a senior Jewish Agency and Israeli government official), Yehuda Tokatly, and others—added details about how the company was planning to work in agriculture, industry, and other domains. Gad Frumkin (an attorney who had been the only Jew to serve on the Mandatory Supreme Court), the president of the company, also participated in the press conference.[99]

Another group of investors founded the Maris Corporation in 1952. In the first stage, it invested about $50,000 to purchase heavy construction equipment, mainly bulldozers, which were used to excavate the canals to drain the Hula marshes. Afterward, Maris invested in the Kedma factory, which produced agricultural machinery and implements. Later still, it set up an independent agricultural machinery plant in Beer Sheva. As of February 1955, the company had invested $300,000 in these projects.[100]

In 1952, another group of investors from Argentina established a rubber-products factory in Netanya, Ingum, which employed about seventy workers. The next year, the same group, centered in Córdoba, acquired 74% of the shares of the Tel Aviv–based Agricultural and Construction Bank (Agrobank) as the basis for a financial institution that would specialize in the various fiscal transactions of immigrants and investors from Spanish-speaking countries.[101] The bank had an initial capital of $200,000 for its parent company, which worked outside Israel with commercial firms that required foreign currency, and another $300,000 for its activities in Israel. In 1954, at the request of the new owners, the economist Dr. Jacobo Blecher moved to Israel to manage the bank, which henceforth served as a financial bridge between Argentinian Jews and the State of Israel.[102]

An example of an initiative by Argentinian Jewish capitalists to create a social foundation for immigration was the Zemorot company, established in May 1953 by fourteen wealthy Argentinian Jews in response to a proposal by Samuel Kaufman, a Jewish viticulture expert from Mendoza.[103] That September, some thirty people from all over Argentina (Buenos Aires, Concordia, Córdoba, and Río Negro) agreed to establish a cooperative venture in Israel, to be named after President Weizmann (who had died the year before). Some members of the group were affiliated with the Argentinian Zionist Federation and belonged to the General Zionist and Progressive parties (which had been Weizmann's political identity). They undertook to invest a total of 20,000 Israel pounds (440,000 pesos) to construct a winery in Israel and acquire agricultural land for vineyards—between 3 and 3.3 hectares for each member. Some of the investors had experience in the wine industry in Argentina; others were middle-class professionals, including several from the Jewish agricultural colonies.[104] This initiative led to the establishment of the first residential neighborhood for Argentinian immigrants in Rehovot.[105]

Dr. A. S. Zeitlin became the Buenos Aires representative of the Jewish Agency Economic Department in June 1953. Upon his arrival there, he opened an office in the same building as the headquarters of the Higher Zionist Council, with active assistance from the legation staff. He developed ties with the Israeli diplomatic missions and Zionist federations in the other Latin American countries where economic councils had been established. His office provided information and explanations to all who inquired about the Israeli economy as well as consulting services for everyone. His assignment was to make contact with economically influential individuals and circles in order to awaken their interest in Israel's economic problems and help them draw up programs for expanding investment and immigration from their countries. Zeitlin also dealt with problems related to capital transfers and exports, in cooperation with the Economic Division of the Foreign Ministry.[106]

Zeitlin's posting to Buenos Aires ended in February 1955. Several days before his return to Israel, he drafted a report summing up his experiences there. He wrote that one of the biggest problems he had faced was in the field of public information, because of the explicit ban on disclosing details, whether orally or in writing, about capital investments in Israel.[107] In an earlier report to the head of his department (November 1953), which contained the news about the establishment of the Israeli bank, Zeitlin wrote that "this information is intended for you only, for various reasons, one of which is the need to keep this secret inside Argentina."[108]

The background for this restriction on Zeitlin's public information activity was the strict limits that the Perón regime placed on capital transfers. Paradoxically, however, when Zeitlin summarized his achievements in Argentina he noted that "the general trend of a drop in the flow of private capital from the Diaspora to Israel in 1953 and even more so in 1954 did not apply to the flow of private capital from Argentina."[109] During these years, Argentinian Jews invested about $1.5 million in various projects in Israel. Zeitlin noted that most of these plans were linked to immigration by the investor or by a family member (usually a halutz son or daughter).[110] This is additional evidence of the great importance of chain migration.

As I argued earlier, the upper class was underrepresented among immigrants from Argentina (less than 2%). It stands to reason that most of those in the category of tourist-residents belonged to those circles. Scholars can only lament that there is little documentary evidence of how the authorities dealt with them. During most of this period, the Maris Corporation encouraged tourism to Israel, so it seems plausible that it made a certain contribution to the tourist-immigration of those years. My data include only two cases of immigration organized by this company. Zemorot, which was supposed to stimulate more than a hundred families to settle in Israel, failed to justify the hopes placed in it; the database lists only eight families whose immigration was organized by that company between 1954 and 1960. One estimate is that, in 1960, there were twenty-seven families living in the neighborhood it built in Rehovot.[111] What all these immigrants have in common is that they arrived in Israel with capitalist visas. Unfortunately, I have not found information in the archives about Argentinian Jews' investments in Israel during this period.

Both Halutzim and Capitalists: Kefar Argentina

In an article published in *Ha'aretz* in July 1953, under the headline "Argentinian Jews Are Making Aliya," the reporter describes the impending establishment of a mixed agricultural and industrial village by Jews from Argentina.[112] The first thirty-five homes in the village, located on the main road between Tel Aviv and Jerusalem, two kilometers northwest of Ramle, were nearly ready for occupancy. The houses were not built using the mass-construction techniques prevalent in the country and were intended for middle-class immigrants from Argentina, who had decided to build their new homes in Israel on their own and with their own funds.[113] The writer emphasized that from the very start these Jews had declined the standard government "treatment" meted out to immigrants from Eastern Europe and the Arab countries. Their solution had been the establishment of a joint stock company, the Colonia Agrícola Industrial República Argentina, or CAIRA.[114]

Moshe Melman, a wealthy Jew from Buenos Aires who was looking for a feasible way to move to Israel, was one of the founders of the company that initiated the Kefar Argentina ("Argentina village") project. To mark the settlement's twenty-fifth anniversary, he published his recollections of the early years, drawing on many letters and primary documents from his personal archives. In the first chapters of his book, Melman traced the background of the idea for a mixed agricultural-industrial village in Israel, at a time when the Jewish Agency did not encourage immigration by members of the middle class, and building one's own home in Israel was seen as a "vision and a dream," as he put it.[115] Melman also explained his own motive for making aliya: "At the time, my two older sons were active in Hashomer Hatza'ir. I was sure that they would soon find their way to Israel; and as for my wife and me and my youngest son—we too were bound to make aliya sooner or later." Given the situation of those years, only the question of the modalities remained unanswered:

> This question bothered me. I don't have a specific occupation. I'm past 50. My health—not exactly the best. True, the aluminum ware factory I owned was blooming and thriving, but all the same I had never risen above the middle class and not even in my rosiest calculations did I have a chance of amassing sufficient capital to guarantee my family a worry-free existence. I thought that at age 50 a man can still accomplish something, but things are quite risky here [in Israel] for people who arrive with few assets. Middle-class families from Argentina were swept up in the vast stream of aliya from every corner of the Earth. They liquidated their businesses and came to Israel without any plans or direction, but within a short time turned into yordim and went back [to Argentina], embittered and disappointed spiritually, physically, and economically. Some of them were active and loyal Zionists who were now embarrassed to be seen outside, and even more so to return to the movement or work in any institution. I knew very well that an overwhelming majority of the potential olim found themselves in a situation similar to mine.[116]

According to Melman, asking the Jewish Agency for help was out of the question. Argentinian Jews were giving generously to fund the immigration and absorption of Holocaust survivors and Jews from Arab countries who were in danger. Given the circumstances, he viewed the option of applying to the Jewish Agency for assistance in acquiring an apartment and finding a job as "stupid and loathsome."[117] As the son of a farmer from one of the ICA colonies, Melman was attracted to the idea of agricultural labor, but his age and health made that problematic. The only business options he thought feasible were in some branch of light industry or operating a store in the city, but his finances were insufficient for ventures of that sort. Melman wrote that when he visited provincial towns in Argentina he saw that many Jews wanted to move to Israel and work in agriculture. This gave him the idea of linking these three elements—farming, industry, and Jews who were willing to live together in certain conditions and certain circumstances—with the goal of starting a new settlement in Israel that was not far from a city or developing town.[118]

Melman held his first meetings in late October 1950. Soon after, he and the others found the solution for their immigration in a joint stock company that would build a mixed agricultural and industrial settlement in Israel for middle-class Jews and others, based on private enterprise. Any Argentinian Jew, even if not a potential immigrant, could purchase one share for a thousand pesos (about $50). Those who purchased more than one share would become members of the association and have the right to vote for and be members of its board. Those who were thinking about immigration in the near future were required to invest fifty thousand pesos.[119]

The two large Yiddish newspapers in Argentina, *Di Idishe Tsaytung* and *Di Presse*, set out to help the group. Melman noted in particular the editor and publisher Mordechai Stoliar, who allowed them to publicize and advertise the project without charge. The activists also contacted Dr. Abraham Mibashan, because they needed a clear and detailed information pamphlet and were aware of his experience as editor of the monthly *Eretz Yisrael*. Mibashan recommended Natan Lerner, a young law student at the National University in Buenos Aires (and later a specialist in international law and professor in Israel) to translate the information booklet into Yiddish, which was then published at nominal charge by H. Kaufman, a well-known Jewish publisher.[120] The two newspapers published the notice with full details about the establishment of the company; this enabled CAIRA's program to reach the periphery as well.[121] Aside from the advertisements, though, there does not seem to have been any coverage of CAIRA in the Argentinian Jewish press. There seem to have been more reports about it in Israel, a comparison that suggests how the Jewish masses in Argentina generally related to (or rather ignored) this social stratum.

In his memoirs, Melman wrote that it was risky to publicize such ventures during the Perón era: "A project like this, which involved removing capital from the country and hoarding dollars, was strictly illegal in those days."[122] But he and his colleagues were not deterred. The strategy they adopted was to create the impression that their goal was to establish a settlement in Israel in honor of

Argentina. The legation, too, did not look kindly on the CAIRA advertisements and issued broad hints to that effect.[123] The various Zionist parties also tended to oppose the plan: "They think that whatever the party doesn't bake in its own oven is doomed to failure," Melman wrote. "This is just an affair of Hashomer Hatza'ir," went one criticism, based on the argument that the leaders' sons were active members of that movement.[124] But in contrast to the cool response by the legation and parties, the central institutions of Argentinian Jewry, especially AMIA and the DAIA, were extremely positive about it.[125]

As noted previously, during that time there was also significant activity by capitalists; they, too, were taking steps to invest and support immigration to Israel. According to Melman, the wealthy had nothing but scorn for the CAIRA project. They insisted that nothing could come of a scheme in which a shareholder's entire investment did not exceed two thousand pesos. The rich Jews had no interest in immigration; the few who consented to purchase a few shares did so only to placate family members: "They agreed to their request but saw the purchase as a gift," Melman recalled in his memoirs:

> They spoke about the bank [Agrobank], in which every share went for tens of thousands of dollars; they spoke about a colony with vineyards producing wine for export. This was an initiative called Zemorot, headed by a wealthy Jew from Mendoza Province, which is known as "Argentina's wine country." There was a project to build a hotel in Herzliyya, the Accadia. A company was established to cooperate with Kibbutz Mefalsim; and so forth. And here we were coming with a plan to establish a settlement for a hundred families, with shares costing 1,000 pesos [$50] each.[126]

Despite the low expectations of their project, Melman and his associates opened an office to handle routine matters. Their initiative thrived, largely because of the economic circumstances in Argentina. The Perón government had flooded the economy with newly printed banknotes and raised the wages of the working masses. As a result, small merchants and industrialists made substantial profits and converted the proceeds into foreign currency—a process that was good for CAIRA. Within eighteen months, the company had five hundred investors. When the first general assembly of the shareholders was convened, in late 1951, one of the main problems raised was that of information. The activists referred some questions to the Jewish Agency emissaries, who could not always answer them. At the general assembly, it was agreed that the time had come to send two delegates to Israel to discuss their project with the government. With great enthusiasm, the shareholders voted overwhelmingly to dispatch Moshe Melman as the agricultural advisor and Shaul Kugler as the industrial expert and instructed them to locate an appropriate place for the future settlement.[127]

Kugler, born in Galicia, was the well-to-do owner of a large carpentry workshop in Buenos Aires. His older son was a member of Kibbutz Gaash and had been one of the defenders of Negba during the War of Independence. Kugler himself was planning to move to Israel; the idea was that he would serve as the CAIRA representative there.[128] Melman and Kugler booked passage on the Italian ship the SS *Conte Grande*, sailing on April 18, 1952. According to Melman, the issue of their luggage was always a headache for immigrants. "Had the officials performed a thorough search, no oleh could have taken out even half his capital," Melman wrote in his memoirs.[129] The solution was to pay off the customs inspectors—the "tried and true" method of bribery, as Melman put it. The procedure became more or less an institution and, irony of ironies, took on an ideological dimension in the case of the immigrants to Israel. The goal justified every means, as can be understood from the following lines:

> The bribery was organized by experts in that line. Because there was a significant aliya to Israel just then, mostly by halutzim, several offices sprang up that functioned as middlemen and made sure that the inspection at the port would be for appearances' sake only. In return for this blind eye, the emigrating passenger paid a handsome sum that found its way to the pockets of the go-betweens and inspectors. In our case, it was the Negba Company, founded by Hashomer Hatza'ir, that handled the matter. It goes without saying that the person harmed most was the oleh, because the company took as much as the traffic would bear for itself; but there was no other way to receive the custom inspector's rubber stamp.[130]

At one of their intermediate stops in Uruguay, Melman and Kugler went into a financial institution, a sort of private bank, through which it was possible to smuggle large dollar sums out of Argentina. They withdrew $6,000, the capital they had accumulated thus far, which was supposed to serve as the initial funding for their project. In Genoa, Kugler bought a small Fiat; Melman, at the request of Kibbutz Mefalsim, bought machinery for a furniture factory. They landed in Haifa on May 27, 1952. Kugler and his wife proceeded to Kibbutz Gaash, while Melman went with his brother-in-law to Ramat Hasharon.[131]

In early June, they met in Jerusalem with the chairman of the Jewish National Fund (JNF), Yosef Weitz, who offered them seven possible locations for their settlement. But Melman and Kugler were looking not only for fertile agricultural land but also for a central location that would be convenient for industry and factories. In the end, they agreed on a suitable site—300 hectares (including a 35-hectare cultivated orchard) about two kilometers from the town of Ramle. The next step was to sign a construction contract. At this stage, the CAIRA representatives consulted with Dr. José Mirelman, who was in Israel just then to work on the Accadia Hotel project. Mirelman, one of the richest Jews in Buenos Aires, was the managing director of ARPALSA. He and his family maintained luxurious offices in the heart of Tel Aviv. The CAIRA delegates deposited the money they brought with them in the Agrobank, which, as noted, was run by Argentinian financiers, including Mirelman.[132]

In consultation with Dr. Mirelman, and after reviewing the construction market, Melman and Kugler began negotiations with the Rassco company. They received the land from the JNF for ninety-nine years, in return for a nominal annual payment. The settlers would receive twenty-five-year low-interest loans from the Jewish Agency and other sources. Rassco would build the entire village and would receive in payment all the financial support intended for the immigrants who settled there as well as any funds invested in the project by CAIRA and the immigrants themselves. The negotiations also included haggling about the cost of the homes, dairy barn, chicken house, storage sheds, and other structures. The issue of the exchange rate held up the signing of the contract, but was finally resolved in a compromise that pegged the dollar at 1.5 Israel pounds. When the signatures were dry, an announcement appeared in Israeli newspapers in early August 1952. This led the Argentinian minister in Israel, Pablo Mangel, to summon the CAIRA representatives and ask them to curtail the publicity, because "the Argentinian government does not look kindly on citizens who abandon their country."[133]

Construction began at a rapid pace right as soon as the contract was signed. Every farming family was to receive a plot of 1.2 hectares. Those who opted for industry would receive quarter-hectare auxiliary farms. The plan called for fifteen public structures, including a cultural center with an amphitheater, a school, a synagogue, offices for the village administration, a social club, a warehouse for supplies, a dairy and storage rooms for agricultural produce, a hatchery, a grocery store, a nursery school, a health clinic, industrial buildings, a hotel, and a swimming pool. Additional land would be set aside for future public buildings. In the village itself, every family would have its own freestanding home and work its land independently. The 35-hectare citrus orchard, which the village received from the Custodian of Absentee Property, would be a communal venture, as would the marketing of the produce. Part of the profits generated by the orchard would be sent back to the shareholders in Argentina.[134]

In mid-1953, the CAIRA offices received a letter from Rassco with the news that the first thirty homes were ready for occupancy. The construction costs came to IL 9,500 per housing unit: each family paid IL 2,500, the Jewish Agency provided a loan of IL 3,000, and CAIRA covered the balance. As of July 1953, twenty-five families had signed up for full-scale farms and ten for auxiliary farms. The plans anticipated that the total population would eventually reach 130 families.[135] Melman asserted that only 10% of the applicants actually moved to Israel in the end, because many were deterred by having to liquidate their assets at a loss and the risk of not being able to get their funds out of Argentina. Even the immigrants who had already signed up to leave were subjected to meticulous screening by the Israeli immigration authorities, similar to that of potential immigrants from other countries.[136]

On November 11, 1953, a farewell party was held in Buenos Aires for the first group of immigrants. The new Israel minister to Argentina, Arieh Kubovy (who had succeeded Tsur in August) congratulated the immigrants and gave every family a Bible as a present.[137] The eight families bound for Kefar Argentina sailed a week later and reached Haifa port in mid-December.[138] Several of them were small-scale industrialists in Buenos Aires who had liquidated their businesses in order to move to Israel. Others were veteran farmers from the ICA colonies. There were also a veterinarian and a truck driver, who shipped his vehicle from Argentina for the villagers to use. The settlers brought tractors, combines, and other agricultural equipment for collective use.[139] With the arrival of the first group, a new chapter in the saga of Kefar Argentina began.

CAIRA ended up organizing the immigration of about 5% of all immigrants from Argentina in the late 1950s. The village was settled in three stages. The first stage, described above, was in 1953 and 1954; the second, in 1956; and the third stage was in 1958. In 1960, Kefar Argentina was home to more than 350 families.[140] The composition of the immigrants to Kefar Argentina, as contained in my database and checked against the figures presented above for all middle-class immigrants, bolsters my case that Kefar Argentina can be seen as a paradigmatic case for the lower-middle-class immigrants. This is most prominent in the occupational breakdown of the settlers there, with a relatively high proportion of merchants, small-scale industrialists, and farmers.

The age breakdown of these immigrants further reinforces my basic assumption. As noted, they were representatives of the lower middle class who tried to overcome the many obstacles to resettlement in Israel by means of an organized joint initiative that would minimize the difficulties that members of this class encountered in the immigration and absorption process. One of those difficulties, for example, was posed by the rules of selective immigration, which disfavored those past age thirty-five. But more than 45% of all the Kefar Argentina immigrants were older than that.[141]

In one of his reports, Dr. Zeitlin, the first representative of the Jewish Agency Economic Department in Buenos Aires, expressed his concern about CAIRA's procedure for approving candidates. "We have not found a maximum willingness to cooperate and receive assistance on the part of CAIRA management," he wrote.[142] Ephraim Avigur (Gorman), too, referred to CAIRA's work method in a March 1956 report to the Absorption Department.[143] He recounted that most of the work in Israel was being done by the JNF, the Jewish Agency Rural Settlement Department, and Rassco. In Argentina, the company continued to sell shares and make loans to immigrants on easy terms, which made it possible to expand the village. Its guiding principle was that it alone would select the candidates.[144] The severe inflation in Argentina had affected CAIRA and left it deeply in debt, mainly to Rassco. Against this background, Avigur suggested that the Jewish Agency step in and find Israelis who would like to move to the village—a proposal that was implemented in the end.[145]

Despite all the difficulties, Kefar Argentina proved to be a strong magnet for immigrants throughout the period under study here.[146] In early 1962, Moshe Kitron wrote in one of his many reports that Kefar Argentina was continuing to develop, despite all the problems and false starts, and was about to expand again.[147] The settlers there exemplified the class that all the sources analyzed thus far identify as harboring the main potential for immigration from Argentina—petty bourgeois families with limited means who found the way to surmount the many hurdles on the road to immigration. These are the difficulties reviewed in chapter 2: the rules of selective immigration, the problem of having to liquidate assets at a loss, fiscal issues such as the exchange rate and protective tariffs, matters of housing and employment, and other social and cultural obstacles.

An interesting aspect of this story of collective immigration from Argentina is the Argentinian Jewish establishment's scornful and dismissive attitude toward this group's achievements, the cold shoulder that the legation gave CAIRA at first, the opposition of the Zionist parties, and even the lack of significant coverage in the local Jewish press. The Zionist public discourse portrayed this group as though it occupied the lowest rung of Zionist endeavor. At the top of the hierarchy were the halutzim, an unchallenged source of pride for all Zionist circles. The capitalists boasted of their productive investments and saw their activity as a form of Zionist pioneering in every sense of the word. But in keeping with the classic Zionist scheme, the lower middle class was a stratum that needed a land of refuge, a class that had to be supported because its immigration was motivated mainly by distress. The saga of Kefar Argentina challenged that perception.

University-Educated Immigrants: The Physicians in the Negev

There was another collective social actor that was prominent among the middle-class immigrants from Argentina in these years—the 15% of them who were university educated and members of the liberal professions. A quarter of those in this category were physicians. An interesting fact that emerges from the database is that a majority of these immigrant-physicians from Argentina settled in the Israeli periphery. The severe shortage of medical professionals there and the organizational and legislative changes introduced to remedy the situation provide a partial explanation for this group's settlement choices. An illustrative example is the case of Dr. Jaime Derechinski (who later Hebraicized his name to Chaim Doron).[148]

In early 1952, the main office of the Histadrut-affiliated General Health Fund (Kupat Holim Kelalit, generally referred to simply as "Kupat Holim") in Israel received an unusual letter from a young physician in Argentina, Dr. Jaime Derechinski, who was planning to make aliya. Dr. Derechinski, who had just graduated from the medical school in Buenos Aires, had been an active Zionist as a teenager and served as the secretary of the Confederation of Zionist Youth in Argentina. In his letter, the young physician and his wife, Naomi, a registered nurse, asked whether positions could be found for them in one of the settlements of the northern Negev. Their request was approved by Dr. Leon Goldman, director of personnel for Kupat Holim. In April 1953, the couple arrived at the headquarters of Kupat Holim's Judea District in Rehovot, full of hope and in expectation of a speedy assignment to their jobs. The Negev was in dire need of doctors, and the population was in great misery. "I studied medicine in Argentina because I knew that the young State of Israel needed doctors," is what Professor Doron told me when I interviewed him.[149] His parents, who had come to an ICA colony in Argentina from Slonin in White Russia in the early twentieth century, followed their son and daughter-in-law to Israel. "I wanted to be near my close friends, but I was not interested in collective life. So I asked to settle near Kibbutz Mefalsim," he recalled. His friends and sister had been among the founders of that kibbutz.[150]

The young couple settled in Beer Sheva. He worked in primary care medicine in the Negev kibbutzim for fifteen years and treated David Ben-Gurion several times while he was living in Sede Boker. He established the first clinic for family medicine in Beer Sheva and trained doctors to work in frontier districts. He was also among the founders of the Institute for Higher Education in the Negev, which later became the Ben-Gurion University of the Negev, and one of the organizers of the Beer Sheva branch of OLEI (the Organization of Latin American Olim in Israel). In 1960, Kupat Holim sent him to study public health at the University of London. This program included visits to Norway and Denmark, where he investigated the structure of community medical services. After his return to Israel, he spent seven years as the senior Kupat Holim physician, served as administrator of Soroka Hospital in Beer Sheva, and finally was appointed executive director of Kupat Holim. He was considered an expert in public health and medical administration and developed these fields at Ben-Gurion University and later at Tel Aviv University. He was also among the founders of the National Institute for Health Policy Research.[151]

Doron's personal and professional background led him to devise a plan to encourage the immigration and absorption of physicians from Argentina and other countries of Latin America. The shortage of medical personnel in the frontier districts posed a major headache for Kupat Holim, which was expected to provide services throughout Israel. The unwillingness of physicians to leave urban centers such as Tel Aviv and Jerusalem for the Negev or Galilee led Doron to the conclusion that the only way to overcome the doctor shortage was to "import" them directly from overseas to the periphery, and especially the Negev. Thanks to his intimate acquaintance with Argentina, Doron came to believe that a project to encourage the immigration of physicians from Argentina and other Latin American countries had good prospects for success if drawn up in a systematic fashion rather than conducted on an ad hoc and individual basis. His plan included a detailed absorption track and was based on young doctors in their first years of residency, who would come to Israel in an organized group so as to ease their social absorption. Implementation of the plan required cooperation between the Jewish Agency (through PATWA) and Kupat Holim. As part of their absorption, the physicians, while learning Hebrew and then taking a special course to acquaint them with the conditions of medical work in Israel, would work in hospitals and be paid a salary that allowed their families to maintain a basic standard of living in Israel. His scheme was approved.[152]

Starting in 1956, groups of young doctors began coming to Israel from Latin America, most of them from Argentina, and the lion's share settled in Beer Sheva.[153] An item published in the *Jerusalem Post* on August 16, 1957, under the headline, "Doctors from Argentina Settle in Beersheba," reported the arrival of the second organized group.[154] In November 1957, the PATWA representative in Argentina, Pinchas Zamir, received permission from Yitzhak Wolfson, the director of PATWA, to begin organizing the third group of doctors, who would come to Israel in February 1958.[155] The flow increased in the 1960s, catalyzed by the program's affiliation with the Negev Central Hospital (today the Soroka Medical Center) in Beer Sheva, which employed the newcomers. In December 1961, Dr. Doron was quoted to the effect that 70% of the Argentinian physicians who had come to Israel in organized groups had settled in the country and were even more successful than anticipated. He noted in particular the four groups that had arrived in the country over the last two years as well as the fifth group of ten doctors, who, after completing their specialized training, had been assigned to frontier and development areas in the north and south.[156] An article published in the daily *Haboker* in March 1963 reported that a group of thirty doctors from Argentina had settled in Beer Sheva:

> The doctors and their wives are now in the family ulpan [Hebrew language classes] in Beer Sheva. Their approximately 30 children are attending the city's kindergartens and elementary schools. The plan for absorbing the doctors is extremely detailed and was prepared in advanced. The absorption track includes a year of study in Hebrew-language classes and an accelerated course to get the doctors used to the conditions of medical work in Israel. At the same time, the doctors are employed in one of the hospitals. Dr. Chaim Doron, the administrator of the Kupat Holim district that includes Beer Sheva, is himself an oleh from South America, and as such, is involved and cooperates unconditionally in their absorption program. There are now 320 families from South America living in Beer Sheva, more than half of them from Argentina. For financial reasons, many families are going to development regions. There are 25 families from South America in Dimona and 30 families in Eilat.[157]

The author of the *Haboker* article, Yitzhak Eisenberg, visited the ulpan in Beer Sheva. He heard details about the physicians from the director of the ulpan, Ophira Levy; from Dr. Chaim Izakovitz, the head of the Negev District of the Absorption Department; and especially from the Negev District coordinator of the Division for Immigrants from Western Countries and the university-educated Gedalyahu Gruman. Gruman, born in Lwow, had lived in Rosario for two decades before settling in Israel seven years earlier. Eisenberg spoke with several of the thirty Argentinian doctors, who told him about the reasons for their immigration and their plans for the coming years. Thirty-three-year-old Dr. Maximo Lionel Friedman had worked at the university hospital in Buenos Aires for eight years. As an identified Zionist, he had been an active member of the Maccabee social club and one of the founders of the Hehalutz-Lamerhav group in Argentina. He told the interviewer that anti-Semitism was on the rise in that country, as the Jewish doctors felt only too well in their daily contact with their non-Jewish colleagues in the hospitals, and that there were many obstacles to their professional advancement as well.[158]

An item that appeared in the daily *Davar* in February 1967 reported the impending arrival of sixty young physicians from South America, in three organized groups.[159] According to the article, this would be the largest group of immigrant-doctors in the past decade. The source for the information was again Dr. Doron (identified as the vice president of OLEI), speaking at a symposium on the history of Argentinian Jewry. Doron noted that 180 physicians had come to Israel in the last ten years, most of them from Argentina. He added that the groups that were on their way consisted of young people who wanted to settle in the Negev and development areas.[160]

"I think that the physicians' program was intended to satisfy two needs in one go," Doron said in our interview, "the need for physicians and the need for an immigrant-absorption infrastructure."[161] Professor Doron's own story is another example of the decisive importance of chain migration, with which we are familiar from other studies of immigration. The immigrant's personal contacts, the communications and relationships among families, friends, or other people from their hometowns, both in Argentina and in Israel, are decisive. Doron is an outstanding illustration of this point as well. His case also embodies an important element of the process, which is totally overlooked by quantitative studies: chain migration by university-educated young adults whose Zionist ideology was reinforced by the prospects for finding work in their field in Israel. Moreover, Doron's story, like the case of Kefar Argentina, reiterates that the most significant projects that drew immigrants from Argentina were those created by the immigrants themselves.

The End of the Pioneer Era

The late 1950s saw the start of a significant change in the aliya of members of Zionist youth movements; both its magnitude and proportion of total Jewish immigration from Argentina declined sharply. According to data of the Aliyah Department office in Buenos Aires, halutzim made up 48% of all immigrants from Argentina in 1956, 43% in 1957, 35% in 1958, 32% in 1959, 28% in the 1960s, and only 20% in 1961.[162] These percentages may be somewhat misleading, because they include not only the halutzim themselves, members of the pioneer youth movements and the young-adult brigades, but also children through age sixteen, processed by Youth Aliyah, and others who came with oleh visas, most of them the parents, siblings, and other relatives of halutzim. Nevertheless, the data indicate that this category of immigrants dropped precipitously as the 1950s progressed.

According to my database, only some 11% of the immigrants from Argentina in 1960 and 1961 were members of the pioneer youth movements. But roughly a fifth of the immigration in those years was organized by these movements. We may infer, then, that about half of the immigrants they processed were actually the families of halutzim. The drop in the pioneer aliya is also reflected in the age distribution of all immigrants in those years, and especially the smaller number of those just out of high school (ages eighteen to twenty). In those years, Argentinian Jewish immigration to Israel consisted mainly of young families, as reflected in the figures for their age, family status, and gender.

While pioneer aliya decreased, total immigration increased in the early 1960s and surpassed the mark of 500 people a year. Many of the immigrants were older and from the middle class, along with young professionals, office workers, and skilled tradesmen of various sorts—"Jewish nationalists without an ideological background," as one community leader put it.[163] This change troubled the officials in charge of immigration, because they had always seen the halutzim as the backbone of Jewish relocation to Israel. This perspective was based on the assumption, which was in fact accurate, that the halutzim "pull their parents and relatives after them."[164]

The historical documents highlight a series of objective difficulties that impeded immigration by halutzim in these years. The primary sources show that one source of the general decline in the ranks of the pioneer youth movements in the late 1950s was related to the parents of those who settled on kibbutzim and were unable to follow them. At a conference of Aliyah Department staff in January 1960, Avigur, himself an immigrant from Argentina, noted that in the first years after independence there were parents who were excited by the fact that their children had settled on to kibbutzim, but when the family pioneer became only "a correspondence child," after ten years of absence, the bitterness increased and began to leave its mark.[165] The Zionist Executive's report on its activities from 1956 to 1960 related that the office in Buenos Aires had taken note of the worrisome phenomenon of Argentinian halutzim who left Israel and returned to South America, mainly "due to the lack of absorption options for their parents, most of whom are members of the middle class."[166] As mentioned above, most prospective immigrants from Argentina came from this class, including a majority of the parents of the pioneers, and no concrete and adequate steps were being taken to accommodate them.

The frustration of the young adults and their parents was not the only cause for the weakening of the Zionist youth movements in the late 1950s and early 1960s. There were also ideological reasons, rooted in the stormy developments on the international scene in those years and especially in Latin America, notably the Cuban Revolution and Fidel Castro's rise to power in 1959. It should be noted that back then, at the height of the Cold War, the magic idea of the socialist liberation of Latin America enchanted many people all over the continent, especially the youth. These events must have influenced young Jews in Argentina as well. The following passage from a letter to the Aliyah Department by engineer Moshe Dayan, who was active in the right-wing Revisionist movement in Argentina, gives an impression of the ideological decay in the Zionist ranks that began in the late 1950s:

> Argentinian Zionist youth are full of admiration for Fidel Castro, because he fought in the Sierra Maestra, and also revere Patrice Lumumba, who was murdered by the colonialists. Only by employing an ideal as a means can we shatter the apathy that afflicts the young people, most of whom tend to affiliate with the non-Zionist Left.[167]

These assessments are liable to mislead the reader. The Zionist youth movements never enlisted all or even a majority of the young Jews in Argentina. In their glory years, the early 1950s, their membership never exceeded 7,000. The late 1950s and early 1960s saw a further weakening of the sector. But it is not true that most of the Jewish youth were affiliated with the anti-Zionist Left. In my opinion, the main factor that diluted the ranks of the halutzim was rooted in Jewish life in Argentina and the changes that took place then. Most young Jews preferred social organizations like Hebraica, Maccabee, and Hakoach, where they could find all the recreational amenities they might want: playing fields, swimming pools, and fancy clubrooms. The Zionist youth movements found themselves on the defensive, confronted by the growing aspiration of all Argentinian Jews, and especially the younger generation, for a comfortable life.

The Journey to Israel: The Immigrants Speak

In sources that document the journey to Israel, we encounter the voices of the immigrants themselves, their lifestyles, their desires, their motives for pulling up stakes and moving to the new country, and so forth. Here they are no longer a statistic. For example, the wealth of recollections and anecdotes about the *Flaminia*'s twenty-seven-day voyage to Israel yields the impression that all sorts of social and public relationships were woven on board the ship. Two days before it reached Haifa port, one of the women gave birth. Their sea passage was the first stage in their long process of absorption and integration into Israel. "The impression emerged that the voyage on the *Flaminia* was the beginning and an inseparable part of their absorption in Israel," noted one of the reports written while the ship was still at sea.[168]

The many experiences that were put into writing after this long journey can provide us with a broad picture of the immigrants. For example, some stories reflect the *Flaminia* passengers' attitudes toward religion and tradition. In the first week of the trip, a few young people wanted to season their meat-filled ravioli with grated cheese. They claimed that they were used to this and could not get used to a kosher diet; there were even voices raised against "religious coercion." The writer added that the graduates of Hashomer Hatza'ir evidently viewed mixing milk and meat as an ideological precept. He added that on the last Friday night of the voyage, about twenty people came to the Sabbath services—twice as many as usual—because "most of the olim have never been to a synagogue." And, he went on,

> These Jews from Argentina, of whom a decisive majority are secular, enjoy the davening of a fine cantor and moving celebrant, just as they melt with pleasure when they hear traditional melodies that stir the heartstrings, but they do not recite the prescribed prayers. At the Friday night Sabbath meal, 33 families sat down to dinner, without the ritual

> hand-washing or kiddush over the wine, without the table hymns and without the grace after meals. When their escort, Yedaya Hacohen from Jerusalem, recited the kiddush to a pleasant melody, precisely on key, dozens of heads were suddenly covered with sheets from newspapers.[169]

The Aliyah Department escort was astounded when the immigrants themselves set up a social committee and surprised by the number of volunteers who ran the activities it planned. They made a very positive impression on him. In his description of life on the ship, he noted that the high points of these activities were the Hebrew-language classes, a nursery school, and the publication of a daily newsletter. There were no fewer than nine Hebrew classes, at both the beginning and advanced levels. All the teachers were immigrants themselves. Two preschool classes were set up, meeting for three hours in the morning and another two after lunch. To mark the Purim festival, the children put on two plays (by the younger and older children) based on the book of Esther; they "stirred great emotion among the passengers and tears of joy could be seen in the eyes of many of those present," the escort wrote in his report. As for the newsletter, in Spanish, it included a daily news column translated from Italian, information about activities aboard the ship, various announcements for the immigrants, a literary corner, and even a humor column. A drama group put on several plays during the voyage.[170]

Representatives of the three kibbutz movements that were going to take in most of the immigrants boarded the *Flaminia* in Naples and accompanied the passengers the rest of the way to Haifa, making use of the time to take a close look at the new recruits. "This was competition for each and every body," reported the daily *Hatzofeh*. According to the article, it was the representative of the Kibbutz Artzi movement affiliated with Hashomer Hatza'ir, a native of Argentina and veteran member a kibbutz in Israel, who introduced himself as the grandson of Rabbi Akiva Rabinowitz-Te'omim of Poltava, one of the founders of the Ultraorthodox Agudat Yisrael, who consistently stood out among the three. "He seems to have inherited his zeal from his grandfather and employs it on behalf of his movement," added the reporter.[171]

The afternoon of Sunday, March 31, 1963, was far from routine in Haifa port. Three passenger ships docked that day, with a total of 1,800 passengers, among them more than a thousand from South America, mostly from Argentina. Many veteran residents who had emigrated from that continent stood waiting for the newcomers inside and outside the passenger terminal; the dominant language that day was Spanish. There had been lively movement around the port from the morning hours. Volunteers from OLEI met at the Shugurevsky department store near the port.[172] Its owners had emigrated from Argentina in 1921, and the father had founded the Haifa branch of OLEI.[173] The volunteers already had alphabetical lists of the new arrivals and where they would be settling. They were told that the passengers would begin disembarking at noon, but in the event the process was delayed until the evening.[174]

Dr. Chaim Bablik, a gastroenterologist who had excellent prospects for obtaining a respectable position in his specialty, emphasized "I am not running away from persecution. I am making aliya because from childhood I was raised in a Jewish nationalist home." Dr. Bablik spoke fondly about his grandfather, born in a Polish shtetl, who used to go around affixing mezuzahs to the doors of Jewish homes in Buenos Aires. His father was an active Zionist, and they had spoken Spanish, Yiddish, and Hebrew at home. "I was a member of a Zionist youth club and my friends and I waited impatiently for our legs to grow longer so we could make aliya." Later Bablik was admitted to medical school. He completed his studies with distinction and his income as a doctor increased from year to year. He was even appointed to a lectureship at the university. "I decided to liquidate all my affairs and make aliya. I will not have a spacious home here as I did in Buenos Aires, and I will have to work much harder here until I become established financially. But this has been my aspiration for my whole life—to live in the land of the Jews."[175]

Yaakov David Bickel, a fifty-eight-year-old building contractor, came to Argentina from Lithuania in 1925. Bickel had visited Israel in 1958 and gone so far as to purchase an orchard near Gedera. He said that he had been motivated to immigrate by both the difficult financial situation and the wave of anti-Semitism in Argentina. His son and daughter-in-law, who were still there, would follow when they finished their studies.[176] Another Jew, speaking a mixture of Yiddish, Russian, and Spanish, related how he had come to Argentina from Russia only four years earlier and was now taking up his wanderer's staff for the last time: "I am tired of imprisonment, persecution, and constant fear. I deserve a little peace. I am trying to find it in Israel. Do they need tailors in Migdal Ha'emeq? I am an expert tailor, 30 years in the trade, and when they send me to Migdal Ha'emeq I want to know whether I will find work there with needle and thread."[177] A young architect, a native of Buenos Aires and the grandson of immigrants from a town near Bialystok, said that he had never been a Zionist and was also far from leading a Jewish life. But one day he decided to leave the country he was born in:

> In the office where I work, a thriving firm of architects in one of the provincial towns of Argentina, a debate erupted about the Eichmann trial in Jerusalem. I said what I said about the Nazi murderer and my colleague, an architect of Spanish ancestry, came up to me during the argument and slapped me in the face, telling me in a voice choked with hostility: "It's too bad that Eichmann didn't burn all the Jews. But sooner or later we'll complete his essential work in our country as well." After my shock, I hit him back. But the blow seared my body and my soul: Is Argentina really my homeland or am I just a stranger there? And is it totally unthinkable the neo-Nazi organization Tacuara Movement, many of whose leaders are the sons of generals and millionaires, will attain key positions in the government? I told my family that I could not breathe the air of a country where I am treated as an inferior. And now I am on my way to Israel. I have signed up for Hebrew studies on one of the kibbutzim, I will obtain elementary knowledge of the language and become somewhat familiar with the architecture sector. The country is making great strides in construction and development and I will certainly find work.[178]

Mauricio Citrinovich, a furrier, whose parents had lived on one of the Baron Hirsch colonies, liquidated his assets and came with his wife and two children to settle on Kibbutz Bahan—a nonpartisan kibbutz with a largely Argentinian population. Citrinovich, who was one of the leaders of the Maccabee Sports Association in Buenos Aires, trembled as he spoke: "In the past year I have been in at least ten fights with Tacuara hooligans. How can one live in constant fear, always having to defend oneself? I do not want my children to be afraid that a swastika will be carved on their faces. In Israel, they will perhaps have to fight against an outside enemy; but in the country itself they will be free men."[179] Something similar was said by Walter Herzfeld, a native of Vienna who had immigrated to Argentina in the early 1950s and gone into the import-export business. Now, though, he had decided to relocate to Israel. In his opinion, Jews had no future in Argentina, neither politically nor economically.[180]

Pascual and Felisa Bichman, a young couple from Buenos Aires with two children, nine-year-old Pablo and three-year-old Monica, had registered in the Jewish Agency office in their hometown; their immigration file was handled by the engineer David Horowitz. In September 1963, the Bichman family came to Israel with 410 other immigrants, on board the Brazilian liner *Ana Neri*. "It was the incident of the Sirota girl [the nineteen-year-old Argentinian Jewish coed kidnapped and tortured by neo-Nazis in June 1962] that spurred us to make aliya," Felisa told me when I interviewed her at her home in Kiryat Ono in 2009. That had been a turning point in their thinking, because it led them to the conclusion that they had nothing to do in Argentina and that their children had no future in the country. "The truth is that we were thinking about our children when we made the final decision to make aliya."[181]

Pascual Bichman was among the ninety-eight tailors who left Argentina for Israel between January and November 1963; tailors were more likely to make the move than other artisans and constituted 20% of all artisan-immigrants. An item in *La Luz* emphasized that unlike the merchants, those who worked with their hands—tailors, silversmiths, welders, carpenters, electricians, and mechanics—were having no trouble finding jobs in Israel.[182] The same article stated that if the sixty office workers who had registered for immigration in the first quarter of 1963 mastered Hebrew quickly, they too would soon find work. Pascual Bichman found a job the day after he finished the ulpan on Kibbutz Givat Hashelosha. David Horowitz, the emissary who had overseen their immigration, had not understood why the Bichmans insisted on a kibbutz ulpan. "As a tailor," Horowitz promised, "you don't have to go through the delay of learning the language in order to make a living." But at the suggestions of their relatives in Israel, the young couple decided that they would spend their initial period in Israel on a kibbutz.[183]

In the last years before the Six-Day War (1964–67), the bulk of the immigrants from Argentina continued to be young working-class families. The proportion of artisans, skilled tradesmen, and laborers remained higher than their share in the Jewish community, while businesspeople were underrepresented. The percentage of liberal professionals rose slightly; most of them were young, and the vast majority settled in development areas. More than two-thirds of the immigrants went to kibbutzim and the periphery, and less than a third to the big cities and center of the country. During these years, the kibbutzim were still the main destination for Argentinian immigrants. The Aliyah Department representative in Buenos Aires reported that the immigrants during this period tended to be halutzim, physicians and their families (most of them headed for development areas), upper-class families, and others whose purpose was reunification.[184] There were also a fair number of capitalists whose immigration was handled by the Economic Department—more than 6% of all immigrants, whereas previously their percentage had not reached even 2% of the total. Nonetheless, the socioeconomic and occupational composition of the immigrations from Argentina in 1964–67 continued to resemble that of the 1950s.

There was some increase in the number of halutzim in those years. They accounted for less than 4% of the immigrants in 1963, but almost 6% during the next four years. An allusion to this rebound is provided by an article by Shraga Har-Gil that appeared in *Maariv* in March 1967, under the headline "Argentinians Are Coming to the Kibbutz."[185] The journalist described his meeting with young immigrants from Argentina, ages twenty to twenty-five, in the members' clubroom on Kibbutz Gazit in the Lower Galilee. They had arrived six months earlier and included six married couples. They were all graduates of universities in South America or had dropped out in order to link their future to the kibbutz:

> They brought with them the enthusiasm of South American students. Kindle a tiny match of an argument among them, and a huge bonfire of biting sharp debate will burn for hours and hours. Like most students at South American universities, they too are leftwing socialists, fans of Fidel Castro, of the sort that can be found at every student demonstration in Buenos Aires. They fought the police there, demonstrated for a larger budget for the universities, against an inflated budget for defense, and against many other issues.[186]

The journalist continued that some of the young people he met at Gazit had been active in the Communist Party, including José Salzman of Buenos Aires, the son of a wealthy textile merchant, who had attended a Jewish school (he later became a professor at the Technion). When he was seventeen, Salzman began looking for an outlet for his idealism. At the university where he studied he found only general revolutionary movements that were not prepared to address his needs as a Jew. So, along with other Jews of his age and status, he joined the Mordechai Anielewicz Brigade, which was affiliated with Hashomer Hatza'ir. Salzman and his comrades took part in protests against the war in Vietnam and in student demonstrations. The young immigrants on Gazit told the journalist that their movement published a monthly newsletter, of which about 9,000 copies were sold on the campuses. Its editors were students who suggested that settling on a kibbutz in Israel was the ultimate revolutionary solution.[187]

Immigration has many faces. There is no doubt that the immigrants' personal stories add an important dimension to the process studied here. Their experiences make it possible to understand the patterns that emerge from the quantitative data. The personal story unveils the immigrant's own perspective, which is essential for appreciating the complexity of the immigration process. The question, however, is whether a specific case is representative? Can it teach us about the general rule, or is it sui generis? We can arrive at an answer to this question only if each case is examined against the background of the bigger picture—the macro picture. For example, the personal details of Dr. Bablik, whose story was told here, are included among the 538 immigrants who sailed on the *Flaminia* and are part of my database. The database tells us that Bablik was thirty-eight, married, came with a "temporary resident" visa, had been processed through PATWA, and was planning to settle in Netanya.[188] The qualitative information provided by his recollections, together with the quantitative information from the database, reveal that his case—including his age, as well as his financial and family status—was not typical of the physician-immigrants from Argentina. He was not like most of the young doctors who had scant financial resources when they came to Israel with the goal of serving the population of the periphery, following the chain migration of physicians for professional and ideological motives.

Only a small fraction of the Argentinian Jewish immigration to Israel during these years was ideological. This was true of the halutzim who claimed to be returning to their old/new homeland, there to take part in the Zionist revolution by creating the new Jew and a new and just society. It was also true of the capitalists, who were proud of their productive investments and saw their economic activity as a Zionist and pioneering act in every sense. It was true of the lower-middle-class Jews who refused to be seen as a group in dire need of a country of refuge and needing to be supported because their motives were rooted in their existential distress. And it was true of the university-educated immigrants whose motives included their job prospects in Israel. But the case of Argentinian Jewry is also first and foremost one of ethnic migrants who, in the specific circumstances, and because of their ethnic and national bond to the national center, immigrated to Israel.

An analysis of the case of Argentinian Jewry reveals that even among the halutzim there were immigrants whose motives were rooted in the Argentinian reality. In all the paradigmatic cases analyzed in this chapter, we cannot miss the decisive importance of chain migration. The immigrant's personal contacts, the communications and relationships among families, friends, or others from their hometowns, acquaintances, members of the same profession or the same Zionist youth movement, both in Argentina and in Israel, were decisive for the decision to leave Argentina and settle in Israel. In the end, it was a personal and subjective choice. The individual stories recounted in this chapter highlight the importance for the decision of the primordial Jewish identity, the Pintele Yid: Zionist ideology and the aspiration to live a full Jewish life without persecution and without assimilation. The personal testimonies are less illustrative of the economic calculations behind aliya. But as we saw in the previous chapter, the demographics of the immigrants from Argentina reveal that, for most of them, it was the economic factor that tipped the scale in favor of immigration to Israel.

Summary and Conclusion

Argentinian Jewry as an Example of an Ethno-National Diaspora

I began this study of Argentinian Jewish immigration to Israel between 1948 and 1967 with the focus on the immigrants' country of origin. I treated Argentina as a separate geographic entity from which immigrants arrived in the period under study. I identified the unique characteristics of the Jewish community of Argentina, including its origins, history, and development. I examined the principle changes in various domains from the late nineteenth century to the 1960s. Finally, I looked at the demographic, economic, and social characteristics of the Jews of Argentina. All of this provided the qualitative and quantitative foundation for the analysis in the subsequent chapters.

My study shows that the ethnic and national element of the collective identity of Argentinian Jewry is undeniable. This element, however, did not prevent Argentina's Jews from leading an active Jewish life in the Diaspora and maintaining their life as an organized community, while at the same time underscoring their membership in the Argentinian nation. Most of them saw Argentina as their country and homeland and not only as the country to which they (or their parents) had chosen to migrate, as "temporary residents" in "a host country." This element of the collective identity of the Jews in Argentina stands out just as strongly as the ethnic component. This is an important conclusion of my study, because the picture that emerges challenges the classic Zionist dichotomy that the Jewish destiny in the Diaspora must lead either to total assimilation or to segregation and ghettoization. My findings indicate that the Jews found their place in Argentinian society but did not assimilate religiously or culturally; they integrated into civil society while finding a way to maintain and refashion their Jewish identity. This process is prominent from the late 1950s onward.

The Factors behind Argentinian Jewish Immigration to Israel

When I turned to why these Jews immigrated to Israel, I considered four main questions: What role was played by economic and political factors, both in Argentina and in Israel? How important was Argentinian anti-Semitism for the decision to relocate? What place did Zionist ideology occupy in the immigrants' considerations? Where did a Jewish education fit into their deliberations?

I found that there was a significant correlation between the situation in Argentina and the decision to leave for Israel. The political climate was a factor that spurred this movement but could also deter it. It was one of the most important motivations when the future was uncertain; on the other hand, it was also one of the main factors that could reduce the traffic significantly in periods of political stability. This was exemplified, for example, by the general elections in July 1963, which one of the emissaries subsequently labeled "the months of cancellations." The relief felt by the public at large after the elections had an immediate impact on the number of Jews who came to register for immigration at the Jewish Agency offices and the actual number of departures. The steep decline in the opening of immigration files when the situation stabilized because of the election results illustrates my point.

The health, good or bad, of the Argentinian economy was also a motivating factor. The documents highlight the decisive influence of the current situation on the decision to leave or stay. One emissary reported that during the strike by the metalworkers, new applicants showed up from among the Jews employed in the metal industry, but they stopped coming when the strike was over; similarly, textile workers were the main visitors to the Aliyah Department office in Buenos Aires when they went out on strike. He added that even the most polished absorption programs did not attract immigrants in the absence of some outside stimulus, which could be economic, political, or something else but was always associated with the applicant's own life.

Among the factors that motivated Argentinian Jews to opt to relocate to Israel, anti-Semitism does not seem to have been near the top of the list. At most it expedited the process in unfavorable economic and political circumstances. This is clear during the period studied here, when manifestations of anti-Semitism proliferated, but the number of those leaving for Israel rate declined. Anti-Semitism, in its various forms, was deeply embedded in all strata of Argentinian society. The anti-Semitic incidents described here were severe and had no parallel elsewhere on the continent. However, and despite the harsh expressions of anti-Semitism, the Jews of Argentina developed in a heterogeneous social milieu as full partners with the majority society, particularly after the late 1950s. Despite the rabid anti-Semitism, Argentinian Jews did not immigrate en masse, whether to Israel or other destinations. Out of a population of 300,000, only 5% moved to Israel in the two decades studied here. Most of them chose to stay in Argentina and participate in the processes of socioeconomic, cultural, and political modernization that marked Argentina during those years.

It turns out that pull factors, too, were not trivial, including the greater prosperity that marked Israel for much of the 1960s as well as the improvements in the absorption processes following the liberalization of the immigration and absorption system and the positive reports sent back to Argentina by tourists, acquaintances, and family members who had moved to Israel. The sources I analyzed give a clear impression of the decisive importance of chain migrations as an analytical category. The immigrant's personal contacts, the media, and the interplay with family, friends, fellow townspeople, professional colleagues, or members of the same Zionist youth movement, both in Argentina and in Israel, were of paramount importance for the process. This can be seen in all the paradigmatic cases presented in chapter 6.

These cases illustrate mainly the importance of the pintele yid, or "Jewish spark," which gives the impression that the germ of the idea to move to Israel came from a Jewish life and social circle. This corroborates another hypothesis of my study—the crucial role of a Jewish education, both formal and informal, in the decision. The most prominent datum in an Aliyah Department survey of the Jews of Buenos Aires is the importance of children's enrollment in Jewish schools: about 80% of those giving favorable consideration to the idea of immigrating to Israel were sending their children to Jewish schools. This point emerges both from the Borochov Youth, a classic example of pioneer aliya, and from the *Flaminia*, a classic case of ethnic immigrants with no strong ideological orientation. It is important to note that the individual element discovered in my study highlights the role of Zionist ideology and the aspiration to live a full Jewish life without persecution and assimilation, and downplays the importance of economic factors. But when we look at the overall composition of the immigrants from Argentina, it turns out that the economic issue was decisive for the majority. We must conclude, then, that there was a significant interaction along the spectrum from a strong Jewish identity to economics.

Analysis of the various cases also reveals that the theoretical assumptions and typological definitions of Zionist historiography are narrow and dichotomous and do not necessarily fit the present case, which is multifaceted. The Argentinian immigrants should be understood as a case of "ethnic immigrants" who, in certain circumstances, because of their ethnic and national ties to the national center immigrated to Israel. At the same time, they were also "migrants" propelled mainly by the push factors in Argentina. Even among the halutzim there were such migrants whose motives were grounded in circumstances in Argentina or in their personal problems.

Israeli Immigration Policy and Its Implementation

Two main questions arise when we track Israeli immigration policy and its implementation in Argentina: What principles were decisive in shaping that policy in the first two decades of the State? How did the policy formulated in Jerusalem by the Zionist Executive and the sovereign institutions of the State of Israel and its implementation affect individuals' decision to move to Israel?

I focused on the immigration policy that prevailed in Israel from 1948 to 1967. The discussion was based on a systematic use and critical analysis of the documents left behind by policy makers in Israel and in Argentina, in pursuit of the principles behind them. My main finding was that the establishment of Israel made absolutely no difference in how the Zionist policy makers viewed the issue. During the entire period covered, the organization and promotion of immigration were based on ideological arguments that called for unrestricted immigration and the ingathering of the exiles, and on the pragmatic necessity of fortifying the country and its security. In the Law of Return, the ideological principles were given a legislative embodiment that gave the final stamp of approval to the national exclusivity of immigration, on the basis of ethno-national principles, and expressed the state's obligation to unrestricted Jewish immigration and the ingathering of the exiles. But the country's citizens and the immigrants were in fact seen as an instrument for building the state; the welfare of the state and its development always took precedence over the welfare of the people.

This view of immigrants as a means for building the state was particularly prominent in the selective immigration policy that prevailed from the early 1950s. During the entire period under discussion here, the dimensions and composition of immigration were limited in accordance with economic, partisan-political, and cultural considerations. They also influenced absorption. A classic illustration is provided by the various absorption schemes, such as the "straight from the boat to the village" program, that were designed to promote population dispersal. This policy was adopted as a national goal and was carried out by the State in order to prevent the concentration of the population in urban areas and to increase settlement in frontier districts.

A significant turning point with regard to immigration and absorption policy came in the early 1960s. For the first time since independence, policy makers drafted concrete absorption programs with formal absorption tracks tailored to different categories of immigrants. The significant increase in immigration from the developed countries at this time illustrates this turning point; in its wake, the immigrants' social, demographic, and economic profile changed as well. The documents indicate that a major impetus for this change was the improvement in the Israeli economy, but even more important was the new attitude of the absorption agencies toward immigrants from the West, a result of the liberalization of the immigration and absorption systems that led to greater consideration of the newcomers' own needs.

The various departments of the Jewish Agency implemented the immigration policies set by the Israeli government and facilitated immigration from Argentina. My initial assumption was that the agency, and particularly its Aliyah Department, strongly influenced the patterns of immigration from Argentina. Its representatives dealt with candidates face to face and handled all the technical details of their immigration. As my study progressed, I reconstructed the work patterns of the bureaucracy in Argentina, with the goal of assessing the influence of immigration policy and its implementation on the actual traffic.

It turned out that the bureaucracy in Argentina did not realize the full immigration potential of that country's Jews. Its deficiencies, including a lack of coordination, tangled bureaucracy, and duplication of roles slowed down, delayed, and reduced the flow. The Aliyah Department's files are a mess. The strong influence of the officials' partisan affiliation is unmistakable. There are real ideological differences between the employees of the aliya apparatus—which was staffed by members of the National Religious Party (Hapo'el Mizrahi)—and representatives of the other departments and the embassy—most of which were under Mapai control.

Many factors that impeded immigration emerged from this study: the lack of readily available and up-to-date information for potential immigrants, the devaluation of the peso and problem of liquidating assets, travel expenses, housing conditions and the high cost of living in Israeli towns, not to mention the quotas that limited immigration from Argentina and the rest of South America. All these curtailed the flow from Argentina at a time when, as my sources indicate, broad circles of Argentinian Jewry, and especially the middle class, evinced increasing interest in coming to Israel.

The case of Argentinian Jewry exemplifies how immigration was organized and encouraged on the basis of doomsday scenarios about "the distressing situation of the Jews" and sometimes "the distressed state of Judaism," as painted by interested parties that represented Israel as a safe haven for all Jews. The representatives of the Aliyah Department, both in Israel and in Argentina, were people with a religious worldview, affiliated with the Religious Zionist movement that controlled the department after the establishment of the State. The documents show them to have been prophets of doom and redemption. In their eyes, aliya was always an escape from existential hardship. They demonstrated an honest and sincere desire for its success, sometimes in the form of plaintive cries to rescue the local Jews from desolation, economic misery, and anti-Semitism. Their reports tended to exaggerate the dangers lurking for Argentinian Jewry. The story of the *Flaminia* highlights the gap between the locals and the observant Israelis who oversaw the immigration process. For the Israelis and the Aliyah Department, the prime directive was to rescue the Jews of Argentina from spiritual annihilation. They simply could not fathom a Jewish community with national and Zionist feelings but a secular Jewish identity, whose members wanted to integrate into the host society while maintaining their Jewish sentiments as part of their Argentinian identity.

The representatives of the socialist parties in Israel, such as Moshe Kitron, also tended to exaggerate the perils lurking for Jews in Argentina. In their case, these assessments cannot be disconnected from their strong Borochovian worldview, a perspective that was widespread in Labor Zionist circles in both Argentina and Israel. It saw the Jews as an ethnic and cultural minority that was not integrated into a hostile Argentinian majority society, living as it were at on the slopes of a volcano, and evaluated their future accordingly. Time and again, however, developments in Argentina and the changes among the Jews proved that, despite the severe economic and political crises and manifestations of anti-Semitism, the Borochovian perspective did not correspond to the real world.

Despite the use of catastrophic arguments as a strategy to encourage immigration to Israel and the attempt to present the country as a refuge, during these years, immigration from Argentina was controlled and limited, mainly due to the policy of selective immigration. The selection procedure and individual processing spawned bureaucratic red tape that interfered with and delayed emigration from Argentina and reduced the number of immigrants. The bureaucracy was excessively cumbersome; the redundancy and foot-dragging generated by the disputes and confrontations over authority and the competition among the various departments interfered with effective implementation of the mission. This fact also significantly damaged the very concept of aliya emissaries and Argentinian Jews' image of the Jewish Agency. The bottom line is that the politicization, selective policy, and bureaucracy that marked the Jewish Agency had a negative impact on emigration from Argentina.

The Social and Demographic Pattern of the Immigrants from Argentina

In order to assess the impact of Israeli immigration policy and its implementation, I juxtaposed them with the number of immigrants and their demographics. Here the discussion was based on processing the aggregate quantitative data found in historical studies, censuses, reports, and surveys, and cross-checking them against the computer database I assembled for my research. The juxtaposition helped me study the selective nature of the immigration from Argentina. A comparison of the immigrants' age, family status, and occupations with those of the entire Jewish community in Argentina and of all immigrants to Israel in those years confirmed a key assumption of my study: the policy of selection affected the demographics of the newcomers, including those from Argentina.

The immigration from Argentina was concentrated among young families. Their distribution by age, origins, family structure, and occupation, as compared to all Argentinian Jewry, reflects economic and selective aliya. More than 60% of the immigrants from Argentina were of prime working age. They fit the traditional socioeconomic pattern—lower-middle-class people who, unlike most Jews, were not managing to advance on the economic ladder. In the 1960s, about two-thirds of all employed Jews in Argentina worked in commerce, petty industry, clerical jobs, and the liberal professions; in other words, they belonged to the white-collar middle class. By contrast, most of the immigrants held blue-collar jobs. This social and occupational pattern coincided perfectly with the goals of Israeli immigration policy in those days. The places in Israel to which the new arrivals from Argentina were directed provides further corroboration of this conclusion: close to two-thirds of them settled on kibbutzim or in development regions, while only one-third went to the cities and the center of the country.

This juxtaposition of immigration policy with the number and demographics of the immigrants from Argentina enhanced my understanding of the key issues. A reconstruction of the sociodemographics teaches us more about the immigrants' motives and characteristics. The case of immigration from Argentina and its social composition suggest the significant weight of push factors during the period covered by this study, especially in the 1960s, and notably the tidal wave of 1963. Here too, the case of Argentinian Jewry disproves the sweeping categories and generalizations and undercuts the terms deeply embedded in the Zionist discourse, such as "countries of distress" and "wealthy countries." The immigrants who came from Argentina were considered to be in the latter group. The assumption behind the uniform treatment of all the wealthy countries was that immigrants from there were not coming to escape disaster but solely for ideological and personal reasons.

As we have seen here, however, the broad and arbitrary distinction between "countries of distress" and "wealthy countries" is not appropriate for Argentina. The aliya bureaucracy classed it as a wealthy country, when it actually showed many features of a country of distress. The truth is that Argentinian Jewry fell somewhere between these two poles. Moreover, as we have seen, only a few Argentinian immigrants came exclusively for ideological reasons; the majority were migrants propelled by other considerations. This was especially prominent in the organization and composition of the mass wave of 1963. Here the attempt to paint it as an organized rescue mission collided with the stubborn refusal by Argentinian Jewry to be seen as a community that was in need of a safe haven and that had to be supported financially because its immigration was rooted in distress. The story of Kefar Argentina, another example of the Jewish middle class with limited means, challenged that perspective in the early 1950s.

The individual story of an immigrant or a group of immigrants, as a key analytical unit for research, was found to be essential for understanding the process in its full complexity. Personal stories add an important aspect—that of the individual—and can provide a better understanding of the patterns that are reflected in the numerical data. In fact, the individual aspect is essential, because it makes it possible to focus on the main social agent—the immigrants themselves. It must not be forgotten that, at the end of the day, the decision to leave Argentina for Israel was personal and subjective. This led me to the additional effort needed to collect primary sources that provide the immigrants' retrospective view of their experience. I probed their initial attitudes and uncovered their characteristics and reasons for immigrating to Israel, as they emerged in paradigmatic cases that represent the various categories of immigrants. The combination of individual stories and quantitative data makes it possible to paint an authentic portrait of an exceptional instance on the Israeli scene of the 1950s and 1960s.

The immigration of Argentinian Jews to Israel between 1948 and 1967 should be understood not only against the background of the social and political realities in their country of origin, but also against that of the mass immigration to Israel in its first decades. The present study aspires to do justice to this relatively small group and give its members their rightful place in history. The annals of immigration to Eretz Israel are incomplete without the Argentinian Jews who came to Israel, settled in, and struck deep roots in the young state.

Finally, it is important for me to note that my research embodies the significant contribution that historians can make to the study of the phenomenon of immigration and especially that to Israel. The individual, unique, and particular aspect that I have tried to reveal is vital for understanding the process of migration, but only if it is set within the general macro and quantitative frame. Separately, the individual picture remains only a collection of anecdotes, and the quantitative picture fails to explain the phenomenon in sufficient depth. The databases I constructed for the present study made it possible for me to overlap the two circles, the quantitative and the qualitative, and probe more deeply into the immigration process, in all its stages and aspects. I believe that this unique methodology demonstrates the need for broader and deeper interdisciplinary cooperation among historians, sociologists, and demographers in the study of Jewish immigration to Israel.

NOTES

Introduction

1. The data are based on the various numbers of the Statistical Abstract of Israel, published each year by the Central Bureau of Statistics.
2. Gur Alroey, *An Unpromising Land: Jewish Migration to Palestine in the Early Twentieth Century* (Stanford, CA: Stanford University Press, 2014), 1–19.
3. www.themarker.com/news/1.2459454.
4. http://hdr.undp.org/en/countries/profiles/ISR.
5. Sergio DellaPergola, "Some Reflections about Migration in Israel: Comparative Aspects," *Hagira* 1 (2012): 6, 13, 20–21 [Heb.], 6. Margalit Shilo, "The Good of the People or the Good of the Land? The Zionist Movement's Attitude towards Aliya in the Time of the Second Aliya," *Katedra* 46 (1987): 109–22 [Heb.]; Aviva Halamish, *Dual Race against Time: Zionist Immigration Policy in the 1930s* (Jerusalem: Yad Ben-Zvi, 2006) [Heb.]; Joseph Heller, *The Struggle for the Jewish State* (Jerusalem: Shazar Center, 1985) [Heb.]; Hagit Lavsky, "The Surviving Remnant and the Establishment of the State: An Opportunity That Was Used," *Katedra* 55 (1990): 175–81 [Heb.]; Yoav Gelber, "From 'Do Not Go Up' to the Law of Return: Vacillation and Changes in the Zionist Attitude towards Aliya," in *Ingathering of Exiles: Aliyah to the Land of Israel Myth and Reality*, ed. Devora Hacohen (Jerusalem: Shazar Center, 1998), 249–81 [Heb.]; Moshe Lissak, Mass Immigration in the *Fifties: The Failure of the Melting Pot Policies* (Jerusalem: Mosad Bialik, 1999); Devora Hacohen, *Immigrants in Turmoil: Mass Immigration to Israel and Its Repercussions in the 1950s and After*, trans. Gila Brand (Syracuse, NY: Syracuse University Press, 2003); Ephraim Yaar and Zeev Shavit, eds., *Trends in Israeli Society* (Tel Aviv: Open University, 2001), 1: 162–78 and 365–486 [Heb.]; Avi Picard, *Cut to Measure: Israel's Policies Regarding the Aliyah of North African Jews, 1951–1956* (Beer Sheva: Ben-Gurion Institute and Ben-Gurion University of the Negev, 2013) [Heb.].
7. "Ingathering of the Exiles Day," *Dappei Aliyah* 7 (1949/50): 13–20.
8. David Ben-Gurion, "We Have Reached a Million," *Dappei Aliyah* 7 (1949/50): 3.
9. "Voice of Israel Broadcasts," *Davar*, December 16, 1949, 27.
10. Yitzhak Rafael, "On Ingathering of the Exiles Day," *Dappei Aliyah* 7 (1949/50): 8–12. See also Rafael, *Not*

Easily Came the Light (Jerusalem: Idanim, 1981), 128–32 [Heb.].

11. Moshe Sicron, "The Mass Aliya: Dimensions, Characteristics, and Influence on the Demographic Structure of Israel," in *Immigrants and Transit Camps, 1948–1952*, ed. Mordechay Naor (Jerusalem: Yad Ben-Zvi, 1986), 31–32. [Heb.]
12. Baruch Duvdevani, "Some Problems of Aliya," *Dappei Aliyah* 30 (1956): 5–6.
13. Shmuel N. Eisenstadt, "Aliyah ve-hagirah, kavim le-tipologia sotziologit" (Aliyah and Hagirah: The Outline of a Sociological Typology), *Metzudah* 7 (1954): 83–91; Roberto Bachi, *The Population of Israel* (Paris: CICRED; Jerusalem: Hebrew University, 1977); Sammy Smooha, *Israel: Pluralism and Conflict* (London: Routledge and Kegan Paul, 1978), 48–69; Sergio DellaPergola, "The Global Context of Migration to Israel," in *Immigration to Israel: Sociological Perspectives*, ed. Elazar Leshem and Judith T. Shuval (New Brunswick, NJ: Transaction, 1998), 51–92; Uzi Rebhun and Chaim Isaac Waxman, "The 'Americanization' of Israel: A Demographic, Cultural, and Political Evaluation," *Israel Studies* 5, no. 1 (2000): 65–91.
14. In recent years, studies in various disciplines (notably sociology, anthropology, and history) have laid the historiographical groundwork and basic research framework for a study of migration as it relates to Israel. See, for example, Rivka Reichman, "Immigration to Israel: A Mapping of Trends and Empirical Studies, 1990–2006," *Israeli Sociology* 10, no. 2 (2009): 339–80 [Heb.]; Adriana Kemp and Rivka Reichman, *Migrants and Workers: The Political Economy of Labor Migration in Israel* (Jerusalem: Van Leer Jerusalem Institute and Hakibbutz Hame'uchad, 2008) [Heb.]; Elana Gomel, *The Pilgrim Soul: Being Russian in Israel* (Amherst, NY: Cambria Press, 2009); Galia Sabar, *We're Not Here to Stay: African Migrant Workers in Israel and Back in Africa* (Tel Aviv: Tel Aviv University, 2008) [Heb.]; Picard, *Cut to Measure*. What all of these have in common is their focus on the individual immigrant as the unit of analysis.
15. William Safran, "Diasporas in Modern Societies: Myths of Homeland and Returns," *Diaspora* 1, no. 1 (1991): 83–99; Gabriel Sheffer, "From Diasporas to Migrants—From Migrants to Diasporas," in *Diasporas and Ethnic Migrants: Germany, Israel, and Post-Soviet Successor States in Comparative Perspective*, ed. Rainer Munz and Rainer Ohliger (Portland, OR: Frank Cass, 2003), 21–36.
16. Jeffrey Lesser and Raanan Rein eds., *Rethinking Jewish-Latin Americans* (Albuquerque: University of New Mexico Press, 2008), 1–22; Haim Avni et al., eds., *Pertenencia y alteridad: Judíos en/de América Latina, cuarenta años de cambios* (Madrid: Iberoamericana, 2011); Judit Bokser-Liwerant, Sergio DellaPergola, Haim Avni, Margalit Bejarano, and Leo Senkman, introduction to "Cuarenta años de cambio: Transiciones y paradigmas," Avni, *Pertenencia y alteridad*, 13–83; Adriana Brodsky and Raanan Rein, eds., *The New Jewish Argentine: Facets of Jewish Experiences in the Southern Cone* (Leiden: Brill, 2013), 1–5.
17. Haim Avni, "Cuarenta años, el contexto histórico y desafíos a la investigación"; Avni, *Pertenencia y alteridad*, 102–11.

18. Raanan Rein, "Waning Essentialism: Latin American Jewish Studies in Israel," in *Identities in an Era of Globalization and Multiculturalism*, ed. Judit Bokser-Liwerant et al. (Leiden: Brill, 2008), 109–24; Jeffrey Lesser and Raanan Rein, "Challenging Particularity, Jews as a Lens on Latin American Ethnicity," *Latin American and Caribbean Ethnic Studies* 1, no. 2 (2006): 249–63.
19. Raanan Rein, ed., *Árabes y Judíos en Iberoamérica: Similitudes, diferencias y tensiones* (Seville: Fundación Tres Culturas, 2008); José Moya, "The Jewish Experience in Argentina in a Diasporic Comparative Perspective," in Brodsky and Rein, *New Jewish Argentine*, 7–29; Margalit Bejarano and Edna Aizenberg, eds., *Contemporary Sepharadic Identity in the Americas: An Interdisciplinary Approach* (Syracuse, NY: Syracuse University Press, 2012); Raanan Rein and Edna Aizenberg, "Introduction: Going Beyond, Going Against—New Studies on Jewish Latin Americans," *Estudios Interdisciplinarios de América Latina y el Caribe* 23, no. 1 (2013): 7–10; Sandra McGee Deutsch, "Changing the Landscape: The Study of Argentine-Jewish Women and New Historical Vistas," in Lesser and Rein, *Rethinking Jewish-Latin Americans*, 161–86.
20. Judit Bokser Liwerant, "Being National, Being Transnational: Snapshots of Belonging and Citizenship," in *Shifting Frontiers of Citizenship: The Latin American Experience*, ed. Mario Sznajder, Luis Roniger, and Carlos Forment (Leiden: Brill, 2013), 343–66; Leonardo Senkman, "Klal Ysrael at the Frontiers: The Transnational Jewish Experience in Argentina," in *Identities in an Era of Multiculturalism: Latin America in the Jewish World*, ed. Judit Bokser Liwerant, Eliezer Ben-Rafael, Yossef Gorny, and Raanan Rein (Leiden: Brill, 2008), 125–50; Leonardo Senkman, "The Latin American Diasporas: New Collectives Identities and Citizenship Practices," in Sznajder, Roniger, and Forment, *Shifting Frontiers of Citizenship*, 385–93; Sergio DellaPergola, "National Uniqueness and Transnational Parallelism: Reflections on the Comparative Study of Jewish Communities in Latin America," *Judaica Latinoamericana* 7 (2013): 79–84.
21. Martin Howard Sable, *Latin American Jewry: A Research Guide* (Cincinnati: Hebrew Union College Press, 1978); Judith Laikin Elkin and Ana Lya Sater, eds., *Latin American Jewish Studies: An Annotated Guide to the Literature* (New York: Greenwood Press, 1990); Judith Elkin, ed., "Bibliography of Books and Articles in Latin American Jewish Studies, 1991–1996" (1997); Judith Elkin, "Recent Publications in Latin American Jewish Studies: Current Bibliography of Latin Jewish Studies 1997–1998" (1999); AMILAT, *Judaica Latinoamericana*, vols. 1–6 (Jerusalem: Magnes Press, 1988, 1993, 1997, 2001, 2005, 2009, 2013); www.utexas.edu/cola/orgs/lajsa/—LAJSA (Latin American Jewish Studies Association), College of Liberal Arts, University of Texas at Austin; www.amia.org.ar/index.php/linker/default/index/area/38—AMIA (comunidad judía), Buenos Aires.
22. D. Schers and H. Singer, "The Jewish Communities of Latin America: External and Internal Factors in Their

Development," *Jewish Social Studies* 39 (1977): 241–58; F. Peñaloza, "Pre-Migration Background and Assimilation of Latin-American Immigrants in Israel," *Jewish Social Studies* 34 (1972): 122–39; Robert Soldinger, *The Absorption of Latin-American Immigrants in Kibbutzim* (Rehovot: Settlement Study Center, 1981), 1–61; Donald L. Herman, *The Latin American Community of Israel* (New York: Praeger, 1984); Luis Roniger, "The Latin American Community of Israel: Some Notes on Latin American Jews and Latin American Israelis," *Israel Social Science Research* 6, no. 1 (1988): 63–72; Batia Siebzehner, "Un imaginario inmigratorio: Ideología y pragmatismo entre los latinoamericanos en Israel," in Avni, *Pertenencia y alteridad*, 389–414.

23. Luis Roniger and Gabriel Jarochevsky, "Los Latinoamericanos en Israel: La Comunidad Invisible," *Reflejos* 1 (1992): 39–49.
24. David Ben Israel, *De América Latina a Israel, al Kibutz* (Merhavia: Merhavia Press, 1978); Florinda Goldberg and Yosef Rozen, eds., *Los Latinoamericanos en Israel: Antología de una aliá* (Buenos Aires: Contexto 1988). See also Shlomo Bar-Gil, *We Started with a Dream* (Beer Sheva: Ben-Gurion University, 2005) [Heb.]; Shlomo Bar-Gil, *Youth: Vision and Reality; From Dror and Gordonia to Ichud Habonim in Argentina, 1934–1973* (Ramat Ef'al: Yad Tabenkin, 2007) [Heb.]; Pedro Goldfarb, *First Latino-American Garin of Hashomer Hatzair: Negba 1946–1949; The Fulfilment of the Dream* (Givat Haviva: Yad Yaari, 2006) [Heb.]; David Horowitz, "The Jewish Community in Argentina and Aliya from It, 1961–1973" (PhD diss., Tel Aviv University, 2006) [Heb.].
25. Jacob Tsur, *The Fourth Credentials: The First Diplomatic Mission in South America* (Tel Aviv: Sifriyat Maariv, 1981), 137 [Heb.].
26. Gur Alroey, "Aliya to America? A Comparative Look at Jewish Mass Migration, 1881–1914," *Modern Judaism: A Journal of Jewish Ideas and Experience* 28, no. 2 (2008): 109–33.
27. Gur Alroey, "'Olim,' 'Immigrants,' and 'Refugees': Semantic Avatars of the Word Oleh in Zionist Thought," in *Milestones: Essays in Jewish History*, ed. Immanuel Etkes, David Assaf, and Yosef Kaplan (Jerusalem: Shazar Center, 2015), 347–61 [Heb.].
28. Ibid., 348–49.
29. Gur Alroey, *Bread to Eat and Clothes to Wear: Letters from Jewish Migrants in the Early Twentieth Century* (Detroit: Wayne State University Press, 2011), 12.
30. *Dappei Aliyah* 15 (1950/51): 31; "Excerpts from Remarks by Yitzhak Rafael at a Press Conference in Jerusalem on July 1, 1951," *Dappei Aliyah* 16 (1950/51): 1–5.
31. Activity Report, 1946/47–1950/51, submitted to the 23rd Zionist Congress, August 1951, CZA K98 XXIII, pp. 500–21; statistics on PATWA activity, 1957–58, CZA S6/6594.
32. Jacob Tsur to Walter Eytan, "Organization and Encouragement of Immigration from the Latin American Countries," October 13, 1949, Israel State Archives (hereafter ISA), gimel-13/5558.
33. "The Coordinating Committee," *Dappei Aliyah* 13 (1949/50): 14–15.
34. During the course of my research I interviewed more than forty individuals, including immigrants of

every category, emissaries, and some who had returned to Argentina. I found more than one hundred letters from immigrants in the personal archives of Dr. Mordechai Ben-Avir. Ben-Avir moved to Israel in the early 1950s and later served as the director of the PATWA office in Buenos Aires in the 1960s. He kindly gave me access to his personal archives, which includes letters from people whose immigration he organized, as well as reports, letters, press clippings, films, and more.

35. Cited henceforth as "10,487 Database."
36. During the stage of collecting materials for this study, I discovered that the Central Zionist Archives (CZA) has the documents of Jewish Agency departments only to the end of 1962. The academic advisor at the CZA informed me that the bulk of the later documents I sought are still at the Jewish Agency Logistics Center in Tserifin (cited hereafter as "JAFI Logistics Center").
37. Samuel L. Baily, "Chain Migration of Italians to Argentina: Case Studies of the Agnonesi and the Sirolesi," *Studi emigrazione/Etudes migrations* 19, no. 65 (1982): 73–91; Samuel L. Baily, *Immigrants in the Lands of Promise: Italians in Buenos Aires and New York City, 1870–1914* (Ithaca, NY: Cornell University Press, 1999); Jose C. Moya, *Cousins and Strangers: Spanish Immigrants in Buenos Aires, 1850–1930* (Berkeley: University of California Press, 1998).

Chapter 1

1. Gino Germani, *Política y sociedad en una época de transición: De la sociedad tradicional a la sociedad de masas* (Buenos Aires: Editorial Paidos, 1966); Francis Korn, *Buenos Aires: Los huéspedes del 20* (Buenos Aires: Editorial Sudamericana, 1974); James R. Scobie, *Revolution on the Pampas: A Social History of Argentine Wheat, 1860–1910* (Austin: University of Texas Press, 1964); Fernando J. Devoto, "Del crisol al pluralismo: Treinta años de historiografía sobre las migraciones europeas a la Argentina," in *Movimientos migratorios: Historiografía y problemas*, ed Fernando J. Devoto (Buenos Aires: Centro Editor de América Latina, 1991), 15–47; Diego Armus, "Diez años de historiografía sobre la inmigración masiva a la Argentina," *Estudios Migratorios Latinoamericanos* 4 (1986): 431–60.
2. Ira Rosenwaike, "The Jewish Population of Argentina, Census and Estimate, 1887–1947," *Jewish Social Studies* 22, no. 4 (1960): 205.
3. J. Lestschinsky, "Jewish Migrations 1840–1946," in *The Jews: Their History, Culture, and Religion*, ed. Louis Finkelstein (Philadelphia: Jewish Publication Society, 1949), 1198–238; Haim Avni, *Argentina and the Jews: A History of Jewish Immigration* (Tuscaloosa: University of Alabama Press, 1991), 241.
4. Avni, *Argentina and the Jews*, 21–44.
5. Ibid.
6. Haim Avni, "A Failed Project? Towards a Balance of Jewish Agriculture in Argentina," in *Emigration and Settlement in Jewish and General History: A Collection of Essays*, ed. Avigdor Shinan (Jerusalem: Shazar Center, 1982), 314 [Heb.].
7. Rosenwaike, "Jewish Population of Argentina," 195–214.
8. Jacob Tsur, "Memorandum on the ICA Settlement Project in Argentina

and Brazil," January 18, 1951, ISA, hettzade 55/1, 6 [Heb.].

9. Sebastián Klor, "Ser judío / sionista / argentino: La experiencia histórica y socioeconómica de los inmigrantes judíos en Córdoba, 1901–1950," *Junta Provincial de Historia de Córdoba* 24 (2007): 55–71; Rosenwaike, "Jewish Population of Argentina," 197–200.

10. Victor A. Mirelman, *En búsqueda de una identidad: Los inmigrantes judíos en Buenos Aires, 1890–1930* (Buenos Aires: Milá, 1988), 7.

11. Margalit Bejarano, "Fuentes para la historia de los sefaradíes en la Argentina," *Sefárdica* 9 (1986): 99–109; Margalit Bejarano, "Sephardic Communities in Latin America: Past and Present," *Judaica Latinoamericana* 5 (2005): 9–26.

12. Avni, *Argentina and the Jews*, 93–127.

13. Ibid., 128–74; Alfredo José Schwarcz, *Los judíos de habla alemana en la Argentina* (Buenos Aires: Grupo Editor Latinoamericano, 1991).

14. Avni, *Argentina and the Jews*, 175–95, 241; Leonardo Senkman, *Argentina: La Segunda Guerra Mundial y los refugiados indeseables, 1933–1945* (Buenos Aires: Grupo Editor Latinoamericano, 1991); Avraham Milgram, ed., *Entre la aceptación y el rechazo: América Latina y los refugiados judíos del nazismo* (Jerusalem: Yad Vashem, 2003).

15. Haim Avni, "Cuarenta años, el contexto histórico y desafíos a la investigación," in *Pertenencia y alteridad: Judíos en/de América Latina, cuarenta años de cambios*, ed. Haim Avni et al. (Madrid: Iberoamericana, 2011), 95.

16. Haim Avni, "'Majority Societies' in Jewish Diasporas: Latin American Experience," in *Transnationalism: Diasporas and the Advent of a New (Dis)order*, ed. Eliezer Ben-Rafael and Yitzhak Sternberg (Boston: Brill, 2009), 337–45.

17. Mordecai Alperson, *Thirty Years of Jewish Settlement in Argentina* (Tel Aviv: Hevrah, 1930), 60 [Heb.].

18. Simón Weill, *Población israelita en la República Argentina: Conferencia pronunciada el 23 de Octubre de 1935* (Buenos Aires: Bene Berith, 1936); Lestschinsky, "Jewish Migrations 1840–1946"; Arieh Tartakower, *Jewish Migration in the World* (Jerusalem: Institute for Jewish Higher Education, 1947) [Heb.].

19. Rosenwaike, "Jewish Population of Argentina," 195–214.

20. Sergio DellaPergola, "Cuántos somos hoy?," in Avni, *Pertenencia y alteridad*, 311.

21. Uziel Schmelz and Sergio DellaPergola, *The Structure of Latin American Jewry: The Demographics of the Jews in Argentina and Other Countries in Latin America* (Tel Aviv: David Horowitz Institute for the Research of Developing Countries, Tel Aviv University, 1974), 23 [Heb.].

22. Ibid., 28.

23. *American Jewish Year Book*, vol. 61 (1960), 183; vol. 72 (1971), 291–92.

24. Sergio DellaPergola, "National Uniqueness and Transnational Parallelism: Reflections on the Comparative Study of Jewish Communities in Latin America," *Judaica Latinoamericana* 7 (2013): 79–84.

25. *Israel Central Bureau of Statistics, Immigration to Israel, 1948–1972*, Part 1: *Annual Data* (Jerusalem: CBS, 1973) [Heb.].

26. Yehoshua Wolberg, "On the Prospects for Aliya from Argentina: An Official Summary of a Visit to Argentina

on Behalf of the Jewish Agency, in August 1963," October 1963, ISA, hettzade 11/2150 [Heb.].

27. Ibid.

28. E. Ross, "A Quick Look at South American Jewry: We Overdid Our Estimates of the Risks and Prospects" (undated), JAFI Logistics Center 2067 [Heb.]. On all emigration from Argentina in those years, to various destinations, see the works cited in note 30 below.

29. Yehoshua Wolberg, "Critical Notes on the Problem of Aliya from Argentina" (Hebrew), October 22, 1965, JAFI Logistics Center 2067.

30. Enrique Oteiza, "Emigración de profesionales, técnicos y obreros calificados argentinos a los Estados Unidos: Análisis de las fluctuaciones de la emigración bruta julio 1950 a junio 1970," *Desarrollo Económico* 10, no. 39/40 (1970–71): 429–54; A. Marshall, "Emigration of Argentines to the United States," in *When Borders Don't Divide: Labor Migration and Refugee Movements in the Americas*, ed. Patricia R. Pessar (New York: Center for Migration Studies, 1988), 129–41; Juan Carlos Zuccotti, *La emigración argentina contemporánea (a partir de 1950)* (Buenos Aires: Plus Ultra, 1987); A. Pellegrino, "Tendencias de la migración internacional en América Latina y el Caribe en la segunda mitad del siglo XX," in *Patrones migratorios internacionales en América Latina*, ed. Enrique Oteiza (Buenos Aires: Eudeba 2010), 27–40.

31. L. Calvelo, "Tendencias y patrones de la emigración argentina entre 1960 y 2010," in *Más allá de la fuga de cerebros: Movilidad, migración y diásporas de argentinos calificados*, ed. L. Luchilo (Buenos Aires: Editorial Universitaria de Buenos Aires, 2011), 69–91.

32. Avni, *Argentina and the Jews*, 15.

33. Schmelz and DellaPergola, *Structure of Latin American Jewry*, 131.

34. Ibid., 135–36.

35. Ibid., 134.

36. Avni, *Argentina and the Jews*, 16–17.

37. For illuminating statistics that exemplify this change, see M. Benarie, *The Historical Development of Jewish Commerce and Industry in Buenos Aires: A Jubilee Book—A Summary of 50 Years of Jewish Life in Argentina* (Buenos Aires: Idische Zeitung, 1940), 267–90 [Yiddish].

38. Moshe Kitron, "Memorandum for David Ben-Gurion, Re: South American Jewry," November 14, 1952, Central Zionist Archives, personal papers A494/11 [Heb.].

39. Schmelz and DellaPergola, *Structure of Latin American Jewry*, 119–20.

40. Leonardo Senkman, "Ser judío en Argentina: Las transformaciones de la identidad nacional," in *Identidades judías: modernidad y globalización*, ed. Paul Mendes-Flohr, Yom Tov Assis, and Leonardo Senkman (Buenos Aires: Centro Internacional para la Enseñanza, Universitaria de la Cultura Judía; Ediciones Lilmod, 2007), 405–7, 429.

41. For a comprehensive survey of these organizations, see Avni, *Argentina and the Jews*, 47–53, 65–67, 70, 86–91.

42. Ibid., 43–47. See also Bejarano, "Los sefaradíes en la Argentina," 143–60.

43. Senkman, "Ser judío en Argentina," 429–36; Tzvi Schechner, "'Kehile,' un concepto común heredado: La creación de organizaciones comunitarias sobre la base de 'Asociación de Entierro' en el judaísmo ashkenazí

de Buenos Aires y México, D.F.," in AMILAT, *Judaica Latinoamericana* (Jerusalem: Magnes Press, 1988), 115–28.

44. Silvia Schenkolewski-Kroll, "La 'conquista de las comunidades': El movimiento sionista y la comunidad Ashkenazi de Buenos Aires (1935–1949)," *Judaica Latinoamericana* 2 (1993): 197–99; Haim Avni, "The Origins of Zionism in Latin America," in *The Jewish Presence in Latin America*, ed. Judith Laikin Elkin and Gilbert W. Merkx (Boston: Allen and Unwin, 1987), 135–55; Judit Bokser Liwerant, "Los judíos de América Latina: Los signos de las tendencias; Juegos y contrajuegos," in Avni, *Pertenencia y alteridad*, 127–28; Senkman, "Ser judío en Argentina," 433.

45. Activity Report, Tevet 5716 to Nisan 5720 (January 1956–March 31, 1960), submitted to the 25th Zionist Congress, Jerusalem, December 1960–January 1961, Central Zionist Archives, K105 XXV, 21–22.

46. "What We Learned from the Elections to the Zionist Congress" [Yiddish], *Di Fraye Yugent*, November 1, 1946, 1–3 (original in Spanish).

47. Silvia Schenkolewski-Kroll, *The Zionist Movement and the Zionist Parties in Argentina, 1935–1948* (Jerusalem: Magnes Press, 1996), 223 [Heb.].

48. "New Methods Yield Great Success among the Jews of South America," *Davar*, September 12, 1948, 2.

49. Jaime Finkelstein, "A Year of My Life," *Argentiner YIVO shriften* 13 (1983): 22–42 [Yiddish]; Efraim Zadoff, *Historia de la educación judía en Buenos Aires, 1935–1957* (Buenos Aires: Milá, 1994), 93–100.

50. Zadoff, *Historia de la educación judía*, 93–100; M. Koren, "Jaime Finkelstein: The Paradigmatic Educator" (an article written to mark the first seventy years of the Scholem Aleijem schools, which I received from its author) [Spanish].

51. M. Koren, "Itzhak Bank, the Enthusiastic Community Activist," 1–2 (an article written to mark the first seventy years of the Scholem Aleijem schools, which I received from its author) [Spanish].

52. Finkelstein, "A Year of My Life."

53. Ibid.

54. Ibid. This fierce struggle paved the way for the establishment of the Argentinian branch of the ICUF (Idisher Cultur Farband = Federación de Entidades Culturales Judías de la Argentina), a Jewish communist organization. See Nerina Visacovsky, "El discurso pedagógico de la izquierda judía en Argentina (1935–1970)" (PhD diss., Universidad de Buenos Aires, 2007).

55. The credit cooperatives, established in the 1930s, became one of the dominant factors on the Argentinian Jewish scene in the 1950s and 1960s, because they served as the main financing source for public activities by the community, especially in the field of education. See Avni, *Argentina and the Jews*, 87–88; Avni, *Emancipation and Jewish Education* (Jerusalem: Shazar Center, 1985), 53 [Heb.]. See also Zadoff, *Historia de la educación judía*, 98–100.

56. Yaacov Rubel, *Las escuelas judías Argentinas (1985–1995): Procesos de evolución y de involución* (Buenos Aires: Milá, 1998), 12–15.

57. Avni, *Emancipation and Jewish Education*, 31–49, 53, 63–64, 69–70, 115; Rubel, *Las escuelas judías Argentinas*, 16–17; Zadoff, *Historia de la educación judía*, 255–88; Senkman, "Ser judío en Argentina," 431–36.
58. Rubel, *Las escuelas judías Argentinas*, 20.
59. Jacob Tsur, *The Fourth Credentials: The First Diplomatic Mission in South America* (Tel Aviv: Sifriyat Maariv, 1981), 45 [Heb.].
60. Moshe Kitron, "After Perón's Victory," December 1951, Central Zionist Archives, personal papers, A494/9 [Heb.].
61. Ibid., 49.
62. Avni, *Argentina and the Jews*, 47–48, 53–55; Avni, *Emancipation and Jewish Education*, 118; Senkman, "Ser judío en Argentina," 427–30.
63. Avni, *Argentina and the Jews*, 50–51.
64. Avni, *Emancipation and Jewish Education*, 117–18, 138; Avni, *Argentina and the Jews*, 92–95; Rubel, *Las escuelas judías Argentinas*, 23–28; Zadoff, *Historia de la educación judía*, 456–62; Senkman, "Ser judío en Argentina," 431–32.
65. M. Kitron to Z. Shazar, March 19, 1963, ISA, het-tzade 11/2150. See also "Memoria y Balance General del 1 de enero al 31 de diciembre de 1963" (Buenos Aires: AMIA, 1964). By 1967, total nationwide enrollment had reached 20,000. See Avni, *Argentina and the Jews*, 89–90; Avni, *Emancipation and Jewish Education*, 69–70, 135; Rubel, *Las escuelas judías Argentinas*, 47, 57, 60.
66. Kitron to Shazar, March 19, 1963.
67. Schmelz and DellaPergola, *Structure of Latin American Jewry*, 106.
68. Jaime Firstater, *Lucha, Moral y Futuro* (Córdoba: Editorial Schalom, 1967), 328–29.
69. Carlos Meirovich, *¿Por qué no te fuiste, papá?: Saga de una familia de argentinos judíos* (Buenos Aires: Milá, 2008).
70. Ibid., 310–11.
71. Berel Lang, "Hyphenated-Jews and the Anxiety of Identity," *Jewish Social Studies*, n.s. 12, no. 1 (2005): 1–15.

Chapter 2

1. J. Tsur to W. Eytan, "Organizing and Encouraging Aliya from the Countries of Latin America," October 13, 1949, ISA, gimel-13/5558.
2. Ibid.
3. Ibid.
4. Moshe Kostrinsky, "We Are Making Aliya from South America," August 22, 1949, CZA S71/205.
5. Kitron papers, CZA, A494/1–52; see also Naomi Kitron, *On Three Continents: The Life of Moshe Kitron* (Jerusalem: Carmel, 2005) [Heb.].
6. Moshe Kostrinsky, "Adiós América," CZA, Kitron papers, A 494/7.
7. Ibid.
8. Moshe Kitron, "Prospects for Aliya from Latin America," *Hador*, October 30, 1951.
9. Moshe Kitron to Y. Raphael, June 30, 1953, CZA, Kitron papers, A494/34.
10. Memo from Moshe Kitron to David Ben-Gurion, "Re: Jews of South America," November 14, 1952, CZA, Kitron papers, A494/11.
11. Kitron, "Prospects for Aliya from Latin America."
12. In the Borochovian view, the economic status of the Jews in the Diaspora resembles an inverted pyramid, because most of them are engaged

in nonproductive occupations and their situation is not "normal." Only in Eretz Israel can the Jews turn the pyramid right-side up and live normal lives based on productive labor. For more on Ber Borochov's ideas, see Gideon Shimoni, *The Zionist Ideology* (Hanover, NH: University Press of New England [for] Brandeis University Press, 1995), 187–94.

13. Gino Germani, *Política y Sociedad en una Época de Transición: De la sociedad tradicional a la sociedad de masas*, 4th ed. (Buenos Aires: Paidós, 1971), 179–232.
14. Diego Armus, "Diez años de historiografía sobre la inmigración masiva a la Argentina," *Estudios Migratorios Latinoamericanos* 4 (1986): 433; Devoto, "Del crisol al pluralismo"; Néstor Tomás Auza, *Católicos y liberales en la generación del ochenta* (Buenos Aires: Ediciones Culturales Argentinas, 1975).
15. Carlos Altamirano, ed., *La Argentina en el siglo XX* (Buenos Aires: Ariel; Quilmes: Universidad Nacional de Quilmes, 1999); David Rock et al., *La derecha argentina: Nacionalistas, neoliberales, militares y clericales* (Barcelona: J. Vergara, 2001).
16. Tulio Halperin Donghi, *La república imposible* (Buenos Aires: Ariel, 2004).
17. Graciela Ben-Dror, *The Catholic Church and the Jews: Argentina, 1933–1945* (Lincoln: University of Nebraska Press, 2008), 41–49. See also Leonardo Senkman, ed., *El antisemitismo en la Argentina* (Buenos Aires: Centro Editor de América Latina, 1989); Daniel Lvovich, *Nacionalismo y antisemitismo en la Argentina* (Buenos Aires: J. Vergara, 2003).
18. Raanan Rein, *Argentina, Israel, and the Jews: Perón, the Eichmann Capture and After*, trans. Martha Grenzeback (Bethesda: University Press of Maryland, 2003), 36–37, 44–45; Ben-Dror, *Catholic Church and the Jews*, 92. See also Leonardo Senkman, "El 4 de junio 1943 y los judíos," *Todo es historia* 193 (1983): 67–78.
19. Daniel James and Luis Justo, *Resistencia e integración* (Buenos Aires: Sudamericana, 1991).
20. Moshe Kitron, "After Perón's Victory," December 7, 1951, CZA, Kitron papers, A494/9.
21. Memo from Moshe Kitron to David Ben-Gurion, "Re: Jews of South America," November 14, 1952, CZA, Kitron papers, A494/11.
22. Ibid.
23. Kitron, "Prospects for Aliya from Latin America," *Hador*, October 30, 1951; Moshe Kitron, "After Perón's Victory," December 7, 1951; memo from Moshe Kitron to David Ben-Gurion, "Re: Jews of South America," November 14, 1952; Moshe Kitron to Y. Raphael, June 30, 1953, CZA, Kitron papers, A494/34; Moshe Kitron, "By Virtue of the Idea and the Force of Reality," *Davar*, February 27, 1955, 3–4.
24. Rein, *Argentina, Israel, and the Jews*, 40–41; Raanan Rein, *Populism and Charisma: Peronist Argentina, 1943–1945* (Tel Aviv: Modan, 1998) [Heb.]. See also Leonardo Senkman, "The Response of the First Peronist Government to Antisemitic Discourse, 1946–1954: A Necessary Reassessment," *Judaica Latinoamericana* 3 (1997): 175–206; Leonardo Senkman, "El antisemitismo bajo dos experiencias democráticas: 1945–1966 y

1973–1976," in El antisemitismo en la Argentina, ed. Leonardo Senkman (Buenos Aires: Centro Editor de América Latina, 1989); Lawrence D. Bell, "In the Name of the Community: Populism, Ethnicity, and Politics among the Jews of Argentina under Perón, 1946–1955," *Hispanic American Historical Review* 86, no. 1 (2006): 93–122.

25. Kitron, "Prospects for Aliya from Latin America," *Hador*, October 30, 1951.
26. Kitron, "After Perón's Victory," December 7, 1951, CZA, Kitron papers, A494/9.
27. Interview with David Dor, April 13, 2008. See also Devora Schachner, *A Political Girl* (Tel Aviv: Hakibbutz Hame'uchad, 2002) [Heb.]; Arieh Vardi, *Between Two Worlds, 1938–1946*, trans. [from Spanish] Peninah Meier (Tel Aviv: Sifre Hemed, 2006) [Heb.]; Horacio Verbitzky, "Cambio Cultural," *Página 12* (May 9, 2010), www.pagina12.com.ar/diario/elpais/1–145363-05-2010-09.html (accessed November 12, 2012).
28. Rein, *Argentina, Israel, and the Jews*, 40. See also Leonardo Senkman, "El peronismo visto desde la legación israelí en Buenos Aires: Sus relaciones con la OIA (1949–1954)," *Judaica Latinoamericana* 2 (1993): 115–36; Bell, "In the Name of the Community."
29. Kitron, "By Virtue of the Idea and the Force of Reality," *Davar*, February 27, 1955, 3–4.
30. Ibid.
31. Ibid.
32. Uziel Schmelz and Sergio DellaPergola, *The Structure of Latin American Jewry: The Demographics of the Jews in Argentina and other Countries in Latin America* (Tel Aviv: David Horowitz Institute for the Research of Developing Countries, Tel Aviv University, 1974), 119–20 [Heb.].
33. It is important to note that, aside from the testimony of the head of the Mossad, there are no records of his trip to Argentina or its objective. See Isser Harel, *Security and Democracy* (Tel Aviv: Idanim, 1989) [Heb.]; quoted by Rein, *Argentina, Israel, and the Jews*, 143.
34. "Excerpt from the Survey of the Recent Coup in Argentina by Our Representative in Buenos Aires," October 5, 1955, CZA S6/6203.
35. Ibid.
36. Ibid.
37. Ibid.
38. Ibid.
39. "Aliya from Argentina Will Grow Stronger," *Hatzofeh*, February 11, 1954, CZA S71/946.
40. Memo from Moshe Kitron to David Ben-Gurion, "Re: Jews of South America," November 14, 1952. See also J. Tsur to W. Eytan, "Organizing and Encouraging Aliya from the Countries of Latin America," October 13, 1949.
41. J. Tsur to W. Eytan, "Organizing and Encouraging Aliya from the Countries of Latin America," October 13, 1949.
42. "Excerpt from the Survey of the Recent Coup in Argentina by Our Representative in Buenos Aires," October 5, 1955, CZA S6/6203.
43. M. Kaufman to S. Z. Shragai, November 15, 1955, CZA S6/6204.
44. Ibid.
45. The Higher Zionist Council in Argentina to S. Z. Shragai, October 23, 1956, CZA S6/6205.

46. M. Armon to the Aliyah Department, Jerusalem, "Summary of a Two-Year Mission," November 15, 1959, CZA S6/6596.
47. Anita Shapira, *Israel: A History* (Waltham, MA: Brandeis University Press, 2013), 265–66.
48. Raanan Rein, "Argentine Jews and the Accusation of 'Dual Loyalty,' 1960–1962," in *The Jewish Diaspora in Latin America and the Caribbean: Fragments of Memory*, ed. Kristin Ruggiero (Brighton: Sussex Academic Press, 2005), 51–71.
49. Y. Israeli to B. Duvdevani, July 26, 1962, CZA S6/7320.
50. M. Gelerter to M. Sharett and Z. Lurie, August 1, 1962, CZA S65/203.
51. Ibid.
52. Y. Barmor to Latin America Department, "Visit to Resistencia and Corrientes," June 27, 1962, CZA S6/7321.
53. Y. Avidar to A. Levavi, "On the Mood of the Jewish Community in Argentina," September 14, 1962, ISA, het-tzade 11/2150.
54. Haviv Kna'an, "In the Face of the Terrorism in South America There Is an Inclination to Make Aliya," *Ha'aretz*, July 30, 1964, CZA S6/7321.
55. Y. Israeli, "Between Passover and Independence Day (Letter from Buenos Aires)," *Dappei Aliyah* 46 (1962): 47–48.
56. Rein, *Argentina, Israel, and the Jews*, 214–19.
57. Y. Israeli, "Between Passover and Independence Day."
58. I. Goldenberg and Z. Feingersh to S. Z. Shragai, June 3, 1962, CZA S65/203.
59. Ibid.
60. Ibid.
61. Avidar to the Foreign Ministry, July 27, 1962, quoted by Rein, *Argentina, Israel, and the Jews*, 215n59.
62. A. Cygel, "Report on My Activities in Argentina," August 23, 1962, CZA S65/203.
63. Ibid.
64. B. Duvdevani to S. Z. Shragai, January 14, 1963, JAFI Logistics Center, file 2058.
65. Ibid.
66. S. Z. Shragai to M. Kitron, October 24, 1962, CZA, Kitron papers, A494/18.
67. Ibid.
68. Quoted by Kitron, *On Three Continents*, 311.
69. These data allowed me to determine the connection between applications at the Jewish Agency offices and actual immigration. See M. Kitron to Z. Lurie, "Report on Registration and Aliya in 1962," January 21, 1963, CZA S64/393.
70. Ibid.
71. M. Kitron to S. Z. Shragai, December 16, 1962, CZA, Kitron papers, A494/18.
72. Activity Report, Tevet 5716 to Nisan 5720 (January 1956–March 31, 1960), submitted to the 25th Zionist Congress, Jerusalem, December 1960–January 1961, CZA, K105 XXV, 211–26.
73. A. Cygel, "Report on My Activities in Argentina," August 23, 1962, CZA S65/203.
74. M. Kitron to S. Z. Shragai, December 12, 1962, CZA, Kitron papers, A494/18.
75. The Economic Department provided information to potential olim, both capitalists and tourists, about the possibilities for establishing factories and the prospects for investments in

commerce and industry. See Activity Report, 1946/47–1950/51, 500–521.

76. M. Kitron to S. Z. Shragai, December 12, 1962, Kitron papers, CZA A494/18.
77. Rein, *Argentina, Israel, and the Jews*, 214–15.
78. M. Kitron to S. Z. Shragai, April 23, 1963, JAFI Logistics Center, 2059–60.
79. M. Kitron, "Aliya from Argentina, January–June 1963" (no date), CZA S65/203.
80. Ibid.
81. M. Cavaliero to A. Dobkin, December 16, 1963, CZA S65/203.
82. M. Kitron, "Emigration to Israel by Jews from Argentina," CZA, Kitron papers, A494/49.
83. "Statistical Summaries of Registration and Aliya from Argentina, January–February–March 1964," April 1964, ISA, het-tzade 3/2153.
84. "Statistical Summaries of Registration and Aliya from Argentina, January–April–June 1964," July 1964, ISA, het-tzade 3/2153.
85. Rein, *Argentina, Israel, and the Jews*, 232.
86. DAIA, *Medio siglo de lucha por una Argentina sin discriminaciones: Todo es Historia* (Buenos Aires, 1985), 14; Eliahu Toker and Ana E. Weinstein, eds., *Trayectoria de una idea: Nueva Sión; 50 años de un periodismo judeo-argentino con compromiso, 1948–1998* (Buenos Aires: Ediciones Fundación Mordejai Anilevich, 1999), 83.
87. Senkman, "El antisemitismo bajo dos experiencias."
88. Y. Israeli to Y. Wolberg, "Report by the Aliya Committees," September 23, 1964, JAFI Logistics Center, file 2065.
89. Ibid.
90. Ibid.
91. D. Hofen and P. Perez, "Willingness to Emigrate among the Jewish Community in Buenos Aires, Sample Report," October 31, 1964, JAFI Logistics Center, file 2054.
92. D. Hoffman, "The Attitude of Buenos Aires Jews to the Question of Aliya," December 1964, JAFI Logistics Center, file 2078, 5.
93. Ibid., 9–10.
94. Ibid., 11–12.
95. Ibid.
96. Ibid., 13.
97. Ibid., 14.
98. Ibid.
99. Ibid., 15.
100. Ibid.
101. Ibid., 16.
102. Ibid., 17.
103. Ibid., 19.
104. Ibid., 20.
105. Ibid., 22.
106. Y. Israeli to S. Z. Shragai, September 23, 1965, JAFI Logistics Center, file 1175.
107. Ibid.
108. Ibid.
109. Ibid. On the Onganía dictatorship, see Guillermo A. O'Donnell, *1966–1973, el estado burocrático autoritario: Triunfos, derrotas y crisis* (Buenos Aires: Editorial de Belgrano, 1982); Liliana de Riz, *La política en suspenso, 1966–1976* (Buenos Aires: Paidós, 2000).
110. M. Tadmor to S. Z. Shragai, "The Military Coup in Argentina and Its Possible Implications for the Jews," July 4, 1966, JAFI Logistics Center, file 2068.
111. Ibid.
112. Ibid.
113. S. Har-Gil, "Argentinians Are Coming to the Kibbutz," *Maariv*, March 5, 1967, 12.

114. Ibid.
115. Haim Avni, "A True Turning Point? The Six-Day War and the Organized Jewish Community in Argentina," *Yahadut zemanenu* 11–12 (1998): 274–75 [Heb.].
116. Ibid., 281–82.
117. *Aliya to Israel, 1948–1972, Part 1: Annual Data* (Jerusalem: Central Bureau of Statistics, 1973), 23.
118. M. Barkai, "The Best, the Loneliest," *Davar*, December 17, 1965, 21–23, 31.
119. Ibid.
120. E. Ross, "A Quick Look at South American Jewry: We Overdid Our Estimates of the Risks and Prospects" (undated), JAFI Logistics Center, file 2067 [Heb.].
121. M. Dayan to B. Duvdevani, October 31, 1964, JAFI Logistics Center, file 2065.
122. Central Bureau of Statistics, 1948–2015.

Chapter 3

1. Activity Report, 1946/47–1950/51, submitted to the 23rd Zionist Congress, August 1951, CZA, K98 XXIII, 184–89.
2. "33,000 Olim Reached Israel in Three Months," *Davar*, August 17, 1948, 4.
3. Activity Report, 1946/47–1950/51, 179.
4. A. T., "Momentum of Aliya and Settlement Frozen," *Davar*, August 29, 1948, 4.
5. Ibid.
6. Ibid.
7. Ibid.
8. Activity Report, 1946/47–1950/51, 184–89.
9. Ibid.
10. Dvora Hacohen, *Immigrants in Turmoil: Mass Immigration to Israel and Its Repercussions in the 1950s and After*, trans. Gila Brand (Syracuse, NY: Syracuse University Press, 2003), 25–31.
11. Yitzhak Rafael, *Not Easily Came the Light* (Jerusalem: Idanim, 1981) 50, 52 [Heb.]. See also Tom Segev, *1949, the First Israelis* (New York: Free Press, 1984), 95–116.
12. Activity Report, 1946/47–1950/51, 184–85.
13. Yitzhak Rafael, "To Gather the Dispersed of the Jewish People," *Dappei Aliyah* 1 (1949): 13–15.
14. Ibid.
15. Activity Report, 1946/47–1950/51, 189–91.
16. "Ingathering of the Exiles Day," *Dappei Aliyah* 7 (1950): 13–20.
17. "The Jewish Agency for Israel, Aliya Department," *Davar*, December 12, 1949, 4.
18. Rafael, *Not Easily Came the Light*, 128.
19. Ibid.
20. "Ingathering of the Exiles Day," *Dappei Aliyah* 7; Rafael, *Not Easily Came the Light*.
21. "Ingathering of the Exiles Day," 44–47.
22. "Voice of Israel Broadcasts," *Davar*, December 16, 1949, 27.
23. Yitzhak Rafael, "On Ingathering of the Exiles Day," *Dappei Aliyah* 7 (1950): 8–12. See also Rafael, *Not Easily Came the Light*, 128–32.
24. Rafael, "On Ingathering of the Exiles Day."
25. Moshe Shapira, "Settle Millions More in the Homeland!" *Dappei Aliyah* 7 (1950): 5–7. Shapira's remarks were broadcast on Israel Radio on Ingathering of the Exiles Day.
26. "Remarks by the President of Israel on Ingathering of the Exiles Day," *Dappei Aliyah* 7 (1950): 1–2.
27. David Ben-Gurion, "We Have Reached a Million," *Dappei Aliyah* 7 (1950): 3.

28. "Ingathering of the Exiles Day," *Dappei Aliyah* 7; "The Jewish Agency for Israel, Aliya Department," *Davar*, December 12, 1949; "Voice of Israel Broadcasts," *Davar*, December 16, 1949.
29. Rafael, *Not Easily Came the Light*, 131; "Hanukkah in Jerusalem under the Sign of the Struggle," *Davar*, December 13, 1949, 4.
30. Rafael, *Not Easily Came the Light*, 132.
31. Shapira, "Settle Millions More in the Homeland!"
32. "Ingathering of the Exiles Day in the Diaspora: Additional Echoes," *Dappei Aliyah* 8 (1950): 23–26.
33. Rafael, "On Ingathering of the Exiles Day," 12; "Ingathering of the Exiles Day in the Diaspora: Additional Echoes," 26.
34. "Day of the Million," *Davar*, December 18, 1949, 1; "Ingathering of the Exiles Day"; Rafael, *Not Easily Came the Light*, 129–30.
35. Hacohen, *Immigrants in Turmoil*, 25–29.
36. "Excerpts from the Remarks by Yitzhak Rafael at a Press Conference in Jerusalem on Aug. 22, 1949," *Dappei Aliyah* 4 (1949): 3.
37. Activity Report, 1946/47–1950/51, 184–89.
38. Ibid.; "Aliya since Independence (May 1948–September 1949)," *Dappei Aliyah* 5 (1950): 31.
39. Israel Central Bureau of Statistics, *Immigration to Israel 1948–1972* (Jerusalem: CBS, 1973) [Heb.].
40. Dvora Hacohen, "Immigrant Settlement Policy during the First Decade of the State: The Attempts to Limit Immigration and their Fate," in *Ingathering of Exiles: Aliya to the Land of Israel Myth and Reality*, ed. Dvora Hacohen (Jerusalem: Shazar Center, 1998), 285–316 [Heb.]. See also Dalia Ofer, "Emigration and Aliya: New Aspects of Jewish Policy," *Katedra* 75 (1995): 150–64 [Heb.]; Yehuda Dominitz, *Aliyah and Migration: From Years of Destruction to an Era of Rebirth (1935–1961)* (Jerusalem: Zionist Library, 2000) [Heb.].
41. Activity Report, 1946/47–1950/51, 192–93.
42. "Twenty Years of Immigration to Israel," *Dappei Aliyah* 69 (1968): 39.
43. Ibid., 35.
44. Moshe Sneh, "The Lack of Aliya from the West," *Dappei Aliyah* 8 (1950): 12–14.
45. J. Tsur to W. Eytan, "Organization and Encouragement of Immigration from the Latin American Countries," October 13, 1949, ISA, gimel-13/5558.
46. M. Yakir, "A Time for Action: On Aliya from America," *Dappei Aliyah* 8 (1950): 6.
47. H. Greenberg, "Possibilities for Aliya from America," *Dappei Aliyah* 20 (1952). See also D. Pines, "Who and How Many Will Make Aliya from America?" *Davar*, January 20, 1950.
48. On the pre-State period, see Gur Alroey, *An Unpromising Land: Jewish Migration to Palestine in the Early Twentieth Century* (Stanford, CA: Stanford University Press, 2014); Margalit Shilo, "What's Good for the People or What's Good for the Country? The Zionist Movement's Attitude towards Aliya during the Second Aliya," *Katedra* 46 (1987): 109–22 [Heb.]; Aviva Halamish, *Dual Race against Time: Zionist Immigration Policy in the 1930s* (Jerusalem: Yad Ben-Zvi, 2006) [Heb.]; Joseph Heller, *The Struggle for the Jewish State*

(Jerusalem: Shazar Center, 1984) [Heb.]; Hagit Lavsky, "The Surviving Remnant and the Establishment of the State: An Opportunity That Was Exploited," *Katedra* 55 (1990): 175–81 [Heb.]; Yoav Gelber, "From 'Don't Come!' until the Law of Return: Vacillations and Changes in the Zionist Attitude towards Aliya" [Heb.], in Hacohen, *Ingathering of Exiles*, 249–82.

49. See Dvora Hacohen, "The Law of Return: Its Content and the Disputes about It," in *Independence: The First Fifty Years*, ed. Anita Shapira (Jerusalem: Shazar Center, 1998), 57–87 [Heb.].
50. "Excerpts from the Remarks in the Knesset by the Prime Minister, David Ben-Gurion, about the Law of Return," *Dappei Aliyah* 13 (1950): 19.
51. Ibid.
52. Ibid. See also Amnon Rubinstein and Barak Medinah, *The Constitutional Law of the State of Israel* (Jerusalem: Schocken, 1996), 1: 109–11 [Heb.].
53. Hacohen, *Immigrants in Turmoil*, 125–28. See also Sergio DellaPergola, "Some Reflections on Migration in Israel: Comparative Aspects," *Hagira* 1 (2012): 25–28 [Heb.].
54. Hacohen, *Immigrants in Turmoil*, 120–22. See also "The Coordinating Committee," *Dappei Aliyah* 12 (1950): 14–15.
55. "On the Battlefields of Aliya," *Dappei Aliyah* 22 (1952): 4–5.
56. Haim Barkai, *The Genesis of the Israeli Economy* (Jerusalem: Mosad Bialik, 1990), 33–44 [Heb.]. See also Hacohen, *Immigrants in Turmoil*, 194–201; Aviva Halamish, "Selective Aliya as an Idea and Practice and in Zionist Historiography," in *The Age of Zionism*, ed. Anita Shapira, Jehuda Reinharz, and Jay Michael Harris (Jerusalem: Shazar Center, 2000), 185–203 [Heb.]; Moshe Lissak, *Mass Immigration in the Fifties: The Failure of the Melting Pot Policies* (Jerusalem: Mosad Bialik, 1999) [Heb.]; Dalia Ofer, ed., *Israel in the Great Wave of Immigration, 1948–1953* (Jerusalem: Yad Ben-Zvi, 1996) [Heb.]; Avi Picard, *Cut to Measure: Israel's Policies Regarding the Aliya of North African Jews, 1951–1956* (Beer Sheva: Ben-Gurion Institute and Ben-Gurion University of the Negev, 2013), 63–110 [Heb.].
57. Activity Report, Nisan 5711 to Tevet 5716 (April 1951–December 1955), submitted to the 24th Zionist Congress, Nisan 5716, CZA, K102 XXIV, 59–61.
58. Lissak, *Mass Immigration in the Fifties*, 19–20; Hacohen, "Immigrant Settlement Policy," 302–3; Picard, *Cut to Measure*, 69–78.
59. "On the Jewish Agency Executive's Decisions about Aliya Matters," *Dappei Aliyah* 22 (1952): 3.
60. Ibid.
61. "Jewish Immigrants by Month of Aliya since the Establishment of the State," *Dappei Aliyah* 22 (1952): 27.
62. Yitzhak Rafael, "We Must Prepare for the Renewal of Mass Aliya," *Dappei Aliyah* 24 (1953): 5–11.
63. Ibid.
64. Activity Report, Nisan 5711 to Tevet 5716, 60.
65. Ibid., 63, 232–33.
66. Ibid.
67. Activity Report, Nisan 5711 to Tevet 5716, 64, 234–35.
68. Ibid., 63. See also "Council for Aliya from the West," *Dappei Aliyah* 28 (1954): 6–7.

69. "Meeting of the Aliya Council, Tel Aviv, June 24, 1953," *Dappei Aliyah* 26 (1953): 5–29. The Aliya Council was established in 1952 to advise the Jewish Agency Aliyah Department. According to Dvora Hacohen, it had no real effect on aliya policy and arrangements. She writes that "it became a debating society for low-level functionaries," while the Coordinating Committee continued to make the decisions. See Hacohen, *Immigrants in Turmoil*, 230 [the quotation appears only in the Hebrew original], (Jerusalem: Yad Ben-Zvi, 1994), 298.
70. Activity Report, Nisan 5711 to Tevet 5716 (April 1951–December 1955), submitted to the 24th Zionist Congress, Nisan 5716, CZA, K102 XXIV, 59–61. See also Lissak, *Mass Immigration*, 19–20; Hacohen, "Immigrant Settlement Policy, 302–4.
71. "The Coordinating Committee at Its meeting of June 14, 1953," *Dappei Aliyah* 26 (1953): 3.
72. Ibid. See also Activity Report, Nisan 5711 to Tevet 5716, 59–61.
73. "A Special Office to Deal with Latin American Immigrants," *Hatzofeh*, February 4, 1953, CZA S71/946.
74. "Aliya from Independence until the End of December 1953," *Dappei Aliyah* 27 (1954): 56–57.
75. "Meeting of the Aliya Council, Tel Aviv June 24, 1953," *Dappei Aliyah* 26 (1953): 5–29.
76. "The Decisions by the Zionist General Council on Matters of Aliya and Absorption," *Dappei Aliyah* 27 (1954): 3.
77. Ibid.
78. "Personnel Changes in the Aliya Department," ibid., 4. See also Rafael, *Not Easily Came the Light*, 162–66.
79. "The Decisions by the Zionist General Council on Matters of Aliya and Absorption," *Dappei Aliyah* 27 (1954): 6–9; S. Daniel, "A Profile of S. Z. Shragai," *Dappei Aliyah* 38 (1960): 4–6.
80. "Activity Report, Tevet 5716 to Nisan 5720," 65–66.
81. Ibid., 64.
82. *Dappei Aliyah* 29 (1956): 3.
83. David Ben-Gurion, "Security Means Aliya and Settlement, Excerpts from His Speech in the Knesset on Nov. 2, 1955," *Dappei Aliyah* 29 (1956): 5.
84. Yehuda Dominitz, "Some Problems of Aliya in 1957," *Dappei Aliyah* 32 (1958): 33.
85. Picard, *Cut to Measure*, 172–82.
86. Baruch Duvdevani, "Some Problems of Aliya," *Dappei Aliyah* 30 (1956): 5–6.
87. *Immigration to Israel 1948–1972*.
88. Ibid.
89. Baruch Duvdevani, "Some Problems of Aliya," *Dappei Aliyah* 30 (1956): 11–12. See also Picard, *Cut to Measure*, 187–238.
90. Baruch Duvdevani, "On Aliya in 1957," *Dappei Aliyah* 32 (1958): 11.
91. Ibid.
92. *Immigration to Israel 1948–1972*.
93. Duvdevani, "On Aliya in 1957," 8.
94. Ibid., 9.
95. *Immigration to Israel 1948–1972*.
96. Y. Edd, "Journalists' Conversations with the Head of the Department, Mr. S. Z. Shragai," *Dappei Aliyah* 37 (1959): 5–7.
97. *Immigration to Israel 1948–1972*.
98. Ibid., 18–23; See also Activity Report, Tevet 5716 to Nisan 5720 (January 1956–March 31, 1960), submitted to the 25th Zionist Congress, Kislev 5721, CZA, K105 XXV, 64–73.
99. Edd, "Journalists' Conversations," *Dappei Aliyah* 37 (1959): 7.

100. S. Z. Shragai, "Problems of Aliya," *Dappei Aliyah* 31 (1956): 20–22.
101. Activity Report, Tevet 5716 to Nisan 5720, 211–26.
102. Ibid.
103. Ibid., 70–73; See also B. Duvdevani to the Zionist Federation in Argentina, Uruguay, and Chile, "The Mission of Mr. A. Avigur (Gorman)," August 2, 1959, CZA, S6/6595.
104. Lev Grinberg, "Social and Political Economy," in *Trends in Israeli Society*, ed. Ephraim Yaar and Zeev Shavit (Tel Aviv: Open University, 2001), 628–30 [Heb.].
105. Activity Report, Tevet 5716 to Nisan 5720 (January 1956–March 31, 1960), submitted to the 25th Zionist Congress, Kislev 5721, CZA, K105 XXV, 118, 128; Activity Report, Nisan 5720 to Nisan 5724 (April 1, 1960–March 31, 1964), submitted to the 26th Zionist Congress, Heshvan 5725, CZA, K109 XXVI, 103–4, 112.
106. "Twenty Years of Aliya and Absorption: Summaries" (no date), ISA, gimel-3/7065; *Immigration to Israel 1948–1972*.
107. "Aliya Department Activity Report, Nisan 5724 to Tevet 5728," *Dappei Aliyah* 69 (1968): 19–33; "Twenty Years of Immigration to Israel," *Dappei Aliyah* 69 (1968): 34–41.
108. "Twenty Years of Immigration to Israel," 39; *Immigration to Israel 1948–1972*.
109. "Rights and Obligations of Olim and Temporary Residents, According to Israeli Law and Procedures," *Dappei Aliyah* 64 (1965): 3–7. See also "New Trends and Phenomena in the Absorption of Immigrants from Developed Countries," *Dappei Aliyah* 67 (1967): 21–22.
110. "Eshkol to Representatives of the Jewish Communities: Increase Aliya from the West," *Dappei Aliyah* 65 (1966): 12.
111. "Aliya Department Report, October 1965–October 1966," *Dappei Aliyah* 65 (1967): 11–14.
112. Guide for the New Immigrant, May 15, 1964, JAFI Logistics Center, file 2066 [in Spanish]. For the original Hebrew, see Guide for the New Immigrant, JAFI Logistics Center, file 1353.
113. Activity Report, Nisan 5720–Nisan 5724 (April 1, 1960–March 31, 1964), submitted to the 26th Zionist Congress, Heshvan 5725, CZA, K109 XXVI, 103.
114. Avraham Cygel, "Changes in Immigrant Absorption," *Dappei Aliyah* 67 (1967): 21–22.
115. Activity Report, Nisan 5720–Nisan 5724, 103.
116. The Joint Government–Jewish Agency Authority for Immigration and Absorption," *Dappei Aliyah* 68 (1968): 4–5. See also "Announcement by the Agency Executive Regarding the Department of Aliyah and Absorption," *Dappei Aliyah* 67 (1967): 2.
117. Activity Report, Nisan 5764 to Tevet 5728 (April 1, 1964–December 31, 1967), submitted to the 27th Zionist Congress, Nisan 5728, CZA, K112 XXVII, 53.
118. "Mr. S. Z. Shragai's Announcement at a Meeting of the Executive of His Resignation as Head of the Aliya Department," *Dappei Aliyah* 65 (1967): 79.
119. S. Har-Gil, "Argentinians are Coming to the Kibbutz," *Maariv*, March 5, 1967, 12.
120. Activity Report, Nisan 5764 to Tevet 5728 (April 1, 1964–December 31, 1967),

submitted to the 27th Zionist Congress, Nisan 5728, CZA, K112 XXVII, 111.

121. "Announcement by the Agency Executive regarding the Department of Aliyah and Absorption," *Dappei Aliyah* 67 (1967): 2.
122. Eli Lederhendler, ed., *The Six-Day War and World Jewry* (Bethesda: University Press of Maryland, 2000).
123. S. Z. Shragai, "Come Fill Up the Land!" *Dappei Aliyah* 67 (1967): 1–2; "Manifesto to Jews in the Diaspora: Rise Up, Make Aliya, and Build the Land," *Dappei Aliyah* 68 (1968): 1; "After the Six-Day War," *Dappei Aliyah* 68 (1968): 3; Activity Report, Nisan 5764 to Tevet 5728, 44.
124. "Growing Stream of Volunteers in the Diaspora," *Dappei Aliyah* 67 (1967): 53–55.
125. Activity Report, Nisan 5764 to Tevet 5728, 44.
126. Ibid.
127. Ibid.
128. *Immigration to Israel 1948–1972.*

Chapter 4

1. Activity Report, 1946/47–1950/51, submitted to the 23rd Zionist Congress, August 1951, CZA, K98 XXIII, 33; Silvia Schenkolewski-Kroll, *The Zionist Movement and the Zionist Parties in Argentina, 1935–1948* (Jerusalem: Magnes Press, 1996), 347 [Heb.].
2. Abraham Mibashan to Jewish Agency Aliya Bureau, September 18, 1945, in *Fifty Years since the Ten Certificates (from Buenos Aires to Mefalsim)* (Mefalsim: Mefalsim Archives, 1995).
3. Activity Report, 1946/47–1950/51, submitted to the 23rd Zionist Congress, August 1951, CZA, K98 XXIII, 33–35.
4. Shlomo Garner to Yitzhak Rafael, "Survey of Agency Activity in South America," July 4, 1951, JAFI Logistics Center, file 1198.
5. Activity Report, 1946/47–1950/51, submitted to the 23rd Zionist Congress, August 1951, CZA, K98 XXIII, 35.
6. Ibid. See also "Latin American Overseas Volunteers in Israel" [original in Spanish], CZA, L62/8; Yaakov Markovitzki, *Machal: Overseas Volunteers in Israel's War of Independence* (Jerusalem: Machal, Association of Overseas Volunteers, 2003), 6–7 [Heb.]; Activity Report, Nisan 5711 to Tevet 5716 (April 1951–December 1955), submitted to the 24th Zionist Congress, Nisan 5716, CZA, K102 XXIV, 135.
7. A. Scheel (Eshel), October 31, 1948, CZA, S6/660.
8. Jacob Tsur, *The Fourth Credentials: The First Diplomatic Mission in South America* (Tel Aviv: Sifriyat Maariv, 1981), 22, 45 [Heb.].
9. Ibid., 55. See also Raanan Rein, *Argentina, Israel, and the Jews: Perón, the Eichmann Capture and After*, trans. Martha Grenzeback (Bethesda: University Press of Maryland, 2003), 76–77.
10. Tsur, *Fourth Credentials*, 45–46.
11. "Aliya Office in Argentina Closes Temporarily," *Davar*, May 9, 1949, 1.
12. J. Tsur to W. Eytan, "The Organization and Encouragement of Aliya from Latin America," October 13, 1949, ISA, gimel-13/5558.
13. Ibid.
14. Ibid.
15. "In the Department," *Dappei Aliyah* 8 (1950): 40; "In the Department," *Dappei Aliyah* 9 (1950): 31; Activity Report, 1946/47–1950/51, submitted to the 23rd Zionist Congress, August 1951, CZA, K98 XXIII, 215–16.

16. Shlomo Garner to Yitzhak Rafael, "Survey of Agency Activity in South America," July 4, 1951.
17. Activity Report, Nisan 5711 to Tevet 5716 (April 1951–December 1955), submitted to the 24th Zionist Congress, Nisan 5716, CZA, K102 XXIV, 239; "Work Plan of Dr. A. S. Zeitlin, the Representative of the Jewish Agency Economic Department in South America," March 16, 1953, CZA, S39/201.
18. To Y. Wolfson, director of PATWA, in Jerusalem, from P. Zamir, director of the PATWA office in Buenos Aires, May 22, 1959, CZA, S6/6594.
19. Activity Report, 1946/47–1950/51, 500–521.
20. "A Special Unit to Deal with Immigrants from Latin America," *Hatzofeh*, February 4, 1953, CZA S71/946.
21. Boletín Informativo no. 1, Junio de 1953, OAL: Oficina para América Latina y Países Anglosajones, Agencia Judía, Departamento de Absorción, CZA, S6/ 7146.
22. M. Kitron, "Aliya" (no date), CZA, Kitron papers, A494/34.
23. Dr. I. Wirklich to Mr. Meir Grossman, February 7, 1955, CZA S39/203.
24. Activity Report, Tevet 5716 to Nisan 5720 (January 31, 1956–March 1960), submitted to the 25th Zionist Congress, Kislev 5721, CZA, K105 XXV, 21–22. See also "The Jewish Agency for Israel, the Israeli Office in Argentina (Zionist Community Center)," May 23, 1956, CZA, S6/6204.
25. Higher Zionist Council in Argentina to S. Z. Shragai, October 23, 1956, CZA, S6/6205.
26. Ibid.
27. M. Armon to the Aliyah Department in Jerusalem, "Summary Report of a Two-Year Mission," November 15, 1959, CZA, S6/6596.
28. "Remarks at a Conference of Aliyah Department Workers," *Dappei Aliyah* 43 (1961): 48–49.
29. E. Avigur, "On the Aliya from South America," *Dappei Aliyah* 40 (1960): 65–69.
30. Los Caminos de la Alia, Publicación Mensual de la Agencia Judía para Palestina, Oficina para América del Sur, Boletín 1–10, October 15, 1950–July 15, 1951, CZA, S6/7146.
31. I. Kashtan to S. Garner, October 20, 1950, CZA, S6/6203.
32. Activity Report, 1946/47–1950/51, submitted to the 23rd Zionist Congress, August 1951, CZA, K98 XXIII, 215–16.
33. N. Bar-Giora to the Aliyah Department in Buenos Aires, "Aliya by Candidates for Kibbutzim," January 10, 1955, CZA, S6/6203.
34. "A Correct Procedure," *Davar*, April 12, 1950, CZA, Kitron papers, A494/8; M. Kitron to Y. Rafael, June 30, 1953, CZA, Kitron papers, A494/34.
35. N. Bar-Giora to the Aliyah Department in Buenos Aires, "Aliya by Candidates for Kibbutzim."
36. M. Kitron to Y. Rafael, June 30, 1953, CZA, Kitron papers, A494/34; "The Aliyah Department in the Diaspora," *Dappei Aliyah* 15 (1951): 31; "The Aliyah Department," 1957, CZA, S6/6206; M. Armon, "General Directives for the WZO Aliyah Department in Argentina," 1957, CZA, S6/6579; Higher Zionist Council in Argentina to S. Z. Shragai, October 23, 1956, CZA, S6/6205.
37. Higher Zionist Council in Argentina to S. Z. Shragai, October 23, 1956, CZA, S6/6205.

38. Higher Zionist Council in Argentina to the Aliyah Department in Jerusalem, December 5, 1956, JAFI Logistics Center, file 1175/67.
39. Dr. I. Wirklich to Mr. Meir Grossman, February 7, 1955, CZA, S39/203.
40. E. Avigur, "On the Aliya from South America," *Dappei Aliyah* 40 (1960): 65–69; E. Avigur to B. Duvdevani, "Report on Activities to Encourage Aliyah: Argentina," August 28, 1959–October 25, 1959, CZA, S6/6596.
41. Y. Green, "Are We Breaking the Law of Return?" *Yedioth Ahronoth*, June 24, 1957, CZA, S71/2610.
42. B. Duvdevani to the Zionist Federation in Argentina, Uruguay, and Chile, "The Mission of Mr. E. Avigur (Gorman)," August 2, 1959, CZA, S6/6595. See also "In the Department," *Dappei Aliyah* 38 (1960): 51.
43. "Summary of the Discussion between Mr. Avraham Ber-Kahan and Mr. Ephraim Avigur, the Special Emissary, about the Future Activities of the Aliyah Office in Buenos Aires," January 11, 1960, CZA, S6/7291; "Mr. B. Duvdevani in South America," *Dappei Aliyah* 40 (1960): 6–7. See also "Conferencia de prensa con el señor Baruj Duvdevani," *La Luz*, May 6, 1960, CZA, S6/7289.
44. "Summary of the Discussion between Mr. Avraham Ber-Kahan and Mr. Ephraim Avigur"; E. Avigur, "Excerpts from a Survey Presented at an Aliyah Department Conference," January 1960, CZA, S6/7291.
45. E. Avigur to B. Duvdevani, "Aliya from South America: Activities to Encourage Aliya," December 8, 1959, CZA, S6/6596.
46. Y. Israeli to B. Duvdevani, July 26, 1962, CZA, S6/7320.
47. S. Z. Shragai to Y. Israeli, October 24, 1962, CZA, S6/7324.
48. A. Cygel, "Report on my Activities in Argentina," August 23, 1962, CZA, S65/203.
49. Ibid.
50. Ibid.
51. M. Gelerter to Moshe Sharett and Zvi Lurie, August 1, 1962, CZA, S65/203.
52. M. Gelerter to Zvi Lurie, "Re: Argentina," August 20, 1962, CZA, S6/7323.
53. A. Cygel, "Report on My Activities in Argentina," August 23, 1962.
54. "In the Department," *Dappei Aliyah* 47 (1962): 52; "Memorandum of a Meeting Held in the Office of S. Z. Shragai," October 16, 1962, CZA, S6/7323.
55. S. Z. Shragai to Y. Israeli, October 24, 1962, CZA, S6/7324.
56. Ibid.
57. S. Z. Shragai to M. Kitron, October 24, 1962, CZA, Kitron papers, A494/18.
58. M. Kitron to Zvi Lurie, "Report on Registration and Aliya in 1962," January 21, 1963, CZA, S64/393.
59. M. Kitron to S. Z. Shragai, December 12, 1962, CZA, Kitron papers, A494/18.
60. Ibid.
61. Ibid.
62. M. Kitron to S. Z. Shragai, April 23, 1963, JAFI Logistics Center, file 2059–2060.
63. M. Kitron to M. Yakir, June 28, 1963, JAFI Logistics Center, file 2062.
64. Y. Israeli to Y. Dominitz, "Funding the Travel of Olim from Latin America," January 17, 1963, JAFI Logistics Center, file 175/67.
65. According to the AMIA report for 1963, that year the community provided financial assistance to 1,202

immigrants. See "Memoria y Balance General del 1 de enero al 31 de diciembre de 1963," Centro Marc Turcow, AMIA, Buenos Aires (1964).

66. Y. Israeli to Y. Dominitz, "Funding the Transport of Olim from Latin America," January 17, 1963.
67. M. Kitron to S. Z. Shragai, January 10, 1963, JAFI Logistics Center, file 2058.
68. A. Sabato to the Finance Department and the Aliyah Department, "A Social Worker for Our Office in Argentina," November 3, 1963, JAFI Logistics Center, file 2063.
69. Sebastian Klor, "Database 10,487."
70. D. Estrich to Y. Dominitz, "Forecast of Berths on Ships for South American Immigrants in 1963," February 10, 1963, JAFI Logistics Center, file 1175/67.
71. Y. Dominitz to Y. Israeli, November 8, 1962, CZA, S6/7324.
72. D. Estrich to Y. Dominitz, "The *Flaminia*," December 31, 1962, JAFI Logistics Center, file 2721.
73. Ibid.
74. M. Kitron to S. Z. Shragai, December 12, 1962, CZA, Kitron papers, A494/18.
75. S. Z. Shragai to A. L. Pincus, "The *Flaminia*," January 14, 1963, JAFI Logistics Center, file 2721.
76. Ibid.
77. M. Kitron to S. Z. Shragai, December 27, 1962, JAFI Logistics Center, file 2059–2060.
78. Leonardo Senkman, "A 25 años del caso Sirota: La comunidad y los sectores democráticos contra el nazismo," in *Trayectoria de una idea: Nueva Sión; 50 años de un periodismo judeo-argentino con compromiso, 1948–1998*, ed. Eliahu Toker and Ana E. Weinstein (Buenos Aires: Ediciones Fundación Mordejai Anilevich, 1999), 84–85.
79. "Con 600 olim zarpará el 4 de marzo para Israel el Buque *Flaminia*," *La Luz*, February 17, 1963, CZA, S65/203.
80. Ibid.
81. S. Z. Shragai, "Aliyah to Rescue Jews from Spiritual Destruction: An Address to the Zionist General Council, Adar 5723/March 1963," *Dappei Aliyah* 49 (1963): 8.
82. M. Dayan to B. Duvdevani, October 31, 1964.

Chapter 5

1. Central Bureau of Statistics, Statistical Abstract of Israel, vols. 1–19 (Jerusalem, 1950–68). See also Immigration to Israel 1948–1972, Part 1. Annual data (Jerusalem: CBS, 1973) [Heb.]; Immigration to Israel 1948–1972, Part 2. Composition by Period (Jerusalem CBS, 1975) [Heb.].
2. Statistical Abstract of Israel, vols. 1–19. There were several types of visas with which immigrants/potential immigrants could enter the country, and thus several immigration tracks. (1) Direct immigration refers to those who came on immigrant visas with the declared intention of settling in Israel and were naturalized upon arrival (olim). (2) Settling tourists arrived in the country on a tourist visa to consider their options and changed their status to olim only later. (3) Starting in 1963, newcomers could also register as temporary residents, an intermediate status that conferred some benefits of aliya but not Israeli citizenship. Their travel expenses to Israel were not covered by the Jewish Agency.
3. Aliya Summaries, Jewish Agency Aliyah Department (Jerusalem, 1956);

"Twenty Years of Aliya and Absorption: Summaries" (no date), ISA, gimel-3/7065.

4. There were a total of sixty-nine issues of *Dappei Aliyah* from April 1949 until it ceased publication in June 1968.
5. Binyamin Zvi Gill, "30 Years of Immigration to Israel," *Dappei Aliyah* 11 (1950): 3–75.
6. *Dappei Aliyah* 21 (1952): 2.
7. "Twenty Years of Aliya and Absorption: Summaries"; Immigration to Israel 1948–1972, Part 1. Annual data; Activity Report 1964–67, submitted to the 27th Zionist Congress (Jerusalem, 1968), CZA K112 XXVII, 31–32.
8. Dvora Hacohen, *Immigrants in Turmoil: Mass Immigration to Israel and Its Repercussions in the 1950s and After* (Syracuse, NY: Syracuse University Press, 2003), 58–94, 267.
9. Statistical Abstract of Israel, vols. 1–19.
10. "Immigration Summary: Twenty Years of Immigration to Israel," *Dappei Aliyah* 69 (1968): 34–39.
11. Ibid.
12. Gill, "30 Years of Immigration to Israel."
13. A historical testimony from the beginning of the British Mandate can be found in S. Zacharin, "Through Argentina to the Land of Israel," in *The Book of the Third Aliyah*, ed. Yehuda Erez (Tel Aviv: Am Oved, 1964), 200–202 [Heb.].
14. Gill, "30 Years of Immigration to Israel."
15. Ibid.
16. Ibid.
17. Immigration to Israel 1948–1972, Part 1. Annual Data.
18. Gill, "30 Years of Immigration to Israel."
19. "The First Oleh from Trinidad," *Hatzofeh*, April 11, 1950, CZA S71/205.
20. Immigration to Israel 1948–1972, Part 1. Annual Data. The data do not include non-native immigrants from Argentina between May 15, 1948, and the end of 1949 (more than four hundred immigrants, according to Gill's estimate), or temporary residents after 1963.
21. Ibid.
22. The statistical data of the Aliyah Department coincide with those of the CBS. According to the data, 13,695 immigrants from Argentina were registered during that period. They were joined by 1,198 tourists from Argentina who settled in Israel and by 1,044 immigrants who first registered as temporary residents. There is a discrepancy of twenty-nine immigrants between the Jewish Agency data and the slightly lower figure of the Central Bureau of Statistics. I assume that this corresponds to the number of non-Jewish immigrants from Argentina during this period.
23. "Twenty Years of Aliya and Absorption: Summaries"; Immigration to Israel 1948–1972, Part 1. Annual Data.
24. Ibid.
25. Sergio DellaPergola, "National Uniqueness and Transnational Parallelism: Reflections on the Comparative Study of Jewish Communities in Latin America," *Judaica Latinoamericana* 7 (2013): 79–84.
26. A. Pellegrino, "Tendencias de la migración internacional en América Latina y el Caribe en la segunda mitad del siglo XX," in *Patrones migratorios internacionales en América Latina*, ed. Enrique Oteiza (Buenos Aires: Eudeba, 2010), 27–40; L. Calvelo,

"Tendencias y patrones de la emigración argentina entre 1960 y 2010," in *Más allá de la fuga de cerebros: Movilidad, migración y diásporas de argentinos calificados*, ed. L. Luchilo (Buenos Aires: Editorial Universitaria de Buenos Aires, 2011), 69–91.

27. Yehoshua Wolberg, "On the Prospects for Aliya from Argentina: An Official Summary of a Visit to Argentina on Behalf of the Jewish Agency, in August 1963," October 1963, ISA, hetzade 11/2150 [Heb.].
28. Uziel Schmeltz and Sergio DellaPergola, *The Social Structure of Latin American Jewry: Demography of the Jews in Argentina and Other Latin American Countries* (Tel Aviv: David Horowitz Institute for the Research of Developed Countries, 1974), 81, 97.
29. Activity Report, Nisan 5711 to Tevet 5716 (April 1951–December 1955), submitted to the 24th Zionist Congress, Nisan 5716, CZA K102 XXIV, 59–61.
30. Moshe Kostrinsky, "We Are Making Aliya from South America," August 22, 1949, CZA S71/205; D. Horowitz, "Statistical Summaries on Registration and Aliya from Argentina: January–March 1964," April 1964, ISA, JZ 2153/3.
31. *Dappei Aliyah* 15 (1951): 25–26; "Ponencia sobre relaciones públicas e información económica pronunciada por el Dr. Abraham Mibashan en el Kinus Sionista Sudamericano, realizado en Buenos Aires entre el 27 de septiembre y el 1 de octubre de 1950," CZA, S39/201.
32. Ibid.
33. "Aliya from Argentina Will Increase," *Hatzofeh*, February 11, 1954, CZA, S71/946.
34. Horowitz, "Statistical Summaries on Registration and Aliya from Argentina: January–March 1964," July 1964, ISA, JZ 2153/3.
35. Ibid.
36. Ibid.
37. Schmeltz and DellaPergola, *Social Structure of Latin American Jewry*, 82.
38. M. Kitron to Z. Lurie, "Report on Registration and Aliya in 1962," January 21, 1963, CZA, S64/393.
39. M. Kitron to Y. Wolberg, "The Problem of Aliya Emissaries in Argentina," May 3, 1965, JAFI Logistics Center 2066.
40. "20 Years of Aliya to Israel in Numbers," *Dappei Aliyah* 69 (1968): 41.
41. Gur Alroey, *An Unpromising Land: Jewish Migration to Palestine in the Early Twentieth Century* (Stanford, CA: Stanford University Press, 2014), 90–96, 112.
42. Schmeltz and DellaPergola, *Social Structure of Latin American Jewry*, 73–77.
43. Gur Alroey, *The Silent Revolution: Jewish Emigration from the Russian Empire in the Early Twentieth Century* (Jerusalem: Shazar Center, 2008), 75 [Heb.].
44. Schmeltz and DellaPergola, *Social Structure of Latin American Jewry*, 90–97.
45. Activity Report, Nisan 5720 to Nisan 5724 (April 1, 1960–March 31, 1964), submitted to the 26th Zionist Congress, Heshvan 5725, CZA, K109 XXVI, 101.
46. *Dappei Aliyah* 15 (1951): 25–26; Kostrinsky, "We Are Making Aliya from South America"; M. Kitron to D. Ben-Gurion, "Memo: South American Jewry," November 14, 1952, CZA, Kitron papers, A494/11.

47. Kitron to Ben-Gurion, "Memo: South American Jewry."
48. Moshe Kitron, "Prospects of Jewish Immigration to Israel from Latin America," *Hador*, October 30, 1951, CZA, S71/205.
49. Gill, "30 Years of Aliya to Israel," 36–38, 43–49, 56–59, 70–71. See also Ezra Mendelsohn, *The Jews of Poland between Two World Wars* (Hanover, NH: University Press of New England, 1989).
50. S. Huzner, "Over 1,000 Olim Have Arrived, Most of Them from South America," *Dappei Aliyah* 49 (1963): 22.
51. "The *Flaminia*'s Passengers and Their Journey," *Dappei Aliyah* 49 (1963): 27; "Mass Aliya in Haifa Port Again," *Dappei Aliyah* 49 (1963): 23.
52. Statistical Abstract of Israel (Jerusalem, 1950), 14–17.
53. Anita Shapira, *Israel: A History* (Waltham, MA: Brandeis University Press, 2012), 208–44.
54. Ibid., 239.
55. Most of the immigrants who arrived in Israel in the mid-1950s were sent to the outlying areas as part of the "Ship to Village" campaign (ibid., 236).
56. Amiram Gonen, "Who Is to Be Dispersed: Rural Pioneers, Disadvantaged New Immigrants, or MiddleClass Exurbanites?" *Studies in the Geography of Israel* 14 (1993): 273–85 [Heb.].
57. M. Barkay, "The Best and the Loneliest," *Davar*, December 17, 1965, 22.
58. Ibid.
59. Ibid.
60. Wolberg, "On the Prospects for Aliya from Argentina: An Official Summary of a Visit to Argentina on Behalf of the Jewish Agency, in August 1963," ISA, het-tzade 2150/11.
61. Ibid.
62. Ibid.
63. Ibid.
64. Ibid.
65. Ibid.
66. "In the Margins: Olim and Immigrants," *Davar*, June 16, 1963, 2.
67. Wolberg, "On the Prospects for Aliya from Argentina."
68. Sergio DellaPergola, "Some Reflections on Migration in Israel: Comparative Aspects," *Hagira* 1 (2012): 5–35 [Heb.].
69. Ibid., 16–17.

Chapter 6

1. Moshe Kostrinsky "Certificates," in *Fifty Years since the Ten Certificates (from Buenos Aires to Mefalsim)* (Mefalsim: Mefalsim Archives, 1995), 65 [Heb.].
2. Abraham Mibashan to the Jewish Agency Aliyah Department, September 18, 1945, in *Fifty Years since the Ten Certificates*, 22–23 [Heb.].
3. "From the Lookout," in *Fifty Years since the Ten Certificates*, 41 [Heb.].
4. David Halperin (Hardan), *Mefalsim: The History of a Cadre* (Jerusalem: World Zionist Organization, 1950), 8 [Heb.]; Shlomo Bar-Gil, *Youth: Vision and Reality; From Dror and Gordonia to Ichud Habonim in Argentina, 1934–1973* (Ramat Ef'al: Yad Tabenkin, 2007), 177 [Heb.].
5. Halperin (Hardan), *Mefalsim*, 8.
6. Haim Kopeloff to the Jewish Agency Aliyah Department, December 6, 1945, CZA, S6/3833; Abraham Mibashan to the Jewish Agency Aliyah Department, September 18, 1945, in *Fifty Years since the Ten Certificates*, 22–23; Halperin (Hardan), *Mefalsim*, 8.
7. M. Katzovitch, "Saying Farewell," in *Fifty Years since the Ten Certificates*, 38.

8. The data are extracted from a letter the halutzim wrote in Madrid en route to Palestine, December 6, 1945, CZA, S6/3833.
9. "Immigrating to Israel," a conversation with Eliyahu Toba of Kibbutz Usha, in Asher Nathan, ed., *The First Buds of Ein Hashelosha: The First Hanoar Hatziyyoni Cadre from Latin America—Formation, Battles, and Casualties* (Ein Hashelosha: Ein Hashelosha Kibbutz Archives, 1996), 7–10 [Heb.].
10. Ibid., 38.
11. Y. Paltitzky, "A Bystander's Sketches (Interpretative Items)," in *Fifty Years since the Ten Certificates*, 37.
12. Pedro Goldfarb, *The First Latino-American Cadre of Hashomer Hatza'ir: Negba 1946–1949; The Fulfillment of the Dream* (Givat Haviva: Yad Yaari, 2006), 39 [Heb.]; Nathan, *First Buds of Ein Hashelosha*; Davar, "Kibbutz Ein Hashelosha Will Celebrate Its 10th Birthday on Monday," September 29, 1960, 6; Halperin (Hardan), *Mefalsim*, 36; Bar-Gil, *Youth: Vision and Reality*, 175; Shlomo Bar-Gil, *We Started with a Dream* (Beer Sheva: Ben-Gurion University, 2005), 63 [Heb.]; Moisés Joselevich, *Jornadas pioneras: Apuntes para una historia del movimiento jalutziano de América Latina* (Jerusalem: Keren Kaiémet Leisrael, 1957), 33.
13. Goldfarb, *First Latin-American Cadre*, 32, 36, 63; Bar-Gil, *We Started with a Dream*, 74, 119; Nathan, *First Buds of Ein Hashelosha*, 5; Davar, "Kibbutz Ein Hashelosha Will Celebrate Its 10th Birthday on Monday," September 29, 1960, 6; Halperin (Hardan), *Mefalsim*, 36.
14. M. Carmi, "Chapters on the Movement's Way," *Davar*, February 27, 1955, 3.
15. A. Puch, "On the Way to Nitzanim," in Natan, *First Buds of Ein Hashelosha*, 16–18.
16. Ibid., 5, 19.
17. Bar-Gil, *We Started with a Dream*, 114–29.
18. Ibid., 108–11. The list includes only the cadre members who were at Negba then.
19. Joselevich, *Jornadas pioneras*, 37. The list of the Negba cadre members for August 1948 includes several from Córdoba province, including Julio (Yehiel) Rosenberg, Esther Eynes, Shulamit Singer, Yitzhak Elias Kramer, Samuel Edelstein, and the physicians Yakov Dolfano and Shemaryahu Menuhin. See Goldfarb, *First Latin-American Cadre*, 110–11; interview with Julio Rosenberg, March 18, 2009; interview with Jaime Kramer, May 19, 2009; interview with Jacobo Katar, December 15, 2009; interview with Rosa Romano, May 4, 2008; interview with José Itzigsohn, October 26, 2009; interview with Rosita Sadan, June 23, 2009. This list and other sources show that as soon as independence was declared, the migration chains of youth movement members expanded throughout Argentina, and especially from the major provincial cities of Córdoba, Tucumán, and Concordia.
20. The most prominent among the teachers was Jaime Finkelstein, mentioned in chapter 1 as a stalwart of Jewish education in Argentina.
21. *Di Fraye Yugent*, "The Second National Conference of the Borochov Jugend," June 1951, no. 30, 4 [Spanish]. On the history of the movement in Poland, see Joel Roizman, "Borochov Youth" and "Dror-Borochov Youth,"

in *Poland after the Holocaust* (Ramat Ef'al: Yad Tabenkin, 1999) [Heb.].

22. *Di Fraye Yugent*, "The Second National Conference of the Borochov Jugend," June 1951, no. 30, 4 [Spanish].
23. Dr. Vardi published his autobiography, *Entre dos mundos*, in 2006. I supplemented the information there and checked it against primary documents from the archives and an interview with Dr. Vardi in August 2008 at his home in Petah Tiqva. See Arieh Vardi, *Between Two Worlds, 1938–1946*, trans. [from Spanish] Peninah Meier (Tel Aviv: Sifre Hemed, 2006) [Heb.]; interview with Arieh Vardi, August 12, 2008.
24. Vardi, *Between Two Worlds*, 21–31.
25. Ibid., 70–85; interview with Giora (Guillermo) Galker, January 26, 2008.
26. Vardi, *Entre dos mundos*, 101–3.
27. Ibid.
28. L. Roizman, "Our Borochovism vis-à-vis Reality" [translated from Spanish]. I would like to thank the author for making the original notebook available to me.
29. *Di Presse*, "Em hot zikh gegrindet in B. Aires organizatsie Ber Borochov," July 21, 1941.
30. *Di Fraye Yugent*, "The Second National Conference of the Borochov Jugend," June 1951, no. 30, 4 [Spanish].
31. The Members of Mishmar Hanegev to the Central Committee of the Borochov Jugend in Argentina, B. Aires, July 10, 1947, Yad Tabenkin Archives, File 2, Lot 14 [Yiddish]. See also *Di Fraye Yugent*, "A Visit to Mishmar Hanegev (Fortress Borochov)," April 1947, no. 2, 15–17 [Spanish].
32. *Di Fraye Yugent*, "A Letter from Mishmar Hanegev," November 1947, no. 4, 7 [Spanish].
33. *Di Fraye Yugent*, "The Second National Conference of the Borochov Jugend," June 1951, June 1951, no. 30, 4 [Spanish].
34. *Di Fraye Yugent*, "New from the Movement, around the World and Local," November 1947, no. 4, 15.
35. *Di Fraye Yugent*, February 1951, no. 26, 6. The original notes that the training farm would be three years old in March 1951.
36. Interview with Sholem and Chaike Or, January 26, 2008; interview with Reuben Cohen, April 13, 2008.
37. *Di Fraye Yugent*, "G. Hazanovitch Arrives," October 1949, no. 13, 7.
38. Interview with David Dor, April 13, 2008; interview with Yoel Eshel, July 22, 2008; interview with Moshe Koren, February 18, 2009; interview with Reuben Cohen, April 13, 2008.
39. *Di Fraye Yugent*, November 1948, no. 7, 12.
40. *Di Fraye Yugent*, "The Second Borochov Jugend Cadre Is En Route to Israel," March 1949, no. 8, 1.
41. Ibid.
42. Jaime Finkelstein, "A Day on Mishmar Hanegev," *Di Fraye Yugent*, March 1950, no. 17, 4–5.
43. Yossel Katz was one of the fifty-three volunteers from Argentina who enlisted in the Jewish Legion in 1918 and were posted with it to Palestine. His brother, Pinie Katz, was one of the most prominent intellectuals of the Jewish Left in Argentina. See Leonardo Senkman, "The First Group of Argentinian Volunteers in the Jewish Legion (1918) and the Commemorative Album Edited by M. Podolsky," *Michael* 8 (1983): 30–42 [Heb.]; Raphael Doron, *Legionnaires from Argentina: Volunteers for the*

Jewish Legion in the First World War; Biographies (Givat Haviva: Yad Ya'ari, 2007) [Heb.].

44. Finkelstein, "A Day on Mishmar Hanegev," 4–5.
45. "Mefalsim: The First Settlement by Halutzim from South America," *Davar*, June 13, 1949, 1. Hashomer Hatzair cadres established Kibbutz Gaash; the Hanoar Hatziyyoni cadre established Kibbutz Ein Hashelosha.
46. Activity Report, Nisan 5711 to Tevet 5716 (April 1951–December 1955), submitted to the 24th Zionist Congress, Nisan 5716 CZA, K102 XXIV, 135.
47. Yaakov Markovitzki, *Machal: Overseas Volunteers in Israel's War of Independence* (Jerusalem: Machal, Association of Overseas Volunteers, 2003), 12–13 [Heb.].
48. Activity Report, 1946/47–1950/51, submitted to the 23rd Zionist Congress, August 1951, CZA K98 XXIII, 35.
49. Dvora Hacohen, *Immigrants in Turmoil: Mass Immigration to Israel and Its Repercussions in the 1950s and After*, trans. Gila Brand (Syracuse, NY: Syracuse University Press, 2003), 17, 50, 119.
50. Markovitzki, *Mahal*, 6–7.
51. "Latin-American Overseas Volunteers in Israel" [Spanish], CZA, L62/8.
52. A. Levin to L. Harris, October 14, 1048, CZA, L62/80.
53. Florinda Goldberg and Yosef Rozen, eds., *Los Latinoamericanos en Israel: Antología de una aliá* (Buenos Aires: Contexto 1988), 44–54.
54. Interview with José Itzigsohn, October 26, 2009; José A. Itzigsohn, *Una experiencia judía contemporánea: Memorias y reflexiones* (Buenos Aires: Editorial Paidós, 1969).
55. Ibid., 11–13; interview with José Itzigsohn, October 26, 2009.
56. Itzigsohn, *Una experiencia judía*, 12.
57. Ibid., 15–16.
58. Ibid., 20.
59. Ibid., 25–26.
60. Ibid., 27–28.
61. Ibid., 31.
62. Ibid., 31–32.
63. Ibid., 34–35.
64. A. Levin to L. Harris, October 14, 1048, CZA, L62/80.
65. Itzigsohn, U*na experiencia judía*, 37–38.
66. I. Penhas, "Col. Pataky's 17th Medal," *Davar*, May 22, 1963, 4.
67. Ibid. See also Itzigsohn, *Una experiencia judía*, 36; Goldberg and Rozen, *Los Latinoamericanos en Israel*, 51–52; Ignacio Klich, "Latin America, the United States, and the Birth of Israel: The Case of Somoza's Nicaragua," *Journal of Latin American Studies* 20, no. 2 (1988): 427–28.
68. Itzigsohn, *Una experiencia judía*, 39.
69. Markovitzki, *Mahal*, 15.
70. "Mahal: Definition of Mahal," November 17, 1948, CZA, L62/7.
71. Itzigsohn, *Una experiencia judía*, 51–52. Itzigsohn started back for Argentina in May 1949. He completed medical school there, did a residency in psychiatry, and launched a splendid professional career. He was one of the founders of the Psychology Department at the National University in Buenos Aires, served as a senior lecturer in the department and as its chair for a number of years. At the same time, he was active in the Argentine Communist Party for some fifteen years, until the outbreak of the Six-Day War. The fierce

disagreements occasioned by the war led to his expulsion from the party. Another contributing factor was his criticism of anti-Semitism in the communist countries, which his comrades viewed as treasonous. When he left the Communist Party, he joined Mapam and became involved with the circle of intellectuals affiliated with it. He published a number of articles in Nueva Sión and was a member of the Society for Peace in the Middle East. His life changed totally on March 24, 1976, with the onset of the military dictatorship in Argentina. The junta dissolved Congress and systematically crushed all political, social, or cultural activity that was not to its liking. Dr. Itzigsohn, along with his wife and sons, fled the country in an emergency rescue operation organized by the Jewish Agency. In less than two weeks he took leave of his seventy-odd patients, asked his close friends to see to the liquidation of his property, gave away his library, and, along with his family, moved to Israel, returning to the country he had fought to establish some twenty-seven years earlier.

72. "Settlement by Mahal Fighters in Israel" [Spanish], CZA L62/8.
73. "Latin-American Overseas Volunteers in Israel" [Spanish], CZA L62/8.
74. Arye Eshel to David Ben-Gurion, February 17, 1950, ISA, gimel-15/5558.
75. CZA, L62/8. Of the other volunteers, 18% came from Brazil, 12% from Uruguay, and 10% from Chile. There were also a few volunteers from Bolivia, Colombia, Costa Rica, Cuba, Mexico, Panama, Paraguay, Peru, and Venezuela.
76. CZA, L62/7–8, L62/80.
77. Benzion Benshalom, *Con los ojos abiertos: Observaciones y reflexiones sobre la vida judía, el sionismo y los movimientos juveniles en América Latina* (Jerusalem: World Zionist Organization, Youth and Hehalutz Department, 1954), 36–46.
78. "Conference of People from Latin America," *Hador*, November 24, 1949, CZA, A494/7. See also "Conference of Community Leaders from Latin America," November 25, 1949, no. 5 (17), Mefalsim Archives.
79. See Bar-Gil, *We Started with a Dream*; Bar-Gil, *Youth: Vision and Reality*; David Horowitz, *Young Dror-Hehalutz in Argentina: The Story of the Movements' Founders* (Tel Aviv: Privately published, 2000) [Heb.]; Iair Rubin, *La memoria del sueño* (Buenos Aires: Milá, 2006); David Ben Israel, *De América Latina a Israel, al Kibutz* (Merhavia: Merhavia Press, 1978).
80. The young people disseminated their worldview in various periodicals, including *Nueva Sión*, *Horizonte*, *Pregón Juvenil*, and *Opinión*.
81. Yerah Greenfield, "The Zionist-Socialist Youth Brigades in 1960s Argentina: Constructing Worldviews" (master's thesis, Hebrew University of Jerusalem, 2006), 94 [Heb.].
82. The Anielewicz Brigade had 120 active members; the Habonim Brigade, 100. See "Informe de los movimientos juveniles mundiales," First World Congress of Jewish Youth, Jerusalem, July 28–31, 26.
83. These estimates appear in most of the primary documents at my disposal. See, for example, Ephraim Avigur, "On the Aliya from South America: Excerpts from a Survey Presented at

a Conference of Aliyah Department Staff, January 1960," CZA, S6/7291. See also Haim Avni, *Argentina and the Jews: A History of Jewish Immigration*, trans. Gila Brand (Tuscaloosa: University of Alabama Press, 1991), 98n121, 99n123; Avni, *Jewish Students and the Argentinian Jewish Community* (Hebrew University of Jerusalem, Institute of Contemporary Jewry, 1971), 9–35 [Heb.]. The number of young Jews affiliated with non-Zionist organizations always exceeded the number of halutzim. Most young Jews in Argentina were drawn to the cultural, social, and sports organizations that attracted the nonobservant, including Maccabee, Hakoach, and Hebraica. These clubs became very important foci of Jewish identity in Argentina and were more compatible with the generally comfortable lives of so many teenagers and young adults. Unlike the Zionist youth movements and the young-adult brigades, the sports and cultural associations blossomed mainly in the 1960s and increased their influence then. Their large memberships attest to the young Jews' interest in finding places for social contact among themselves rather than in Jewish content or an aspiration for personal, political, or ideological fulfillment.

84. Joselevich, *Jornadas pioneras.*
85. Ibid., 12.
86. Ibid., 158–59.
87. Devorah Schachner, *A Political Girl* (Tel Aviv: Hakibbutz Hame'uchad, 2002).
88. Ibid., 189–90.
89. Ibid.
90. Bar-Gil, *We Started with a Dream*, 89–90.
91. Of the 1,184 applicants accounted pioneer youth, 240 (about 20%) came to Israel on regular immigrant visas or through Youth Aliyah.
92. Raanan Rein, *Argentina, Israel, and the Jews: Perón, the Eichmann Capture and After*, trans. Martha Grenzeback (Bethesda: University Press of Maryland, 2003), 94–95.
93. S. Ades (Hadas), ed., *Latin Americans in Israel* (Tel Aviv: OLEI and the World Jewish Congress, 1960), 32 [Heb.].
94. Ibid. See also Moshe Melman, *The Beginnings of Kefar Argentina* (N.p., 1979) [Heb.].
95. Ades (Hadas), *Latin Americans in Israel*, 32.
96. Ibid., 34.
97. "Plan to Bring 2000 Families from Argentina," *Ha'aretz*, June 4, 1952, CZA S71/946.
98. Ibid.
99. Ibid.
100. "Maris Capital Investments in Industrial Plants, Ltd.," CZA S39/203; Ades (Hadas), *Latin Americans in Israel*, 33.
101. Y. Zeitlin to Dr. E. Neumann, "An Israeli Bank for Latin America," November 18, 1953, CZA S39/201. See also A. S. Zeitlin, "Report on the Economic Department's Activities in South America" (undated), CZA S115/473.
102. Zeitlin, "Report on the Economic Department's Activities in South America." See also Ades (Hadas), *Latin Americans in Israel*, 33. In Córdoba, Blecher had been a lecturer at the National University. He also managed the Jewish City Bank and was one of the leaders of the local Jewish community. Later he was a

senior economist in Israel, a lecturer in statistics at Tel Aviv University, and prominent in the Latin American community in Israel. See Rafael Aldor, *Perfiles de éxito: Reportajes a olim latinoamericanos* (Buenos Aires: Jewish Agency Economic Department, 1964), 17–20.

103. Ades (Hadas), *Latin Americans in Israel*, 28; "The S. Kaufmann Group—South American Company for Settlement and Industry, Ltd.," CZA S39/203.
104. Dr. A. S. Zeitlin to Y. Katz, "Establishment of a Cooperative Society with Capitalization of 600,000 Pounds," September 17, 1953, CZA S115/473.
105. Ibid. See also Ades (Hadas), *Latin Americans in Israel*, 28.
106. "Work Plan of Dr. A. Z. Zeitlin, the Jewish Agency Economic Department's Representative in South America," March 16, 1953, CZA S39/201.
107. "Summary of the Mission of Dr. A. S. Zeitlin for the Jewish Agency Economic Department in South America, 1953–1955," CZA, S39/203.
108. To Dr. E. Neumann, Economics Department, Jerusalem, from Y. Zeitlin, "An Israeli Bank for Latin America (confidential)," November 18, 1953, CZA, S39/201.
109. Ibid.
110. Ibid.
111. Ades (Hadas), *Latin Americans in Israel*, 28.
112. Y. Kotler, "Argentinian Jews are Immigrating to Israel," *Ha'aretz*, July 2, 1953, CZA, S71/205.
113. Ibid.
114. Melman, *Beginnings of Kefar Argentina*, 25.
115. Ibid., 7.
116. Ibid., 10.
117. Ibid., 11.
118. Ibid.
119. Ibid., 13–15; Kotler, "Argentinian Jews Are Immigrating to Israel," *Ha'aretz*, July 2, 1953, CZA, S71/205.
120. Kotler, "Argentinian Jews Are Immigrating to Israel," 24. Natan Lerner was the vice president of the DAIA in 1957–59. See his testimony in the Oral Documentation Section, Institute of Contemporary Jewry, the Hebrew University of Jerusalem, 1994 (228), 4.
121. Melman, *Beginnings of Kefar Argentina*, 20–30.
122. Ibid.
123. Ibid., 31.
124. Ibid.
125. Ibid., 21.
126. Ibid., 29.
127. Ibid., 32–40; Kotler, "Argentinian Jews Are Immigrating to Israel," *Ha'aretz*, July 2, 1953, CZA S71/205.
128. Ibid.
129. Melman, *Beginnings of Kefar Argentina*, 44.
130. Ibid., 45–46.
131. Ibid., 54–56.
132. Ibid., 60–76.
133. Ibid., 77–90; G. Israel, "Settlement for Argentinian Olim to Be Established Near Ramle," *Al Hamishmar*, August 6, 1952. See also "Industrial Village for Argentinian Olim," *Davar*, March 11, 1953, CZA, S71\946.
134. Kotler, "Argentinian Jews Are Immigrating to Israel."
135. Ibid.
136. Melman, *Beginnings of Kefar Argentina*, 87.
137. "Jewish Families from Argentina Settling in Israel," *Davar*, November 19, 1953, CZA, S71/946.

138. Melman, *Beginnings of Kefar Argentina*, 115; "Olim from Argentina Arrive in Haifa," *Al Hamishmar*, December 16, 1953, CZA, S71/946.
139. Kotler, "Argentinian Jews Are Immigrating to Israel."
140. Melman, *Beginnings of Kefar Argentina*, 149–71; T. Weinstock, "Argentina Was a Nachtasyl: Residents of Baron Hirsch's Colonies Are Settling in Israel," *Davar*, June 3, 1954, 2; "From the Fields of the Baron Hirsch to the Fields of Israel: Kefar Argentina—an Example of City-to-Village Settlers," *Davar*, March 1, 1957; Ades (Hadas), *Latin Americans in Israel*, 26–27.
141. See the testimony of Moshe Ben-Yosef, "Our Agricultural Experience in Nir Zevi (Kefar Argentina)," in *Del Campo al Campo: Colonos de Argentina en Israel*, ed. Haim Avni and Leonardo Senkman (Buenos Aires: Milá, 1993), 92–107.
142. "C.A.I.R.A.," December 31, 1945, CZA, S39/201.
143. E. Gorman to Absorption Department Executive, March 4, 1956, CZA, S6/6204.
144. Ibid.
145. Ibid.
146. A. Peleg, "Kefar Argentina on the Verge of Despair," *Maariv*, June 27, 1961, 5.
147. M. Kitron, "Aliya from Latin America: Situation and Prospects," February 1962, ISA, het-tzade 11/2150.
148. Chaim Doron and Shifra Schwartz, *Medicine in the Community* (Beer Sheva: Ben-Gurion University of the Negev Press, 2004) [Heb.].
149. Interview with Chaim Doron, August 19, 2008.
150. Ibid.
151. Ibid. See also Doron and Schwartz, *Medicine in the Community*.
152. Ibid., 91–92.
153. Ibid.
154. "Doctors from Argentina Settle in Beersheba," *Jerusalem Post*, August 16, 1957, CZA, S71/2610.
155. Doron and Schwartz, *Medicine in the Community*, 92; "Statistics on PATWA's Activity, 1957–1958," CZA, S6/6594.
156. "Doctors from Argentina Who Came to Work for a Year Settling in Israel," *Dappei Aliyah* 44 (1962): 6.
157. Yitzhak Eisenberg, "30 Doctors from Brazil and Argentina Settle in Beer Sheva," *Haboker*, March 6, 1963, JAFI Logistics Center, file 2059–60.
158. Ibid.
159. "60 Young Doctors from Latin America to Settle in the Negev This Year," *Davar*, February 6, 1967, 4.
160. Ibid.
161. Interview with Chaim Doron, Augsut 19, 2008.
162. CZA, S6/6205 (1956–57); S6/6206 (1957–58); S6/6593 (1958–59); S6/6594 (1959); S6/6595 (1959); "Aliya from Argentina, 1959–1961," CZA, S6/7322.
163. M. Kitron, "Aliya from Latin America: Situation and Prospects," February 1962, ISA, het-tzade 11/2150.
164. A. Bar-Kahn to Z. Shazar, July 10, 1961, CZA, S6/7314.
165. E. Avigur, "On the Aliya from South America," *Dappei Aliyah* 40 (1960): 65.
166. Activity Report, Tevet 5716 to Nisan 5720 (January 31, 1956–March 1960), submitted to the 25th Zionist Congress, Kislev 5721, CZA, K105 XXV, 222–226.

167. M. Dayan to B. Duvdevani, October 31, 1964, JAFI Logistics Center, file 2065.
168. D. Estrich to Y. Dominitz, "Report on the *Flaminia* Escorts," March 11, 1963, JAFI Logistics Center, file 2051.
169. "The *Flaminia* Passengers en Route," *Dappei Aliyah* 49 (1963), 26–27.
170. B. Z. Fixler, "Report on the *Flaminia* from South America" (undated), JAFI Logistics Center, file 61–2060.
171. Ibid., 30.
172. Y. Bezalel, "The First 12 Hours on the *Flaminia*," *Dappei Aliyah* 49 (1963): 31.
173. M. Ben-Abir, "La primera familia Argentina que llego a Palestina," unedited handwritten text about the Shugurevsky family—Abraham and Feiga and their sons Shlomo and Uriel (M. Ben-Abir, personal archives).
174. Bezalel, "First 12 Hours on the *Flaminia*," 32.
175. "The *Flaminia* Passengers en Route," *Dappei Aliyah* 49 (1963): 26–27.
176. A. Reuveni, "Haifa Port Again Sees Large Aliya," *Dappei Aliyah* 49 (1963): 23.
177. "*Flaminia* Passengers en Route," 24.
178. Ibid.
179. Ibid., 27.
180. Ibid.
181. Interview with Felisa Rubinstein de Bichman, July 29, 2009; Klor, "The 10,487 Database."
182. "Los inmigrantes de la Argentina son muy apreciados en Israel," *La Luz* 18 (date missing), CZA S65/203.
183. Interview with Felisa Rubinstein de Bichman, July 29, 2009.
184. Har-Gil, "Argentinians Arriving at the Kibbutz," March 5, 1967.
185. Ibid., 12. On Shraga Har-Gil, see "Obituary: Shraga Har-Gil—the Boy with His Back to the Camera," *Ha'aretz*, October 9, 2009.
186. Har-Gil, "Argentinians Arriving at the Kibbutz."
187. Ibid.
188. Klor, "The 10,487 Database."

BIBLIOGRAPHY

Archives

Central Zionist Archives, Jerusalem (CZA)
Israel State Archives, Jerusalem (ISA)
Jewish Agency Logistics Center, Tserifim
Kibbutz Mefalsim
Yad Tebenkin Archives, Ramt Efal

Official Documents and Publications

Central Bureau of Statistics. Immigration to Israel 1948–72, Part 1. Annual Data. Jerusalem: CBS, 1973 [Heb.].

Central Bureau of Statistics. Immigration to Israel 1948–72, Part 2. Composition by Period. Jerusalem, 1975 [Heb.].

Central Bureau of Statistics. Statistical Abstract of Israel, vols. 1–19. Jerusalem, 1950–68.

Jewish Agency for Israel. Activity Report, 1946/47–1950/51, submitted to the 23rd Zionist Congress, August 1951, CZA K98 XXIII, 500–521.

Jewish Agency for Israel. Activity Report, Nisan 5711 to Tevet 5716 (April 1951–December 1955), submitted to the 24th Zionist Congress, Nisan 5716, CZA, K102 XXIV, 59–61.

Jewish Agency for Israel. Activity Report, Tevet 5716 to Nisan 5720 (January 1956–31 March 1960), submitted to the 25th Zionist Congress, Kislev 5721, CZA, K105 XXV, 64–73.

Jewish Agency for Israel. Activity Report, Nisan 5720 to Nisan 5724 (April 1, 1960–March 31, 1964), submitted to the 26th Zionist Congress, Heshvan 5725, CZA, K109 XXVI, 101.

Jewish Agency for Israel. Activity Report, Nisan 5764 to Tevet 5728 (April 1, 1964–December 31, 1967), submitted to the 27th Zionist Congress, Nisan 5728, CZA, K112 XXVII, 111.

Jewish Agency for Israel. Aliya Summaries. Jewish Agency Aliya Department. Jerusalem, 1956.

Newspapers

Al Hamishmar
Davar
Di Fraye Yugent
Ha'aretz
Haboker
Hador
Hatzofeh
Maariv
La Luz
Di Presse

Books and Articles

Ades (Hadas), S., ed. *Latin Americans in Israel.* Tel Aviv: OLEI and the World Jewish Congress, 1960 [Heb.].

Aldor, Rafael. *Perfiles de éxito: Reportajes a olim latinoamericanos.* Buenos Aires: Jewish Agency Economic Department, 1964.

Alperson, Mordecai. *Thirty Years of Jewish Settlement in Argentina.* Tel Aviv: Hevrah, 1930 [Heb.].

Alroey, Gur. "Aliya to America? A Comparative Look at Jewish Mass Migration, 1881–1914." *Modern Judaism: A Journal of Jewish Ideas and Experience* 28, no. 2 (2008): 109–33.

———. *The Silent Revolution: Jewish Emigration from the Russian Empire in the Early Twentieth Century.* Jerusalem: Shazar Center, 2008) [Heb.].

———. *An Unpromising Land: Jewish Migration to Palestine in the Early Twentieth Century.* Stanford, CA: Stanford University Press, 2014.

Altamirano, Carlos, ed. *La Argentina en el siglo XX.* Buenos Aires: Ariel; Quilmes: Universidad Nacional de Quilmas, 1999.

AMILAT, *Judaica Latinoamericana*, vols. 1–6. Jerusalem: Magnes Press, 1988, 1993, 1997, 2001, 2005, 2009, 2013.

Armus, Diego. "Diez años de historiografía sobre la inmigración masiva a la Argentina." *Estudios Migratorios Latinoamericanos* 4 (1986): 431–60.

Auza, Néstor Tomás. *Católicos y liberales en la generación del ochenta.* Buenos Aires: Ediciones Culturales Argentinas, 1975.

Avni, Haim. *Argentina and the Jews: A History of Jewish Immigration.* Translated by Gila Brand. Tuscaloosa: University of Alabama Press, 1991.

———. "Cuarenta años, el contexto histórico y desafíos a la investigación." In *Pertenencia y alteridad: Judíos en/de América Latina, cuarenta años de cambios*, edited by Haim Avni, Judit Bokser-Liwerant, Sergio DellaPergola, Margalit Bejarano, and Leonardo Senkman. Madrid: Iberoamericana, 2011.

———. *Emancipation and Jewish Education.* Jerusalem: Shazar Center, 1985.

———. "A Failed Project? Towards a Balance of Jewish Agriculture in Argentina." In *Emigration and Settlement in Jewish and General History: A Collection of Essays*, edited by Avigdor Shinan. Jerusalem: Shazar Center, 1982.

———. *Jewish Students and the Argentinian Jewish Community.* Hebrew University of Jerusalem, Institute of Contemporary Jewry, 1971 [Heb.].

———. "'Majority Societies' in Jewish Diasporas: Latin American Experience." In *Transnationalism: Diasporas and the Advent of a New (Dis)order*, edited by Eliezer Ben-Rafael and Yitzhak Sternberg, 337–45. Boston: Brill, 2009.

———. "The Origins of Zionism in Latin America." In *The Jewish Presence in Latin America*, edited by Judith Laikin Elkin and Gilbert W. Merkx, 135–55. Boston: Allen and Unwin, 1987.

Avni, Haim. "A True Turning Point? The Six-Day War and the Organized Jewish Community in Argentina." *Yahadut Zemanenu* 11–12 (1998): 274–75 [Heb.].

Avni, Haim, Judit Bokser-Liwerant, Sergio DellaPergola, Margalit Bejarano, and Leonardo Senkman, eds. *Pertenencia y alteridad: Judíos en/de América Latina, cuarenta años de cambios.* Madrid: Iberoamericana, 2011.

Avni, Haim, and Leonardo Senkman, eds. *Del Campo al Campo: Colonos de Argentina en Israel.* Buenos Aires: Milá, 1993.

Bachi, Roberto. *The Population of Israel.* Paris: CICRED; Jerusalem: Hebrew University, 1977.

Baily, Samuel L. "Chain Migration of Italians to Argentina: Case Studies of the Agnonesi and the Sirolesi." *Studi emigrazione/Etudes migrations* 19, no. 65 (1982): 73–91.

———. *Immigrants in the Lands of Promise: Italians in Buenos Aires and New York City, 1870–1914*. Ithaca, NY: Cornell University Press, 1999.

Bar-Gil, Shlomo. *We Started with a Dream*. Beer Sheva: Ben-Gurion University, 2005.

———. *Youth: Vision and Reality; From Dror and Gordonia to Ichud Habonim in Argentina, 1934–1973*. Ramat Ef'al: Yad Tabenkin, 2007 [Heb.].

Barkai, Haim. *The Genesis of the Israeli Economy*. Jerusalem: Mosad Bialik, 1990 [Heb.].

Bejarano, Margalit. "Fuentes para la historia de los sefaradíes en la Argentina." *Sefárdica* 9 (1986): 99–109.

———. "Sephardic Communities in Latin America: Past and Present." *Judaica Latinoamericana* 5 (2005): 9–26.

Bejarano, Margalit, and Edna Aizenberg, eds. *Contemporary Sephardic Identity in the Americas: An Interdisciplinary Approach*. Syracuse, NY: Syracuse University Press, 2012.

Bell, Lawrence D. "In the Name of the Community: Populism, Ethnicity, and Politics among the Jews of Argentina under Perón, 1946–1955." *Hispanic American Historical Review* 86, no. 1 (2006): 93–122.

Ben Israel, David. *De América Latina a Israel, al Kibutz*. Merhavia: Merhavia Press, 1978.

Benarie, M. *The Historical Development of Jewish Commerce and Industry in Buenos Aires: A Jubilee Book—A Summary of 50 Years of Jewish Life in Argentina*. Buenos Aires: Idische Zeitung, 1940 [Yiddish].

Ben-Dror, Graciela. *The Catholic Church and the Jews: Argentina, 1933–1945*. Lincoln: University of Nebraska Press, 2008.

Ben-Rafael, Eliezer, and Yohanan Peres. *Is Israel One? Religion, Nationalism, and Multiculturalism Confounded*. Leiden: Brill, 2005.

Ben-Rafael, Eliezer, and Yitzhak Sternberg, eds. *Transnationalism: Diasporas and the Advent of a New (Dis)order*. Boston: Brill, 2009.

Benshalom, Benzion. *Con los ojos abiertos: Observaciones y reflexiones sobre la vida judía, el sionismo y los movimientos juveniles en América Latina*. Jerusalem: World Zionist Organization, Youth and Hehalutz Department, 1954.

Ben-Yosef, Moshe. "Our Agricultural Experience in Nir Zevi (Kefar Argentina)." In *Del Campo al Campo: Colonos de Argentina en Israel*, edited by Haim Avni and Leonardo Senkman, 92–107. Buenos Aires: Milá, 1993.

Bokser-Liwerant, Judit. "Being National, Being Transnational: Snapshots of Belonging and Citizenship." In *Shifting Frontiers of Citizenship: The Latin American Experience*, edited by Mario Sznajder, Luis Roniger, and Carlos Forment, 343–66. Leiden: Brill, 2013.

———. "Los judíos de América Latina: Los signos de las tendencias; Juegos y contrajuegos." In *Pertenencia y alteridad: Judíos en/de América Latina, cuarenta años de cambios*, edited by Haim Avni, Judit Bokser-Liwerant, Sergio DellaPergola, Margalit Bejarano, and Leonardo Senkman, 127–28. Madrid: Iberoamericana, 2011.

Bokser-Liwerant, Judit, Eliezer Ben-Rafael, Yossef Gorny, and Raanan Rein, eds. *Identities in an Era of Multiculturalism: Latin America in the Jewish World*. Leiden: Brill, 2008.

Bokser-Liwerant, Judit, Sergio DellaPergola, Haim Avni, Margalit Bejarano, and Leo Senkman. Introduction, "Cuarenta años de cambio: Transiciones y paradigmas." In *Pertenencia y alteridad: Judíos en/de América Latina, cuarenta años de cambios*, edited by Haim Avni, Judit Bokser-Liwerant, Sergio DellaPergola, Margalit Bejarano, and Leonardo Senkman, 13–83. Madrid: Iberoamericana, 2011.

Brodsky, Adriana, and Raanan Rein, eds. *The New Jewish Argentine Facets of Jewish Experiences in the Southern Cone*. Leiden: Brill, 2013.

Calvelo, L. "Tendencias y patrones de la emigración argentina entre 1960 y 2010." In *Más allá de la fuga de cerebros: Movilidad, migración y diásporas de argentinos calificados*, edited by in L. Luchilo, 69–91. Buenos Aires: Editorial Universitaria de Buenos Aires, 2011.

DAIA. *Medio siglo de lucha por una Argentina sin discriminaciones: Todo es Historia*. Buenos Aires, 1985.

DellaPergola, Sergio. "Cuántos somos hoy?" In *Pertenencia y alteridad: Judíos en/de América Latina, cuarenta años de cambios*, edited by Haim Avni, Judit Bokser-Liwerant, Sergio DellaPergola, Margalit Bejarano, and Leonardo Senkman, 311. Madrid: Iberoamericana, 2011.

———. "The Global Context of Migration to Israel." In *Immigration to Israel: Sociological Perspectives*, ed. Elazar Leshem and Judith T. Shuval, 51–92. New Brunswick, NJ: Transaction, 1998.

———. "National Uniqueness and Transnational Parallelism: Reflections on the Comparative Study of Jewish Communities in Latin America." *Judaica Latinoamericana* 7 (2013): 79–84.

———. "Some Reflections on Migration in Israel: Comparative Aspects." *Hagira* 1 (2012): 5–35.

Deutsch, Sandra McGee. "Changing the Landscape: The Study of Argentine-Jewish Women and New Historical Vistas." In *Rethinking Jewish-Latin Americans*, edited by Jeffrey Lesser and Raanan Rein, 161–86. Albuquerque: University of New Mexico Press, 2008.

Devoto, Fernando J. "Del crisol al pluralismo: Treinta años de historiografía sobre las migraciones europeas a la Argentina." *Movimientos migratorios: Historiografía y problemas* (1991): 15–47

Dominitz, Yehuda. *Aliyah and Migration: From Years of Destruction to an Era of Rebirth (1935–1961)*. Jerusalem: Zionist Library, 2000 [Heb.].

Doron, Haim, and Shifra Schwartz. *Medicine in the Community*. Beer Sheva: Ben-Gurion University of the Negev Press, 2004 [Heb.].

Doron, Raphael. *Legionnaires from Argentina: Volunteers for the Jewish Legion in the First World War; Biographies*. Givat Haviva: Yad Ya'ari, 2007 [Heb.].

Eisenstadt, Shmuel N. "Aliyah ve-hagirah, kavim le-tipologia sotziologit" (Aliyah and Hagirah: The Outline of a Sociological Typology). *Metzudah* 7 (1954): 83–91.

Elkin, Judith. "Recent Publications in Latin American Jewish Studies: Current Bibliography of Latin Jewish Studies 1997–1998." 1999.

Elkin, Judith, ed. "Bibliography of Books and Articles in Latin American Jewish Studies, 1991–1996." 1997.

Elkin, Judith Laikin, and Gilbert W. Merkx, eds. *The Jewish Presence in Latin America*. Boston: Allen and Unwin, 1987.

Elkin, Judith Laikin, and Ana Lya Sater, eds. *Latin American Jewish Studies: An Annotated Guide to the Literature*. New York: Greenwood Press, 1990.

Erez, Yehuda, ed. *The Book of the Third Aliyah*. Tel Aviv: Am Oved, 1964 [Heb.].

Fifty Years since the Ten Certificates (from Buenos Aires to Mefalsim). Mefalsim: Mefalism Archives, 1995.

Finkelstein, Jaime. "A Year of My Life." *Argentiner YIVO shriften* 13 (1983): 22–42 [Yiddish].

Firstater, Jaime. *Lucha, Moral y Futuro*. Córdoba: Editorial Schalom, 1967.

Gelber, Yoav. "From 'Don't Come!' until the Law of Return: Vacillations and Changes in the Zionist Attitude towards Aliya." In *Ingathering of Exiles: Aliyah to the Land of Israel Myth and Reality*, edited by Devora Hacohen, 249–82. Jerusalem: Shazar Center, 1998).

Germani Gino. *Política y sociedad en una época de transición: De la sociedad tradicional a la sociedad de masas*. Buenos Aires: Editorial Paidos, 1966.

Goldberg, Florinda, and Yosef Rozen, eds. *Los Latinoamericanos en Israel: Antología de una aliá*. Buenos Aires: Contexto 1988.

Goldfarb, Pedro. *First Latino-American Garin of Hashomer Hatzair: Negba 1946–1949; The Fulfilment of the Dream*. Givat Haviva: Yad Ya'ari, 2006 [Heb.].

Gomel, Elana. *The Pilgrim Soul: Being Russian in Israel*. Amherst, NY: Cambria Press, 2009.

Gonen, Amiram. "Who Is to Be Dispersed: Rural Pioneers, Disadvantaged New Immigrants, or MiddleClass Exurbanites?" *Studies in the Geography of Israel* 14 (1993): 273–85 [Heb.].

Greenfield, Yerah. "The Zionist-Socialist Youth Brigades in 1960s Argentina: Constructing Worldviews." Master's thesis, Hebrew University of Jerusalem, 2006 [Heb.].

Grinberg, Lev. "Social and Political Economy." In *Trends in Israeli Society*, edited by Ephraim Yaar and Zeev Shavit, 628–30. Tel Aviv: Open University, 2001 [Heb.].

Hacohen, Dvora. "Immigrant Settlement Policy during the First Decade of the State: The Attempts to Limit Immigration and Their Fate." In *Ingathering of Exiles: Aliyah to the Land of Israel Myth and Reality*, edited by Devora Hacohen. Jerusalem: Shazar Center, 1998).

———. *Immigrants in Turmoil: Mass Immigration to Israel and Its Repercussions in the 1950s and After*. Syracuse, NY: Syracuse University Press, 2003.

———. "The Law of Return: Its Content and the Disputes about It." In *Independence: The First Fifty Years*, ed. Anita Shapira, 57–87. Jerusalem: Shazar Center, 1998 [Heb.].

Hacohen, Dvora, ed. *Ingathering of Exiles: Aliya to the Land of Israel Myth and Reality*. Jerusalem: Shazar Center, 1998 [Heb.].

Halamish, Aviva. *Dual Race against Time: Zionist Immigration Policy in the 1930s*. Jerusalem: Yad Ben-Zvi, 2006 [Heb.].

———. "Selective Aliya as an Idea and Practice and in Zionist Historiography." In *The Age of Zionism*, edited by Anita Shapira, Jehuda Reinharz, and Jay Michael Harris, 185–203. Jerusalem: Shazar Center, 2000.

Halperin (Hardan), David. *Mefalsim: The History of a Cadre*. Jerusalem: World Zionist Organization, 1950 [Heb.].

Halperin Donghi, Tulio. *La república imposible*. Buenos Aires: Ariel, 2004.

Harel, Isser. *Security and Democracy*. Tel Aviv: Idanim, 1989.

Heller, Joseph. *The Struggle for the Jewish State*. Jerusalem: Shazar Center, 1985 [Heb.].

Herman, Donald L. *The Latin American Community of Israel*. New York: Praeger, 1984.

Horowitz, David. "The Jewish Community in Argentina and Aliya from It, 1961–1973." PhD diss., Tel Aviv University, 2006.

———. *Young Dror-Hehalutz in Argentina: The Story of the Movements' Founders*. Tel Aviv: Privately published, 2000 [Heb.].

Itzigsohn, José A. *Una experiencia judía contemporánea: Memorias y reflexiones*. Buenos Aires: Editorial Paidós, 1969.

James, Daniel, and Luis Justo. *Resistencia e integración*. Buenos Aires: Sudamericana, 1991.

Joselevich, Moisés. *Jornadas pioneras: Apuntes para una historia del movimiento jalutziano de América Latina*. Jerusalem: Keren Kaiémet Leisrael, 1957.

Kemp, Adriana, and Rivka Reichman. *Migrants and Workers: The Political Economy of Labor Migration in Israel*. Jerusalem: Van Leer Jerusalem Institute and Hakibbutz Hame'uchad, 2008 [Heb.].

Kitron, Naomi. *On Three Continents: The Life of Moshe Kitron*. Jerusalem: Carmel, 2005 [Heb.].

Klich, Ignacio. "Latin America, the United States, and the Birth of Israel: The Case of Somoza's Nicaragua." *Journal of Latin American Studies* 20, no. 2 (1988): 427–28.

Klor, Sebastián. "Ser judío / sionista / argentino: La experiencia histórica y socioeconómica de los inmigrantes judíos en Córdoba, 1901–1950." *Junta Provincial de Historia de Córdoba* 24 (2007): 55–71.

———. "The 10,487 Database."

Koren, M. "Itzhak Bank, the Enthusiastic Community Activist." Unpublished [Spanish].

———. "Jaime Finkelstein: The Paradigmatic Educator." Unpublished [Spanish].

Korn, Francis. *Buenos Aires: Los huéspedes del 20*. Buenos Aires: Editorial Sudamericana, 1974.

Kostrinsky, Moshe. "Certificates." In *Fifty Years since the Ten Certificates (from Buenos Aires to Mefalsim)* (Mefalsim: Mefalsim Archives, 1995).

Lang, Berel. "Hyphenated-Jews and the Anxiety of Identity." *Jewish Social Studies*, n.s. 12, no. 1 (2005): 1–15.

Lavsky, Hagit. "The Surviving Remnant and the Establishment of the State: An Opportunity That Was Used." *Katedra* 55 (1990): 175–81 [Heb.].

Lederhendler, Eli, ed. *The Six-Day War and World Jewry*. Bethesda: University Press of Maryland, 2000.

Leshem, Elazar, and Judith T. Shuval, eds. *Immigration to Israel: Sociological Perspectives*. New Brunswick, NJ: Transaction, 1998.

Lesser, Jeffrey, and Raanan Rein. "Challenging Particularity, Jews as a Lens on Latin American Ethnicity." *Latin American and Caribbean Ethnic Studies* 1, no. 2 (2006): 249–63.

Lesser, Jeffrey, and Raanan Rein, eds. *Rethinking Jewish-Latin Americans*. Albuquerque: University of New Mexico Press, 2008.

Lestschinsky, J. "Jewish Migrations 1840–1946." In *The Jews: Their History, Culture, and Religion*, edited by Louis Finkelstein, 1198–238. Philadelphia: Jewish Publication Society, 1949.

Lissak, Moshe. *Mass Immigration in the Fifties: The Failure of the Melting Pot Policies*. Jerusalem: Mosad Bialik, 1999 [Heb.].

Lvovich, Daniel. *Nacionalismo y antisemitismo en la Argentina*. Buenos Aires: J. Vergara, 2003.

Markovitzki, Yaakov. *Machal: Overseas Volunteers in Israel's War of Independence*. Jerusalem: Machal, Association of Overseas Volunteers, 2003 [Heb.].

Marshall, A. "Emigration of Argentines to the United States." In *When Borders Don't Divide: Labor Migration and Refugee Movements in the Americas*, edited by Patricia R. Pessar, 129–41. New York: Center for Migration Studies, 1988.

Meirovich, Carlos. *¿Por qué no te fuiste, papá?: Saga de una familia de argentinos judíos*. Buenos Aires: Milá, 2008.

Melman, Moshe. *The Beginnings of Kefar Argentina*. N.p, 1979 [Heb.].

Mendelsohn, Ezra. *The Jews of Poland between Two World Wars*. Hanover, NH: University Press of New England, 1989.

Milgram, Avraham, ed. *Entre la aceptación y el rechazo: América Latina y los refugiados judíos del nazismo*. Jerusalem: Yad Vashem, 2003.

Mirelman, Victor A. *En búsqueda de una identidad: Los inmigrantes judíos en Buenos Aires, 1890–1930*. Buenos Aires: Milá, 1988.

Moya, Jose C. *Cousins and Strangers: Spanish Immigrants in Buenos Aires, 1850–1930*. Berkeley: University of California Press, 1998.

Moya, José. "The Jewish Experience in Argentina in a Diasporic Comparative Perspective." In *The New Jewish Argentine: Facets of Jewish Experiences in the Southern Cone*, edited by Adriana Brodsky and Raanan Rein, 7–29. Leiden: Brill, 2013.

Munz, Rainer, and Rainer Ohliger, eds. *Diasporas and Ethnic Migrants: Germany, Israel, and Post-Soviet Successor States in Comparative Perspective*. Portland, OR: Frank Cass, 2003.

Nathan, Asher, ed. *The First Buds of Ein Hashelosha: The First Hanoar Hatziyyoni Cadre from Latin America—Formation, Battles, and Casualties*. Ein Hashelosha: Ein Hashelosha Kibbutz Archives, 1996 [Heb.].

O'Donnell, Guillermo A. *1966–1973, el estado burocrático autoritario: Triunfos, derrotas y crisis*. Buenos Aires: Editorial de Belgrano, 1982.

Ofer, Dalia. "Emigration and Aliya: New Aspects of Jewish Policy." *Katedra* 75 (1995): 150–64.

Ofer, Dalia, ed. *Israel in the Great Wave of Immigration, 1948–1953*. Jerusalem: Yad Ben-Zvi, 1996.

Oteiza, Enrique. "Emigración de profesionales, técnicos y obreros calificados argentinos a los Estados Unidos: Análisis de las fluctuaciones de la emigración bruta julio 1950 a junio 1970." *Desarrollo Económico* 10, no. 39/40 (1970–71): 429–54.

Paltitzky, Y. "A Bystander's Sketches (Interpretative Items)." In *Fifty Years since the Ten Certificates (from Buenos Aires to Mefalsim)*, 37. Mefalsim: Mefalsim Archives, 1995.

Pellegrino, A. "Tendencias de la migración internacional en América Latina y el Caribe en la segunda mitad del siglo XX." In *Patrones migratorios internacionales en América Latina*, edited by Enrique Oteiza, 27–40. Buenos Aires: Eudeba, 2010.

Peñaloza, F. "Pre-Migration Background and Assimilation of Latin-American Immigrants in Israel." *Jewish Social Studies* 34 (1972): 122–39.

Picard, Avi. *Cut to Measure: Israel's Policies Regarding the Aliyah of North African Jews, 1951–1956*. Beer Sheva: Ben-Gurion Institute and Ben-Gurion University of the Negev, 2013 [Heb.].

Rafael, Yitzhak. *Not Easily Came the Light*. Jerusalem: Idanim, 1981 [Heb.].

Rebhun, Uzi, and Chaim Isaac Waxman. "The 'Americanization' of Israel: A Demographic, Cultural, and Political Evaluation." *Israel Studies* 5, no. 1 (2000): 65–91l.

Reichman, Rivka. "Immigration to Israel: A Mapping of Trends and Empirical Studies, 1990–2006." *Israeli Sociology* 10, no. 2 (2009): 339–80 [Heb.].

Rein, Raanan. *Argentina, Israel, and the Jews: Perón, the Eichmann Capture and After*. Translated by Martha Grenzeback. Bethesda: University Press of Maryland, 2003.

———. "Argentine Jews and the Accusation of 'Dual Loyalty,' 1960–1962." In *The Jewish Diaspora in Latin America and the Caribbean: Fragments of Memory*, edited by Kristin Ruggiero, 51–71. Brighton: Sussex Academic Press, 2005.

———. *Populism and Charisma: Peronist Argentina, 1943–1945*. Tel Aviv: Modan, 1998 [Heb.].

———. "Waning Essentialism: Latin American Jewish Studies in Israel." In *Identities in an Era of Globalization and Multiculturalism*, edited by Judit Bokser-Liwerant et al., 109–24. Leiden: Brill, 2008.

Rein, Raanan, ed. *Árabes y Judíos en Iberoamérica: Similitudes, diferencias y tensiones*. Seville: Fundación Tres Culturas, 2008.

Rein, Raanan, and Edna Aizenberg. "Introduction: Going Beyond, Going Against—New Studies on Jewish Latin Americans." *Estudios Interdisciplinarios de América Latina y el Caribe* 23, no. 1 (2013): 7–10.

Riz, Liliana de. *La política en suspenso, 1966–1976*. Buenos Aires: Paidós, 2000.

Rock, David, et al. *La derecha argentina: Nacionalistas, neoliberales, militares y clericales*. Barcelona: J. Vergara, 2001.

Roizman, Joel. *"Borochov Youth" and "Dror-Borochov Youth" in Poland after the Holocaust*. Ramat Ef'al: Yad Tabenkin, 1999 [Heb.].

Roizman, L. "Our Borochovism vis-à-vis Reality." Unpublished.

Roniger, Luis. "The Latin American Community of Israel: Some Notes on Latin American Jews and Latin American Israelis." *Israel Social Science Research* 6, no. 1 (1988): 63–72.

Roniger, Luis, and Gabriel Jarochevsky. "Los Latinoamericanos en Israel: La Comunidad Invisible." *Reflejos* 1 (1992): 39–49.

Rosenwaike, Ira. "The Jewish Population of Argentina, Census and Estimate, 1887–1947." *Jewish Social Studies* 22, no. 4 (1960).

Rubel, Yaacov. *Las escuelas judías Argentinas, 1985–1995: Procesos de evolución y de involución*. Buenos Aires: Milá, 1998.

Rubin, Iair. *La memoria del sueño*. Buenos Aires: Milá, 2006.

Rubinstein, Amnon, and Barak Medinah. *The Constitutional Law of the State of Israel*. Jerusalem: Schocken, 1996 [Heb.].

Sabar, Galia. *We're Not Here to Stay: African Migrant Workers in Israel and Back in Africa*. Tel Aviv: Tel Aviv University, 2008 [Heb.].

Sable, Martin Howard. *Latin American Jewry: A Research Guide*. Cincinnati: Hebrew Union College Press, 1978.

Schachner, Devora. *A Political Girl*. Tel Aviv: Hakibbutz Hame'uchad, 2002 [Heb.].

Schechner, Tzvi. "'Kehile,' un concepto común heredado: La creación de organizaciones comunitarias sobre la base de 'Asociación de Entierro' en el judaísmo ashkenazí de Buenos Aires y México, D.F." In AMILAT, *Judaica Latinoamericana* (Jerusalem: Magnes Press, 1988), 115–28.

Schenkolewski-Kroll, Silvia. "La 'conquista de las comunidades': El movimiento sionista y la comunidad Ashkenazi de Buenos Aires. 1935–1949." *Judaica Latinoamericana* 2 (1993): 197–99.

———. *The Zionist Movement and the Zionist Parties in Argentina, 1935–1948*. Jerusalem: Magnes Press, 1996 [Heb.].

Schers, D., and H. Singer. "The Jewish Communities of Latin America: External and Internal Factors in Their Development." *Jewish Social Studies* 39 (1977): 241–58.

Schmelz, Uziel, and Sergio DellaPergola. *The Social Structure of Latin American Jewry: Demography of the Jews in Argentina and Other Latin American Countries*. Tel Aviv: David Horowitz Institute for the Research of Developed Countries, 1974.

Schwarcz, Alfredo José. *Los judíos de habla alemana en la Argentina*. Buenos Aires: Grupo Editor Latinoamericano, 1991.

Scobie, James R. *Revolution on the Pampas: A Social History of Argentine Wheat, 1860–1910*. Austin: University of Texas Press, 1964.

Segev, Tom. *1949, the First Israelis*. New York: Free Press, 1984.

Semyonov, M., and N. Lewin-Epstein. "Immigration and Ethnicity in Israel: Returning Diaspora and Nation-Building." In *Diasporas and Ethnic Migrants: Germany, Israel, and Post-Soviet Successor States*, edited by Rainer Munz and Rainer Ohliger, 327–37. Portland, OR: Frank Cass, 2003.

Senkman, Leonardo. "A 25 años del caso Sirota: La comunidad y los sectores democráticos contra el nazismo." In *Trayectoria de una idea*, edited by Eliahu Toker and Ana E. Weinstein, 84–85. Buenos Aires: Ediciones Fundación Mordejai Anilevich, 1999.

———. *Argentina: La Segunda Guerra Mundial y los refugiados indeseables, 1933–1945*. Buenos Aires: Grupo Editor Latinoamericano, 1991.

———. "El antisemitismo bajo dos experiencias democráticas: 1945–1966 y 1973–1976." In El antisemitismo en la Argentina, edited by Leonardo Senkman. Buenos Aires: Centro Editor de América Latina, 1989.

———. "El 4 de junio 1943 y los judíos." *Todo es historia* 193 (1983): 67–78.

———. "The First Group of Argentinian Volunteers in the Jewish Legion (1918) and the Commemorative Album edited by M. Podolsky." *Michael* 8 (1983): 30–42 [Heb.].

———. "Klal Ysrael at the Frontiers: The Transnational Jewish Experience in Argentina." In *Identities in an Era of Multiculturalism: Latin America in the Jewish World*, edited by Judit Bokser Liwerant, Eliezer Ben-Rafael, Yossef Gorny, and Raanan Rein, 125–50. Leiden: Brill, 2008.

———. "The Latin American Diasporas: New Collectives Identities and Citizenship Practices." In *Shifting Frontiers of Citizenship: The Latin American Experience*, edited by Mario Sznajder, Luis Roniger, and Carlos Forment, 385–93. Leiden: Brill, 2013).

———. "El peronismo visto desde la legación israelí en Buenos Aires: Sus relaciones con la OIA. 1949–1954." *Judaica Latinoamericana* 2 (1993): 115–36.

———. "The Response of the First Peronist Government to Antisemitic Discourse, 1946–1954: A Necessary Reassessment." *Judaica Latinoamericana* 3 (1997): 175–206.

———. "Ser judío en Argentina: Las transformaciones de la identidad nacional." In *Identidades judías, modernidad y globalización*, edited by Paul Mendes-Flohr, Yom Tov Assis, and Leonardo Senkman, eds. Buenos Aires: Centro Internacional para la Enseñanza, Universitaria de la Cultura Judía, 2007.

Senkman, Leonardo, ed. *El antisemitismo en la Argentina*. Buenos Aires: Centro Editor de América Latina, 1989.

Shapira, Anita. *Israel: A History*. Waltham, MA: Brandeis University Press, 2013.

Shapira, Anita, ed. *Independence: The First Fifty Years*. Jerusalem: Shazar Center, 1998 [Heb.].

Shapira, Anita, Jehuda Reinharz, and Jay Michael Harris, eds. *The Age of Zionism*. Jerusalem: Shazar Center, 2000 [Heb.]

Sheffer, Gabriel. "From Diasporas to Migrants—From Migrants to Diasporas." In *Diasporas and Ethnic Migrants: Germany, Israel, and Post-Soviet Successor States in Comparative Perspective*, edited by Rainer Munz and Rainer Ohliger, 21–36. Portland, OR: Frank Cass, 2003.

Shilo, Margalit. "The Good of the People or the Good of the Land? The Zionist Movement's Attitude towards Aliya in the Time of the Second Aliya." *Katedra* 46 (1987): 109–22 [Heb.].

Shimoni, Gideon. *The Zionist Ideology*. Hanover, NH: University Press of New England [for] Brandeis University Press, 1995.

Shinan, Avigdor, ed. *Emigration and Settlement in Jewish and General History: A Collection of Essays*. Jerusalem: Shazar Center, 1982 [Heb.].

Sicron, Moshe. "The Mass Aliya: Dimensions, Characteristics, and Influence on the Demographic Structure of Israel." In *Immigrants and Transit Camps, 1948–1952*, edited by Mordechay Naor, 31–32. Jerusalem, Yad Ben-Zvi, 1986 [Heb.].

Siebzehner, Batia. "Un imaginario inmigratorio: Ideología y pragmatismo entre los latinoamericanos en Israel." In *Pertenencia y alteridad: Judíos en/de América Latina, cuarenta años de cambios*, edited by Haim Avni, Judit Bokser-Liwerant, Sergio DellaPergola, Margalit Bejarano, and Leonardo Senkman. 389–414. Madrid: Iberoamericana, 2011.

Smooha, Sammy. *Israel: Pluralism and Conflict*. London: Routledge and Kegan Paul, 1978.

Soldinger, Robert. *The Absorption of Latin-American Immigrants in Kibbutzim*. Rehovot: Settlement Study Center, 1981.

Tartakower, Arieh. *Jewish Migration in the World*. Jerusalem: Institute for Jewish Higher Education, 1947 [Heb.].

Toker, Eliahu, and Ana E. Weinstein, eds. *Trayectoria de una idea: Nueva Sión; 50 años de un periodismo judeo-argentino con compromiso, 1948–1998*. Buenos Aires: Ediciones Fundación Mordejai Anilevich, 1999.

Tsur, Jacob. *The Fourth Credentials: The First Diplomatic Mission in South America*. Tel Aviv: Sifriyat Maariv, 1981 [Heb.].

Vardi, Arieh. *Between Two Worlds 1938–1946.* Translated from the Spanish by Peninah Meier. Tel Aviv: Sifre Hemed, 2006 [Heb.].

Verbitzky, Horacio. "Cambio Cultural." *Página 12* (May 9, 2010).

Visacovsky, Merina. "El discurso pedagógico de la izquierda judía en Argentina (1935–1970)." PhD diss., Universidad de Buenos Aires, 200.

Weill, Simón. *Población israelita en la República Argentina: Conferencia pronunciada el 23 de Octubre de 1935.* Buenos Aires: Bene Berith, 1936.

Weinstock, T. "Argentina Was a Nachtasyl: Residents of Baron Hirsch's Colonies Are Settling in Israel." *Davar*, June 3, 1954.

Yaar, Ephraim, and Zeev Shavit, eds. *Trends in Israeli Society.* Tel Aviv: Open University, 2001 [Heb.].

Zadoff, Efraim. *Historia de la educación judía en Buenos Aires, 1935–1957.* Buenos Aires: Milá, 1994.

Zuccotti, Juan Carlos. *La emigración argentina contemporánea (a partir de 1950).* Buenos Aires: Plus Ultra, 1987.

INDEX

Page numbers in *italics* indicate illustrative tables and figures.

CPSIA information can be obtained
at www.ICGtesting.com
Printed in the USA
BVOW04*1626160717
488758BV00014B/12/P